William Haggar

William Haggar
(1851-1925)
fairground film-maker

Peter Yorke

Published by Accent Press 2007

ISBN 1905170874 / 9781905170876

Printed and bound in the UK

Cover Design by Red Dot Designs

The publisher acknowledges the financial
support of the Welsh Books Council

In loving memory of my Granny, Violet Haggar Yorke, and

To my beloved wife, Betsy

CONTENTS

Acknowledgements

"WHEREVER POSSIBLE.....I HAVE used the protagonists' own words, or those of others closely associated with them. This to my mind gives the authentic atmosphere and feeling of the period.....in a way no modern re-rendering can do."

I am indebted for this maxim to the late Professor Roger Manvell, who stated it in his own acknowledgements prefacing his book, "The Trial of Annie Besant". I had instinctively adopted this approach for its vividness, and was delighted, therefore, to find it thus commended by so eminent a predecessor.

Thus my greatest indebtedness is to those who first brought to my notice the memoirs compiled by the Haggar children of my grandmother's generation: to David Berry, film critic and chronicler of the film in Wales, who sent me a copy of my great-aunt Lily's biography of her father; to my cousin Caroline Hill for giving me a report of great-uncle Henry's speech; and especially to my cousin Roy Haggar, for giving me copies of great-uncle Walter's two reminiscences, of the Haggars' theatre and bioscope days. Roy has given me so much more, including videos of the surviving films, photographs, and memories passed on from his grandma, that without his kindness and his and Maggie's hospitality, this book could not have been written.

David Berry also gave me copies of Geoffrey Hill's article on William Haggar for the Cynon Valley History Society, and of chapter three of his book, "Wales and the Cinema – the first hundred years", and was the first to fire me by his own enthusiasm. It was David Cleveland, of the East Anglian Film Archive at the University of East Anglia, Norwich (UEA), who alerted me to the existence of the Welsh Film Archive (where I contacted David Berry), and for that I am very grateful.

During my subsequent researches, I have been delighted to meet many relatives of whose existence I was previously unaware, including Moya England, Gloria Haddock, Dai Thomas, and Barbara and Frank Perkins in Australia, Siddie and Doreen Roberts in Norfolk, and Tom and May Booth in the Isle of Wight: all have given me kindness, hospitality and reminiscences. I have also spoken on the telephone with, but have not met Grace

Greenland, Roy Haggar Senior, (sadly both died before my researches were complete), and Edward Roberts. I have met Guy Rastall at Roy's home in Tenby, and corresponded with David Greenland in North Carolina, and with other members of the Perkins family in Queensland. June Bilous and her late husband Rudy, it was a particular joy to meet, as June, aged 10, had been a bridesmaid at my parents' wedding in 1937. June provided me with memories of my grandmother and my father, and introduced me to her niece Caroline Hill, who gave me, as well as the report of Henry Haggar's speech, wonderful hundred-year-old photographs of my grandmother and her brothers and sisters.

I have also received great help from Margaret Wilby, Maggie Shufflebottom's daughter; from Vanessa Toulmin of the National Fairground Archive; from the late Paul Lawrence Newman, the great-grandson of Tom Lawrence, and, like me, researching his great-grandfather's travelling theatre days; and from Michael Sanderson at UEA on possible sources of information about the Victorian theatre in the Provinces.

Staff at the Aberdare, Dorchester, Neath and Norwich Public Libraries have pointed me in the right direction from time to time; as have those of the Norfolk, Suffolk and Essex County Record Offices, the Westminster Reference Library, the Family Records Centre in Islington, the British Library at Colindale, the British Film Institute and the Cinema Museum in Kennington. To all of them, and to Stephen Herbert at *Projection Box*, to Jessica Gardner and Michelle Allen at the Bill Douglas Centre, University of Exeter, and to Gwenno Ffrancon at the University of Wales, Bangor, my thanks are due. Appendix 8 contains a list of all of the sources for this book, published or unpublished, which I must acknowledge.

Then of course I owe many thanks to Hazel and Bob Cushion of Accent Press for believing in my manuscript sufficiently to take the risk of publishing a not obviously commercial prospect, and for guiding me gently through the, to me, unfamiliar process of getting it into print; and to Karen Smart for making many last-minute corrections. I am glad to record my gratitude, too, to Undeg Griffiths, Catrin Jenkins and John Reed of The National Screen and Sound Archive of Wales for their encouragement and help with the stills, to Stephen Smith and Neil Watson for allowing me to use other photographs, and to my son-in-law Alex Everard for devising the website.

Last but not least, my wife, Betsy has cheered me on with

advice from her own writing experiences, has read my drafts and corrected my frequent mistakes, and has encouraged me whenever I have felt like flagging. She has my enormous gratitude and love.

Note: spellings adopted are, for the most part, those current at the time of the events narrated; for example, Llanelly, not Llanelli, and Will Hopkins, not Wil Hopcyn.

William Haggar, his children and grandchildren

William and Mary Hagger at Badley, Suffolk

William Hagger, bap. 2.5.1798, gardener of Dedham, m. Hellen Southgate 30.6.1824

James Hagger (1800-1870) wheelwright of Frating m. Sarah (d.1848)

- Samuel James b.1826
- Sarah b.1828
- Mary Elizabeth b.1830, afterwards m.(1)R. Bridgstock (2) J.Taylor
- six other children b.1831 – 1842

Arthur William Haggar (10.3.1851-4.2.1925) = (1) Sarah Hemming (Walton) (1851 – 1909) = (2) Mary Jane ("May") Davies (1884 – 1924)

- Will Jnr (1871-1935) m.27.1.1893 Jane Emily Silverton (1874-1954)
  - Jennie, Gladys, Phyllis, Dorothy, Billy, Josephine & Patrick Haggar
- Frederick (1873-1913) m.30.3.92 Catherine Waldron (1873-1906)
  - Frederick, Robert, & Donald Haggar
- George (1875-79)
- Ellen Elizabeth (1877-1890)
- James (1879-1925) m4.4.1900 Kate Silverton (1877-1955)
  - Lily Kate, James & Gwyneth Haggar
- Walter (1880-1953) m 21.11.06 Ada Rosina Roberts (1884-1969)
  - Grace, Madge, Leonard, Roy & Mary Haggar
- Archibald (1882-1895)
- Rose (1885-1967) m 24.8.1908 Sidney Moses (1886-1960)
  - George Haggar Moses
- Violet (1887-1979) m.15.1.12 Cyril Sydney Yorke (1887-1959)
  - Cyril H. Yorke (1913-1994)
  - William, Queenie, Connie, David & Joyce Moses
- Henry (1889-1945)
- Lily May (1891-1973) m28.8.12 Bertie Richards (b. 1886)
  - Eileen, Colin, Walter, William, & June Richards (b.1926)

/ Note

Note: in 1924, William was said to have 11 children, 40 grandchildren and 3 great-grandchildren.
This should have been 11 children and 29 grandchildren (totalling 40), with June Richards, the 30th grandchild, born after his death.
The 3 great-grandchildren were Will Junior's daughter Jennie's children Moya, William Arthur and Betty.

List of illustrations

The Haggar family
1. William holding Violet aged 2 (1889)
2. William and Sarah at Walter and Ada's wedding (1906) (Will, Lily and Violet behind them)
3. William as a 'Man at the wheel' (1924)
4. Walter, Archie and Henry (1892)
5. Lily aged 2 (1893)
6. Violet in Boer War costume (1902)
7. Rose dressed as a parader (1907)
8. Henry when manager of the Castle Cinema, Merthyr (1930's)
9. Will Junior and his theatrical company (1906)

The Victorian Theatre
10. Sir Henry Irving
11. Lillah McCarthy as Mercia in **The Sign of the Cross**
12. Dan Leno, comedian: William sang his songs

The early British Cinema
13. Robert Paul, inventor of the 'Maltese Cross' projector (*British Film Institute*)
14. William's friend Charles Urban (*British Film Institute*)
15. Cecil Hepworth filmed **Rescued by Rover** (*British Film Institute*)

Bioscope Shows
16. Haggar's Royal Electric Bioscope, 1902
17. Haggar's Royal Bioscope, 1908 (the Marenghi organ showfront)
18. Haggar's Electric Coliseum (the Gavioli organ showfront)
19. Walter's traction engine *King George V*
20. Chipperfield's Electric Theatre on the road in 1911 (*Morton's Media Group Archive*)
21. A Bioscope Show from above: Aspland's Pictureland at Boston Fair in 1912 (*Neil Watson*)

Films comparable with The Maid of Cefn Ydfa

22.   **Richard III (1911)**: Richard wooing Lady Anne (*British Film Institute*)

23.   **East Lynne (1913)**: A dramatic moment shared by Richard, Cornelia, Lady Isabel and a maid (*British Film Institute*)

24.   **David Copperfield (1913)**: Peggoty and David in Barkis' cart (*British Film Institute*)

Stills from William Haggar's films

25.   **Outside the Works**: Workers in the street (*National Screen and Sound Archive of Wales*)

26.   **Outside the Works**: William advertises the show (*National Screen and Sound Archive of Wales*)

27.   **Desperate Poaching Affray**: The Poachers (Sid Griffiths and Will Haggar) surprised by the gamekeepers (*National Screen and Sound Archive of Wales*)

28.   **Desperate Poaching Affray**: The gamekeepers fire (*National Screen and Sound Archive of Wales*)

29.   **Desperate Poaching Affray**: The chase through the pond (*National Screen and Sound of Wales*)

30.   **Desperate Poaching Affray**: Dragged away 'desperate and exhausted' past the camera (*National Screen and Sound Archive of Wales*)

31.   **The Bathers' Revenge**: "Phew" says Walter, spurning the bathers' clothes (*National Screen and Sound Archive of Wales*)

32.   **The Bathers' Revenge**: The spooning couple being tipped into the water (*National Screen and Sound Archive of Wales*)

33.   **The Life of Charles Peace**: Peace at Dyson's House (James, Walter and Violet Haggar) (*National Screen and Sound Archive of Wales*)

34.   **The Life of Charles Peace**: Peace cocks a snook as the third policeman arrives (*National Screen and Sound Archive of Wales*)

35.   **The Life of Charles Peace**: Peace hurling himself from the train (*National Screen and Sound Archive of Wales*)

36.   **The Life of Charles Peace**: The execution scene (*National Screen and Sound Archive of Wales*)

The author and the publishers wish to thank the National Screen and Sound Archive of Wales, the British Film Institute, Morton's Media Group and Neil Watson for permission to use the photographs credited to them above. Other photographs are from the author's collection, and he wishes to thank Roy Haggar and Caroline Hill for their gifts and loans of family items.

Extant Haggar films

Outside the Works / Haggar's Bioscope Camera (?1902/3)

Desperate Poaching Affray (1903)
also known as The Poachers

The Bathers' Revenge (1904)

The Life of Charles Peace (1905)

A Message from the Sea (1905)
The first scene only survives

The Sheep Stealer (1908)

The Stepney Wedding at Llanelly (1911)

The Maid of Cefn Ydfa (1914)
38 minutes of a film originally 50 minutes long

Also –
   The Plumber and the Lunatics (1908)
   not positively identified as a Haggar film.

Copies of these films are held in The National Screen and Sound Archive of Wales, where they can be viewed by appointment, and in the British Film Institute.

Preface

This Film Was a Sensation 28 Years Ago

By 'The Prompter'

AT THE CARDIFF OLYMPIA Cinema the other night, I saw a film which should be preserved in the Welsh National Museum. **The Maid of Cefn Ydfa** was produced in 1910 – 28 years ago – by the late William Haggar, senior, who was, in his day, one of the best-known travelling showmen.

The film put on the screen for my benefit is the only copy in existence. The negative and all other copies were destroyed at the Haggar travelling cinema in Aberdare 9 years since, and the three reels left are so shrunken and worn that they cannot be exhibited on many more occasions.

Mr. W. J. Key, the Olympia manager, is going to show **The Maid** publicly on Friday evening next. He feels, as I do, that this old 'silent' will provide an interesting comparison with the present day talking pictures and methods of making pictures.

Amused and Amazed

Mr. Key and I saw **The Maid** without any sort of musical accompaniment. We were both amused and amazed at the ingenuity of Old Man Haggar, his family (the principal characters) and members of the stock company who made up the 'crowd'.

Scenes were 'shot' during the company's travels in various parts of Wales. For instance, the opening sequence was taken outside the Vicarage, Pontardulais; interior shots – at the home of Ann Thomas (the Maid) – were taken on a nearby cabbage patch. Haggar placed floor-boards on the ground over the cabbages, propped up canvas scenery around them, and there stood the room where Ann, with many melodramatic expressions of distrust, spurned the villain, Anthony Maddocks. In the absence of oval mirrors to adorn the walls, Haggar used white paper in wooden frames, and had I not told you this, you might easily mistake paper for glass.

Message Written in Blood

When Ann wrote a message in 'blood' pricked from her hand on a large ivy leaf, Haggar used white lime as the only method he could think of to show up 'red' on green. Ann throws the leaf from the window of the Old Dulais Arms, Pontardulais.

Perhaps the most amusing episode explained to me by Mr. Key occurred when the villainous Maddocks (I'll bet they hissed him in days gone by) and his co-conspirators pushed the unconscious lover, Will Hopkins, over a waterfall at Llanelly. The water was only a foot deep and the company dug for hours trying to increase the depth. All they did was to strike solid rock a couple of feet down. However, Will Hopkins managed to fall flat and make a big splash, which was all the producer wanted.

Pioneer Effort

Bridgend, Bargoed, and other centres of South Wales figure in **The Maid of Cefn Ydfa**, which, regarded as a pioneer effort, may cause cinema goers to reflect that in some respects, cinematography has not progressed so very far in 28 years. I have seen worse scenes in modern pictures than that in the hermit's retreat where Maddocks commits a foul murder. Lighting effects are excellent; in fact there is very little flicker throughout the film. The only thing that struck me very forcibly was the paucity of close-up 'shots'. Perhaps the old producers were afraid to show too much at close quarters.

In any case, see **The Maid** – it lasts 50 minutes – if you've a mind, and try to imagine what an enormous attraction it was, played to 1d, 2d, and 3d. admission prices all over the country. 'Tis said that when Haggar first put on **The Maid** in the first travelling cinema Wales ever knew, any opposition show could close down. One showman went bankrupt; another introduced a bunch of 'Can Can' girls – they wore frilly knickers and showed their suspenders – but not even this exhibition of feminine daring could beat the business that Haggar did.

2

It is generally agreed that old pioneer showmen of his type had the cinema business – in this country at least – in the palm of their hands at the time **The Maid** was produced. How could they imagine that the financiers were to 'tie-up' with the technicians and create the world-wide entertainment octopus Talking Pictures we know today?

Thus, in the *South Wales Echo* on 16 April 1938, its film critic penned the only known review of a Haggar film before, in more recent years, the surviving films were re-issued on vhs and dvd as monuments of the early cinema. Since 1938, 'Old Man Haggar' has appeared in various film books, but as a bit part extra only, confusingly named William Haggar in some and (erroneously) Walter Haggar in others. This book, telling his story in full, sets the record straight.

1. Ancestry and upbringing

WILLIAM HAGGAR WAS BORN on 10 March 1851,[1] at the home of his great-uncle William in Dedham, Essex.[2] Twelve months later his mother, Elizabeth, took him home to nearby Frating, where she had him baptised at the parish church on Mothering Sunday.[3] There she left him to be brought up by his grandfather James.

The Haggars, first mentioned in the Hundred Rolls,[4] were by now spread throughout the eastern counties.   The Haggards of Bradenham, Norfolk derived their descent from David Haggard who lived in Ware, Hertfordshire, in the 1530s: their most famous son was the barrister, colonial civil servant and writer, Rider Haggard.[5] There was a Haggar estate at Bourn, Cambridgeshire. A Hagger family lived in Great and Little Chishill, where Cambridgeshire, Essex and Hertfordshire meet, from the 1540s until the 1970s, when the last survivor moved to live with his daughter in Reigate; farmers and shopkeepers, they served the community as churchwardens and Overseers of the Poor.[6] Haggars lived in Hitchin, Hertfordshire, working on the land. Cousins of William's lived at Epping, in Essex; Henry and Betsy Hagger's daughter Elizabeth was a scullery maid at Windsor Castle in 1881:[7] the families were in touch, for William's great-grandchildren in Australia remembered, a century later, that a relative of theirs had worked for the Royal Family.[8] Many Hagger families lived in Ipswich and the surrounding Suffolk countryside. Among them were William and Mary, one of three Hagger couples who had children baptised at the church at Badley, near Stowmarket.[9] [10]

Their son, William's grandfather James Hagger[11] lived in Frating, a small village at the cross-roads where the road from Dedham to Brightlingsea meets that from Colchester to Clacton.[12]   A tithe map of 1835 shows James' cottage on the green, in a plot one rood and ten perches in area, at the end of the lane which today bears his name: 'Haggar's Lane'. He was the village wheelwright and carpenter.[13] His wife, Sarah, died at the early age of 38, in September 1848, after bearing 9 children: Samuel, born in 1826,[14] Sarah, Elizabeth, Harriett, who died only six months later, Martha,

Joseph, Mary, and finally twins, Robert and William, in April 1842 – but both the twins died that August.[15] Sarah, Elizabeth and Martha each had an illegitimate child during the years 1850-55: marriage, it seems, was not contemplated, or at least, none of them got married in Frating church. By 1861, only Martha was left to keep house for her father. James died in the spring of 1870, as a result of being kicked by a donkey, the blow breaking a leg which had been bad for some time: he never recovered.[16]

At the time of her mother's death, Elizabeth Hagger, who was said to be 'stunningly pretty', with ginger hair,[17] got a job in Dedham. Later family tradition said that she was in service at a 'big house' there.[18] She lived with her uncle and aunt in Stratford Road, where her son, Arthur William was born – like his mother, William never used his first name. Who his father was, has never been ascertained. Perhaps the son of the 'big house', maybe his name was Arthur, as that was not a Hagger family name. Years later, Elizabeth's daughter Harriet Taylor confided in her niece Lily[19] that her mother received money every month from a solicitor's office, the inference drawn by Lily being that it was 'hush money' for the illegitimate William.[20]

After returning home to Frating with her son in 1852, Elizabeth did not stay long. She found her way to Bury, in Lancashire, marrying there in September 1861 a journeyman bricklayer named Robert Bridgstock: their son James Robert was born in Liverpool in 1862. A year later, they were in Hornsey, North London, where Robert died in July 1863. In May 1868, Elizabeth married James Taylor, a stonemason, at St. Paul's Church in Islington. Their daughter Harriet was born in 1871. Ten years later, the Taylors were living at 2 Park Terrace, Prittlewell, Essex, with their three children, Elizabeth's son James Robert and daughter Harriet, and Elizabeth Taylor, aged 26, James Taylor's daughter by a previous marriage. By the time of the 1891 census, Elizabeth was widowed and keeping a lodging-house at Gordon House, 13 Buckley Road, Kilburn, then a new development: it had not been built in 1881.[21] She was still there fifteen years later.

Lily Richards, Elizabeth's youngest granddaughter, records that both she and her elder brother, Will Junior[22] were sent to her grandmother's house in Kilburn for schooling. Both children hated living with their grandmother: Lily found her a hard taskmaster, and says that Elizabeth blamed her daughter-in-law, Sarah, for enticing William into the theatrical profession, considering that such a way of life was degrading.[23] Elizabeth, like her son William later, had outlived her early disgrace and become respectable. In 1891, her lodgers were professional people, and her granddaughter, six-year old Rose,[24] Lily's elder sister, was staying with her. Clearly Elizabeth had maintained contact with her son, despite her disapproval of his way of life. Indeed, William's business cards and letter heads give her home, 13 Buckley Road, as his business address, for, always on the move, he needed a permanent address for his post to reach him. Ten years later, in 1901, Elizabeth was hosting not only her granddaughter Lily, but also her great-granddaughter Jennie Haggar.[25] She called them both her 'nieces'.[26] She was in her mid-seventies when she did William perhaps her last favour. Lily had left her at Easter 1905, to return home for good. Next year, on 1 April 1906, Rose Haggar had her illegitimate son, George, in the house in Kilburn.[27] Whispers pointed the finger at an Irish actor in the family theatre company: his picture was said to be on the front page of *The Showman*.[28] Probably Rose needed to get away from the family living wagons, so grandmother Elizabeth provided her with sanctuary.

Thus William grew up in his grandfather James' house in Frating, looked after by his aunt Martha.[29] There are two family accounts of William's childhood and early life. One is William's own version, given to a reporter from the *Aberdare Leader* in 1924, the year before his death.[30] The other is in Lily Richards' biography of her father, composed towards the end of her life.[31] For that, she relied heavily on her brother Walter's account of William's film-making days,[32] which she copied, altering personal pronouns as appropriate. She also included her own reminiscences, recollections of what her parents had told her, and stories of William's early life told to her by her grandmother Elizabeth during her stay in Kilburn. When all these sources failed, she filled in gaps from her own imagination. Her daughter June Bilous took dictation from her mother, spent long hours editing out many hesitations and repetitions, and produced the final typed biography.[33]

According to William's account, his parents paid the village schoolmaster a penny a week for his education. Then, when eleven years old, he went to work in the dockyard at Wivenhoe, a small port on the River Colne, only three or four miles from Frating. Later he drifted to Southwold, was apprenticed to a watchmaker, learnt to play the cornet, founded a band,[34] was engaged to play for a travelling theatre, and married a member of the same theatre company. This account has been composed for public consumption – as were William's statements of his father's name and occupation on his marriage certificates: 'Taylor Haggar, Timber Merchant' on the first, (his mother's name was Taylor by that time), and 'William Haggar deceased' on the second. He needed a father and 'parents' for respectability, instead of the grandfather and aunt with whom his mother had left him. It seems that they did not want him. His daughter-in-law Ada said long afterwards that he had had a very bad time: they were cruel to him.[35]

Lily's account is much more circumstantial, although it too shows traces of her father's disguising his real situation: an otherwise unknown uncle appears on the scene to replace his grandfather James, who is never mentioned. Lily wrote:

> His mother had little time for him, and farmed him out to various uncles and aunts who did their best to give him an upbringing. One of Father's uncles owned a sawmill, and took him to live with him for five years teaching him carpentry, which he picked up very quickly, but he was never paid any wages for his work, his uncle telling him how lucky he was to have a home at all. Father worked hard at the sawmill. His day began at 6.30 a.m., and he worked a twelve-hour day with hardly enough to eat and only cast-off clothes to wear. He had a good ear for music and, when he was twelve years old, he joined the local Salvation Army Band, and learned to play every brass instrument, but his favourite was the big trombone.[36]

After a time, some of the older boys suggested that they should form a band of their own, so, in 1869, the eighteen-year old William left his uncle and the sawmill, and set off with three companions to seek their fortune. But after a year, the others tired of this adventure:

> Things looked pretty grim, but his luck held out. At this
> time they were playing at Colchester, and a travelling
> crowd of theatricals were playing in the local Town Hall.
> They needed a stage hand with knowledge of carpentry,
> so Father applied for the job and got it. Financially he was
> no better off, the crowd of players was only third-class and
> often went hungry when business was bad, but at last his
> ambitions crystallised – he suddenly knew he wanted to
> be an actor and run his own company. He was now twenty
> years old, and was very attracted to Sarah Walton, the
> daughter of the theatre company owner, who was just
> eighteen. She was a well-made girl with dark curly hair
> and merry brown eyes. She had a kind heart and had
> never known anything but a hard life on the stage. She
> had no formal education, but she knew almost every line
> of Shakespeare's plays, and could play most of the parts,
> both men's and women's. She had a grand sense of
> humour, as did my father, so they were well suited. They
> decided to marry and leave the Waltons' company, and try
> to get work with a more go-ahead show. It was a bright,
> frosty day in January when William and Sarah were
> married, and their only wedding breakfast was a drink at
> the local pub and some sandwiches. All the Walton
> company came to the wedding, which took place in the
> village church. The bride could not afford a new dress, but
> she made herself a new bonnet with some old silk and
> lace given her by her mother. They were very much in
> love, and Sarah was proud of her handsome husband. It
> was Father's boast in later years that, after paying for the
> marriage licence, all the money he had left was twopence-
> halfpenny![37]

In point of fact, William Haggar and Sarah Hemming[38] were
married in the Register Office at Fakenham, Norfolk, on 31 March
1871.[39]

2. Travelling mummers and portable theatres

IT WAS TO BE a hard life. Walter Haggar, who had grown up in his father's theatre, recalled that a company of actors would consist of about eight gentlemen, four ladies and a few children. They could, and did visit a town and perform a fresh play every night for three or four months.[1] The Haggars' theatre as Walter remembered it was portable, made up of shutter boards, planks and canvas. When the company's stay in one venue was finished, it fell to the actors themselves to 'pull down' and re-erect the theatre in the next place. 'Then', as Lily Richards relates, 'there was continual travelling always to be done on Sundays, finding lodgings – no advance agencies in those days'. Early in their marriage, William and Sarah found employment both with travelling companies playing in rented halls or small theatres, and with those who owned their own show or booth.[2] Such companies were called 'Mummers', and their portable theatres, 'Mumming Booths': William, even in his later film-exhibiting years, was known as 'the old mummer', from his portable theatre days. It was not a glamorous life: the actors' existence could be precarious and uncomfortable, with a regime of hard work, late nights and early mornings, for irregular and uncertain rewards.[3]

At that time, there were four kinds of theatre company operating in the provinces: London companies on tour with celebrated actors and plays; 'stock companies', attached to a theatre or group of theatres; travelling theatres, who toured with a repertoire of plays but performed in permanent buildings; and portable theatres, who toured with their own temporary premises. The portable theatre company which William joined in Southwold or Colchester consisted of six people only, Mr. & Mrs. Richard Julius Walton, their two daughters Sarah and Louie, and two men, one of whom played lead and the other juvenile lead. Richard and his wife, members of the Walton family, at that time well known in the theatre world, were experienced actors, but easy going people with little ambition, rather lazy and fond of liquor and satisfied if they made enough to make ends meet.[4] At that time they had been operating their own company for a few years: in 1868,

Richard Walton placed advertisements as proprietor in *The Era* during a tour of South Wales and the Forest of Dean.[5] But by 1871, these Waltons had thrown in their lot with others. Walter Haggar recalled his grandfather Dick Walton's unique double-handed swordfight act: 'he would hold two cutlasses and had a stage-fight with six opponents: it was an impromptu fight such as might be seen on the films and gained round after round of applause. Dick Walton was the only actor I knew who could do this'.[6] During the 1880s, they remained with William and Sarah's company;[7] and Sarah's sister Louie was with Will Haggar Junior's company in South Wales in the summer of 1912, when she turned down the opportunity of a part in **Little Miss Llewelyn** on the London stage.[8]

At Fakenham in March 1871, Dick and Sarah Walton and William and Sarah Haggar were members of Goree's Portable Theatre Company, then on a tour of Norfolk, Suffolk and Essex.[9] The proprietors, 33-year-old James Goree, 'artist', and his wife, Emmeline (or Emily), 28, originally from Twickenham and Halesworth respectively, had their own caravan, parked in the Cattle Market. The other company members were in lodgings. Two musicians boarded with a widow, and William, Sarah, and Edward Ebley[10] put up at an inn in Oak Street. Dick and Sarah Walton, three other 'comedians', a musician, eleven-year-old Louie Walton and another child dancer, James Goree's daughter Emily, lodged at the Sun Beerhouse.[11] Fifteen in all, they were just the size which Walter gives for a travelling company, and, typically, they had come together from all over the country.[12]

From the pages of *The Era*, it has been observed[13] that, in 1872, over forty portable theatres were providing entertainment up and down the country, outside London. Often these were 'penny theatres', which magistrates, who had to consider whether to grant them licences to perform, might dislike, but which some at least recognised as a better alternative to the beerhouse. Many places welcomed the portables. They provided entertainment, and a view of the outside world. Whitby's reviewer deplored the fact that a company did not turn up for an engagement, so the populace of 20,000 had no amusement.[14] Trowbridge's correspondent celebrated the arrival of three first-class entertainments, but then had to lament that no audience attended.[15] But the *Ilkeston Pioneer* regarded Johnny Noakes' Theatre, which the Haggars met later in South Wales, as a nuisance. 'Why should a whole neighbourhood be almost drummed and blown out of their houses, and infested by all the scum of the town this place attracts?', the paper asked. [16]

The Era published advertisements of all kinds: 'The Zoetrope – this marvellous American toy, the greatest wonder of the age, with 24 coloured engravings'.[17] 'For sale – a very curious monkey beautifully stuffed, once belonging to Bostock and Wombwell's menagerie'.[18] 'Lorenzo, the great sensational one-legged gymnast' sought an engagement.[19] So did the 'Inimitable Walton Company', who used the ads column to blow their own trumpet. The Company:

> Having concluded their brilliant and highly successful pantomime season, open at Barnard's Music Hall, Chatham, on Monday 7th February 1870. New and original spectacular ballets, Burlesques etc., with Magnificent and Costly dresses; also refined Operatic and Characteristic Divertissements. The Troupe Ten in number. Immense change of business. Two entertainments nightly. Proprietors please address as above.[20]

It is not possible to glean much from *The Era* about the way of life of those engaged with portable theatres. But what these adverts portray, and what Walter narrates in his *Theatre Recollections,* is a life little different from that of the Strolling Players of the eighteenth century, of whom there are more detailed descriptions.[21] Bands of unlicensed players eked out a precarious existence by touring the smaller towns. Their life was a hard one; they were often at the mercy of an unscrupulous manager who saw that the bulk of the profits went into his own pocket. They frequently went without food, and after a week's hard work, their only share of the profit would be a stock supper 'which was generally ended in a Quarrel by way of Dessert.' Travelling was difficult for the poorest companies in the eighteenth century, each man having to carry a share of the scenery or wardrobe on his back. Usually, however, at least one wagon was employed, and, of course, it was generally the manager who claimed the privilege of riding on it so that he could keep an eye on the properties. In bad weather, the wagon could get stuck on the poor roads: there was always the danger of being overturned. On arrival at a town, they had first to get permission to perform from the mayor or magistrates. Then the players would put on their smartest clothes (generally borrowed from the company's wardrobe) and gather in the centre of a town, beat a drum and distribute playbills. Performances had to be given wherever accommodation could be found: inn-yards, barns, town halls and so forth. If their luck was out, they would have to resort to a stable. Properties were as meagre as the costumes, though in **The Strollers**[22] a character proudly proclaims: 'we have a second-hand Dragon that lost a wing and two claws in an opera last winter'. Smaller companies had to be content with engaging whatever musicians they could find in the towns they visited: 'generally a motley crowd whose efforts would distress even the most hardened ear. More often than not, a couple of fiddlers would represent the entire musical talent of the town, and it would indeed be fortunate if both were found to be sufficiently capable and sober to play the music required of them.'[23] A hundred years later, little had changed: the Haggars, throughout their years as travelling theatricals, had many similar experiences.

The front of the Haggars' portable theatre was built up from two living wagons, set apart with a small front stage or parade built between them. On each side of the living wagons were steps leading into the theatre known as the 'walk-up'. The sides and roof of the theatre were constructed of frames carrying wooden panels, the whole covered with a canvas tilt and pegged down firmly with guys and stakes. The stage consisted of two flat trucks run together, with a proscenium built round them. Lighting was either by gas or oil lamps. Effects such as dimming were easier with gas-light, but with oil lamps dimming had to be done by passing a piece of semi-transparent paper in front of each lamp. The seating capacity was about two hundred, the seats being bare boards raked down towards the stage. There was a piano, and a good stock of scenery.

Audiences could be restless and unruly. Before the curtain was raised for the opening of the performance or after any interval, a handbell was rung to signal the need for quiet. If the bell had no effect after repeated applications, the Manager would make an appeal from the stage for attention, and if this failed, the actors would leave the stage, go among the audience and forcibly eject any hooligans. They would then return to the stage and, after an apology was made to the audience for the interruption, the play could proceed. On one occasion during a Welsh coal strike, William himself had to go on stage and make an impassioned oration on the grievances of the working man, in order to calm the audience, mostly of striking miners: he managed to get them singing.[24]

By the 1850s, companies attached permanently to a theatre or a small circuit of theatres became known as 'stock companies'. This name persisted until after the Great War, when these enterprises were replaced by repertory companies, which reformed both the repertoire of plays and the manner of acting them. Stock companies and portable theatres had much in common. They had a nightly change of bill: to facilitate this, each player undertook some special line of business. The Leader was generally a tragedian, playing Hamlet or Macbeth. There would be a Leading Lady, a Juvenile Lead, an Old Man, an Old Woman, a Heavy Father, who played tyrants and villains, and a Heavy Woman. The Low Comedian was next in importance to the Leader. All of these acting roles were advertised for in the columns of *The Era*. William Haggar advertised in 1887 for a 'Leading lady: long and profitable engagement to a lady that understands the business of a good Portable', and for a 'Leading Lady and Gent, also Leader of Band'.[25] William became an accomplished low comedian, and earned the nickname, 'Haggarout', when, on one occasion in Tredegar, a new comedian was being tried out. This unfortunate was hissed off the stage, and a cry arose, 'send Haggar out, Haggar out, Haggar out', which promptly stuck. So, initially to William's chagrin, he became typecast in this role. On another occasion, due to the absence of an actor, he had to play the villain, William Corder, in **Maria Martin**. The audience was in hysterics: it was said in the company that this was the only time **Maria** had been played as a comedy! Will Haggar Junior, cast as a villain, was once attacked in the streets of Llanelly by an old lady who berated him for a drunken womaniser. Rising to the occasion, Will replied, in his best stage voice, 'Madam, at least you will never have the good fortune to become one of my victims!

Good day.'[26]

The system of type-casting allowed the actors to memorise and perform a large number of plays in each town:

The actors could, and did, visit a town and perform a fresh play every night for three or four months. It followed that if their type of role changed, they might be somewhat lost. Each player memorised as part of his stock-in-trade the major portion of the dialogue of these plays, and it was no trouble at all, after the usual 11 o'-clock rehearsal, to go on and perform the part. There was a series of what were known as 'stock plays', such as **East Lynne**, **Uncle Tom's Cabin, Maria Marten, Sweeney Todd, Temptation**, and many others. Any one of these plays could be put on at a moment's notice and, when it was, would proceed with no undue hitches, stage waits or 'gagging', and with very little prompting. There was no prompter as such, but if the play was a difficult one, owing to the fact that there were new members or other circumstances, any actor who was not actually on the stage would stand in the wing with the script, so that he could give a guiding word where necessary. But the players were, in any case, never stuck for words. If they forgot their lines, they would make up their own words, and it did not really matter what they said as long as it fitted in with the play, although this was frowned on by the management. The words, 'Stick to the script' were often heard during rehearsals.

Our library of plays consisted mostly of hand-written scripts. When a new play was contemplated, a rehearsal was called, and the script was passed around. The leading man would write out his part, probably staying up half the night to do it, then he would pass it on to the comedian, who passed it on to the villain, and so on until everyone had written out his part and learnt it. On rare occasions, they may have had as many as three rehearsals before this new play was produced. To enable the management to acquire a repertoire of plays to last up to four months, they had to encroach on many copyright plays on which a fee should have been paid. They got away with this by changing the names of the plays; for instance, **The Silver**

King was billed as **The Silver Ring**, **The Sign of the Cross** was renamed **The Shadow of the Cross**, and so on. At 9 o'-clock each Monday morning, all the actors were given a number of bills and were detailed to a certain district, where they would post the bills in a prominent position.[27]

A favourite speciality of the company was a fencing duel between six ladies and a similar number of gentlemen. This was performed to a formal and precise movement, and to a musical accompaniment, provided, over the years, by bands of varying numbers and quality, including among their members the Haggar children, each of whom could play one or more instruments. The company contrived to produce as realistic special effects as possible within their limited means. Thunder was produced with the time-honoured aid of a large piece of tin, and dried peas poured upon the same utility simulated the effect of heavy rain. Snow could be made by using paper confetti or, on one occasion in a Christmas pantomime, the feathers of a goose ready for the Christmas pot. Strong wind was produced by a hand-operated wind machine, and smoke by the simple but dangerous and uncomfortable expedient of burning damp rags in a brazier. Actors and actresses had not only to act. The gentlemen had to be carpenters, painters, labourers and jack-of-all-trades. They had to build, pull down and move the portable theatre, repair it after storm damage, construct and paint scenery and props, and make furniture and other effects. The ladies of the company made costumes, drapes, wigs and masks.[28]

Actors were paid under the so-called 'Commonwealth' system of shares. Walter describes it, and its consequences:

> While we travelled through the English Counties, the pay was divided in what was known as the 'Commonwealth' system; i.e. the takings were made into equal shares. The leading man would get, say, a share and a half, the villain a share and a half, the comedian a share and a half, the leading lady a share and a quarter, utility man one share, and the actresses pro rata, perhaps one share. There would be four shares kept aside for the upkeep of the theatre, two for the costumes, two towards travelling

expenses to the next town, one for gas and two for sundries. There was a total of between twenty and thirty shares each night. The pianist had the job of counting the cash, another would count the ticket counterfoils or 'checks'. When these tallied, the sum was done, and the shares were announced. 'Shares 9d.', it was called out, 'shares 2s.' 'shares 3d.' or whatever it may have been. I have seen the players dozens of times rushing to where the money was being counted, wiping off their grease-paint with their face-cloths as they went. Some would have changed out of their costumes, and all would be anxiously awaiting the announcement of the shares. When the shares were called, the players would hurriedly claim their pence and run – not home, but to the nearest Public House, where they would all assemble in the same room and fight their battles over again. They would go over the play in detail and discuss 'how I brought the house down', 'the end of the first act', or 'the embarrassing situation that cropped up in the second act' etc., all over their 3d. pints of beer.[29]

The company would consist of a mixture of family and non-family members. By the early 1890s, the Haggars had eight of the family to take parts, play instruments, or tumble about to act as attractions. Of the non-family members, some stayed with the company for years. Others came and went: youngsters gained experience and went on to greater things. London actors, who did not get paid when London shows closed for the summer, earned extra pay by appearing in the provinces during the summer vacation. Walter names various performers, including Harry, George and Charlie Lloydall[30] ('three of the finest actors, and the biggest scamps I know'), Clarence Mangau and George Butler,[31] 'well known in Wales', and Kate Tansley, Doris Hare's mother.[32] Henry Selby, Horace Mair and his wife were among those who had parts in **The Test of Truth** in Chepstow in 1890.[33] Will Desmond,[34] Kate Sylvester and John Freeman acted in the Haggar film, **The Sign of the Cross** in 1904, when they were members of Will Junior's company. Will Fyffe[35] joined the Haggars in 1897, having already made his stage debut as Little Willie in **East Lynne** with his father's company. By the time he was fifteen, he was playing Polonius in **Hamlet**. He acted in **The Maid of**

Cefn Ydfa in 1913, and went on to become famous as a music-hall star. It is even said that Charlie Chaplin himself worked with Will Junior's company: a lady in Llanelly recalled him lodging with her mother while on stage with them there.[36]

Sarah Haggar was said to know the whole of Shakespeare, and to be able to play any part: but Shakespeare could be put on in a variety of ways. George Bernard Shaw criticized producers for not playing Shakespeare as originally written.[37] At one end of the spectrum, actor-managers customised plays to suit themselves: typical of this sort of production was Sir Herbert Beerbohm Tree's **The Tempest** in 1904, in which Tree played Caliban, the play being drastically cut in order to render the monster, as far as possible, its hero; this would have made it impossibly short, but for the very long waits needed while the stage-hands shifted the solid scenery, which with sumptuous realism displayed the wonders of Prospero's isle.[38] At the other extreme, Fred Bertram, who joined Hendry's Booth on a fairground circuit, recalled that, in the 1850s, 'Richard the Third runs his wicked career, offers his kingdom for a horse, has his go at Richmond, and gets killed off-hand in twenty minutes', so that several performances each with more than one turn could be got into the time available.[39]

But the Haggars put on more varied drama: their evening's entertainment comprised a melodrama, two comic songs and a laughable farce...'all this for 3d and no entertainment tax!'.[40] Their repertoire, the very stuff of Victorian melodrama, incorporating both the latest from the West End stage and stock plays which could be put on at a moment's notice,[41] could be arranged to last up to four months, with a different play every night.[42] The Haggars would add a dash of local interest. The Welsh melodrama, **The Maid of Cefn Ydfa** became their speciality and, when first filmed, it made their fortune. Another local thriller was **The Fair Maid of Neath, or, The Maniac Lover**.[43] Moliére's well-known adaptation of Plautus was relocated from Rome to Wales, to become **The Miser of Newport**. Welsh pride could be aroused by **The Druid's Curse**, or **Llewelyn, the last Prince of Wales**.[44] It was a dictum of the company that the audience should leave the theatre laughing; so the show always concluded with a comic sketch or song, which relieved any tensions created by the preceding melodrama. Then there was the annual pantomime: as Walter

Haggar remarked:

Each year as Christmas approached, there would be the worry of an impending pantomime. For six hard weeks before Christmas, the entire company would be studying songs, making new scenery, props, costumes, wigs, and other things preparatory to putting over a first-class show, from which we got, in fact, very little profit. I never could understand in my childhood days why they would all work so hard for so long, and produce a pantomime for only one week. I suppose it must have been just love of the game.[45]

3. Struggling to survive

FOR THIRTY YEARS, THE life of a travelling mummer was to be William and Sarah's world, from their marriage in 1871 until the time came when William could finally show films all the year round. At first, they worked in a circuit from Kent up the east of England to Yorkshire and across to Lancashire. They were married in Fakenham, in Norfolk. Nine months later at Gorleston, near Great Yarmouth, the birth of their first son, Arthur William[1] took place two days before Christmas.[2] Fred[3] was born seventeen months later, in May 1873, at Sutton-in-Ashfield, Notts. George[4] arrived two years after that, in June 1875, in Snowden's Yard, Colne, Lancashire, and Ellen[5] was born on the Market Ground at Glossop, in Derbyshire, in April 1877. Jim[6] followed, two years later again, in May 1879, at the Crown Wharf in Erith, in Kent. Tragically, George died at nearby Bexley Heath a month later. At this point the family's fortunes were at a low ebb: Walter, son number five, was born in Burnley, in November 1880, in the 'Union', the local workhouse, in the 'outdoor relief' rooms provided there for those who had no proper lodging. Walter's birth certificate, for the first and only time, shows his father's occupation as having no necessary connection with the theatre or fairground. Previously William had described himself as 'travelling musician', 'travelling showman', 'comedian', or, when Ellen was born, 'Shooting Gallery Proprietor'. Now, 'carpenter' was all he could declare. But a few months later the family was in Heckmondwyke, in Yorkshire, for the famous 'feast' there, with William a 'comedian' again,[7] a description which he was to maintain for the next fifteen years.

After the end of their employment with the Gorees, William acted as carpenter and painter for the next company, making the scenery and props, and setting out on his career as a comic actor. Sarah, a good seamstress, combined acting every sort of part with being the wardrobe mistress. She was also an economical housewife:

Luckily, Mother knew how to make one shilling do the work of two. She would go out hunting for the cheapest butcher, baker or grocer. She learned to buy sheep's heads at threepence each, rabbits for sixpence, bought with their skins on, and hearts and liver and all kinds of offal, which butchers practically gave away in those days. When they were in living wagons, in each new place she had to find a washerwoman to wash and iron all their clothes, and she paid a shilling for a dozen garments, large and small. Neither she nor Father had many clothes, apart from stage costumes which did not belong to them, so the washerwomen never made a fortune out of them![8]

William contributed to the need for economy by making their living wagon, buying only the chassis, four wheels in an iron and timber framework, with a pair of shafts to be fixed to a horse with leather straps when they wanted to move on. The horse always had to be hired, as they could not afford to buy one – and later, Walter remarked that horses were the bane of their life; so, if they were going a long distance, they would send the wagon by rail. William built the wagon-top himself, complete with all fitments except the iron coal-burning stove. Wagons were not luxurious: they contained a cupboard for crockery, a bed with a mattress that folded up to the end of the wagon during the day, and very little else. When the family joined a portable theatre company, everyone lived in wagons, so there were no charges for lodgings or hire of halls.

When Fred, his second son, was a year old, William decided that it was time to start on his own. He and Sarah had been scraping and saving for this since their wedding day, but, even so, they could not afford a fully-fledged theatre. They decided to begin with a marionette show, William carving the puppets and Sarah dressing them. They bought a big drum to beat to attract customers, but now having no more than £1 left, they stayed on with the theatre company until it had grown to £5. Then, when the company moved on, they stayed behind to go it alone – but disaster struck: Will and Fred caught scarlet fever, and had to be nursed in the wagon. They were then at Colne, where there was no hospital. They could not open their show, and were not allowed to move. For six weeks they would have no income; and

20

Sarah was imminently expecting another baby, their third son, George. First they sold the drum, then the marionettes. William scraped a few pence together by selling picture frames from door to door, making them from odd scraps of wood. He would walk miles to snare a rabbit, and spent hours fishing, just to keep body and soul together. When the boys recovered and William and Sarah could move again, they got back their old jobs with the travelling theatre: at least they could eat regularly once more.

Two years later, they tried again, this time with a shooting gallery, a novelty at that time. At first they did well, even making enough money to afford a second wagon for the three boys to sleep in when their sister, Nell, was born at Glossop.[9] After another two years, however, in 1879, they were back in the theatre: evidently there was not enough money in a shooting gallery alone. These were hard years, with young George's death just before he became four, and a new baby every two years. Sarah must have been at her wits end to keep the family together. Having to go into a workhouse to have Walter late in 1880 was a grim experience: perhaps, as happened again later, they had had to sell their second living wagon, and Sarah could not have her baby in a wagon in which William and the four other children also had to sleep.

But now there came a decisive change of direction: the family moved south-west, to Wotton-under-Edge in Gloucestershire, where Archie[10] was born in November 1882. From then on, apart from one last foray with marionettes a few years later, they stayed with the portable theatre, in a circuit through Gloucestershire, Somerset, Dorset, Hampshire and Wiltshire, for almost the rest of that decade. Two more sisters for Nell were born: Rose[11] at Taunton in 1885, and Violet at Poole in 1887.[12]

The family's stories set at the beginning of Lily's biography had not necessarily been in sequential order. From the mid-1880s, however, there is a second account of the family's travels which does deal with its subject in sequence: Walter Haggar's *Theatre Recollections*, which begin when he was not yet five years old, in 1885, and the family theatre, now owned and managed by his father, moved from Bridport to Dorchester. There he remembers the Lloydall brothers getting drunk and fighting soldiers from the local regiment: they had to be discharged from the theatre and smuggled out of Dorchester in a hurry to save their skins. William was friendly with the Pay Sergeant, 'who on Fridays would issue to the soldiers, whether they wanted it or not, a 3d. ticket for the "Gaff" (theatre). Consequently on Friday night there was always a good house and, I may say, the "tommies" were a very good and attentive audience. Of course, the Pay Sergeant benefited accordingly.'[13]

From Dorchester, they moved on to Wimborne, where Walter's young cousin fell into a stream. Walter's uncle managed to pull the lad out, but caught pneumonia as a result, and died shortly afterwards. Walter himself had a spell in bed after falling into a stream at Bridgwater while helping to rescue a circus horse. From Wimborne, they travelled the short distance to Poole, stopping on Poole Quay, where the Gas Works stood when Walter dictated his recollections in 1952. Their stays at Poole, in May-June 1886 and the following winter, were long enough for Jim to be enrolled at the Poole British School,[14] although during the summer they were at Taunton, Bridgwater and Sherborne, where a great feature was made of Guy Fawkes Day: the organisers borrowed from the Haggars every costume and truck they had for their tableaux, wending their way through the torchlit streets. After that, the company returned to Poole for the winter. Parked on the Quay, they made many friends among the fishermen, who helped them to keep the theatre standing in a raging storm one dark night in March 1887. 'At the time', commented Walter, 'we quite thought the entire structure would be blown to smithereens, so strong was the wind.' But instead of the theatre, the wind blew the roof off Sarah's living wagon that night, just as she gave birth to Violet.[15]

During the summer of 1887, they had engagements in Salisbury, Winchester,[16] and Andover at the time of the Queen's Golden Jubilee,[17] where Walter recalled his public debut. Outside the theatre, a temporary platform was arranged, and between each performance the actors would assemble to attract the attention of the crowds. Walter was dressed as a clown, and two of the actors pitched him into each other's arms from end to end with about twenty feet between them, gathering a large crowd of onlookers in the process.[18]

They went on to 'Romsey-in-the-mud', but business was so poor that they were near starvation. Three of the children, including Walter, were sent home from school because William could not afford the 2d. a week fee for schooling.[19] From Romsey, they returned to Dorchester again, William advertising for actors in the The Era in August and September.[20] When no recruits materialised, for the second time William closed the theatre and reverted to marionettes. Walter heard him say to a Police Sergeant who was watching him at work carving the figures, 'I can put these actors away and take them out when I want them. They will get no pay, and they will always be sober', 'something', Walter comments, 'not always the case among live actors!' But the marionettes were equally unsuccessful, the problem being the lack of money in the countryside,[21] and during 1888 and 1889, the Haggars' fortunes fluctuated. Returning to the theatre in Thornbury,[22] they did well there, but badly in Swindon. William engaged in another sideline, returning to making picture frames to supplement their meagre income: these were sought after, not for photographs, but for illuminated texts given by tradesmen to their customers at Christmas, 'The Rock of Ages', 'The Lord's Prayer', 'The Creed' and quotations from speeches by Mr. Gladstone[23] being particularly popular. From Swindon they went on to Wotton-under-Edge, Stroud, and Ledbury, in Herefordshire. At Ludlow in July 1889, Henry,[24] William and Sarah's seventh and last son, was born: he was named after Harry Lloydall, who was still with the company. From there, they toured the Forest of Dean.[25]

The next year, in April 1890, they were back in the same territory, at Chepstow. The theatre was pitched on 'The Meads', a flat grassy area near the mouth of the River Wye, close to the landing stage where P. & A. Campbell's paddle steamers disembarked excursion passengers who had to pass the theatre on their way to the town; but their stay at Chepstow of only about forty minutes was too short for them to attend any performances.[26] William organised a cricket team, made up of members of the company, to play the local cricket club, all the Haggar team being dressed as Ally Sloper, a character in a popular comic, and his family. The gate receipts were given to charity.[27] There was also, as usual during an extended stay, a charity gala performance in the theatre.[28] A special souvenir programme was printed on silk for Major Fothergill Evans, the Patron.[29] The performance comprised

'The Sparkling Comedy entitled **The Test of Truth**; Songs by Mr. W. Haggar Sen.,[30] and the celebrated laughable farce, **The Quiet Family'**.

But before the laughter had died away, a tragedy befell the family. Nell, the apple of her father's eye, slipped out of the living wagon early one morning, and was never seen alive again. The story is told in the account of the inquest reported in the *Chepstow Weekly* Advertiser:[31]

> On Tuesday morning of last week, a girl named Ellen Haggar, the daughter of William Haggar, proprietor of a travelling theatre at present located at Chepstow, left her home, a caravan on the Meads, near the River Wye. Subsequently her boots and stockings were found on the river bank, and her hat in the water. An old grey peaked cap and a couple of odd stage shoes were missing, and it was thought probable that the leaving of the shoes &c. on the river bank was a ruse on the part of the girl, and that she had probably gone to Bristol or Hereford, or some other place where the company had been staying. Enquiries were instituted by the police, but without avail. On Monday afternoon, however, at between two and three o'clock, the body of the unfortunate girl was found in the river.

> The first witness, Wm. Haggar, deposed: I am the father of the deceased Ellen Haggar. I last saw her alive on Tuesday morning last at about half past seven o'clock; she was then in her usual health and spirits. We had a performance at the Theatre that evening. She took part in the performance on the previous evening, and was to have done so that evening. The deceased went out in the morning to procure provisions and milk for breakfast, and brought them back. She had not been away twenty minutes before we missed her. At about nine o'clock I heard my wife scream, and upon going out saw her coming up from the direction of the landing stage, with the boots and stockings in her hand. My wife said, "Here's Nellie's boots and stockings on the mud, and her hat is in the water." With that, we ran at all speed down to the

landing stage. There were prints of her naked feet going towards the landing stage, till the mud was two or three inches deep, and then as though she had returned to the bank. We were on the landing stage and saw her hat in the water. The tide was running at the time.

William concluded with the statement, 'I have always treated my daughter with the utmost kindness. My wife is the girl's own mother. I know no reason why the girl should destroy herself.' Sarah's testimony reiterated this point: 'I did not chastise her. I did not speak harshly to her. We lived happily with her. I had no reason to suppose that she had anything on her mind that might lead her to destroy herself.' After hearing other witnesses, the coroner addressed the jury. 'Every day they heard of suicides, but that such a child — she was only 13 — as the deceased should commit suicide seemed extraordinary. There was no evidence of suicide; she might have fallen into the water accidentally; how she got there was only known to One. The only verdict he thought they could come to was "Found drowned". The jury returned a verdict of "Found drowned in the River Wye".'

They shook the mud of Chepstow off their feet. But to go back to England was to return to the lands of the agricultural depression. Sarah had a different idea. Twenty years before, she had accompanied her parents on a tour of Monmouthshire. Perhaps the Haggars should now try the South Wales Valleys. 'Wild Wales' it had been to George Borrow of Norwich, when he toured it on foot in 1854. Painting sombre pictures of the South Wales scenery, he compared an ironworks working on a Sunday next to the ruins of Neath Abbey to Hieronymus Bosch's *Last Judgment*, and marvelled at the glare from the burning dross of a large forge in Merthyr Vale, lighting his way in the dark.[32]

Thirty-six years later, Borrow would have seen yet more industrial activity, and much more coal-mining than he describes. To every valley had come the pit, the railway, the chapel, the rugby pitch, and the male voice choir. Speculative builders flung jerry-built terraces up the steep sides of the narrow valleys to house the vastly increased population: during the thirty years 1871-1901, the population of the United Kingdom grew by nearly a third, from 31.8 to 41.9 millions, and South Wales, with its booming industry, had a disproportionately large share in this increase. In the Rhondda Valley, only 16 miles long, there were at one time no fewer than 53 working collieries, and its population increased from less than 1,000 in 1851 to 169,000 in 1924. This boom was a result of local initiative: the Cyfartha Fawr iron works in Merthyr, which Borrow visited, belonged, he reports, to the Crawshays, a family 'distinguished by a strange kind of eccentricity, but also by genius and enterprising spirit, and by such a strict feeling of honour that it is a common saying that the word of any one of them is as good as the bond of other people.'[33] The same was true of the railways: each valley had, at that time, its own company, formed to carry coal from the pits to the Bristol Channel Ports of Newport, Cardiff, Penarth, Barry and Swansea, and named for its location: the Taff Vale Railway, the Rhymney Railway, and the Burry Port and Gwendraeth Valley Light Railway, for example. During the decade 1871 to 1881, Great Britain raised 1,305 million tons of coal, out of 2,855 million tons mined worldwide. British coal production was 373 tons per miner in 1871, rising to 403 tons per miner in 1881, although in 1891 it fell back to 358 tons. Exports of coal rose rapidly in the same period, from 12 million tons in 1870 to 29 millions in 1889, by far the greatest in the world. South Wales coal was especially suitable for smelting and for export, but mining there was developed by large concerns, taking over from the original family-owned pits, with no personal relationships between masters and men – which stored up trouble for the future.[34] An advertisement for Poole's Theatres in 1904 catches the excitement of the times: 'Opera house, Treherbert: another fine theatre. Extensive building going on opposite. The pits sunk, coal found. Directly they start, the population doubles. Now good, then excellent.'[35] Such was the booming South Wales to which the Haggars now turned. Their new prosperity gave William the opportunity he had been awaiting:

There was a well-known saying, 'Stick to the coal', and this proved true, for there was money there. Business was so good that the 'shares' were sometimes as much as 7s. 6d., the result of this being that the actors were nearly always drunk! They would be incapable of acting their parts – what happened? Two weeks' Notice on the notice board. Nobody left, they recommenced on salaries, say

26

30s. and 25s. each, or 35 shillings joint. So the salaries were established, they never went back to share terms, and there was only one recognised boss: W. Haggar, senior, whereas in the 'commonwealth' days, everyone shared, so everyone bossed, hence they were always arguing.[36]

Since 1871, William had been, first, an apprentice, learning his trade as comedian and scenery–painter. Next, he had provided the portable theatre, and, with it, the organisation needed to attract a company to him. But the actors had still been free to turn up or not as they pleased, and the democratic nature of the 'commonwealth' system had meant that he could not rely on their following his lead. Now, as employer, he was undeniably in charge of their fortunes. His word was law.

The Haggars were not by any means the only theatre company touring South Wales. Others there at about this time included Jackson's Victoria Theatre, Edward Ebley's Palace of Varieties, John E. Noakes, who was at one time in Aberdare for as long as two years, and built the Royalty Theatre in Llanelly, and the Alexandra Theatre, based in Bargoed. Cedric Price, recalling these and others, preserves memories of William Haggar's travels through South Wales, from Haverfordwest to Abergavenny. At Porth, his theatre was erected in front of the Llwyncelyn Hotel; at Tonypandy on the Pandy Field; at Llwynypia in the Partridge Field; and at Ferndale on the Salisbury Ground. Its nearness to the public houses gave the nonconformists cause for complaint. When their playhouse was burned down in Neath, the Haggars procured more timber, and set to work on a Monday morning to refashion and rebuild: they opened again the following Saturday night. In addition, they were always ready to tour the Halls of South Wales, whenever that course would pay them better than travelling with their portable theatres.[37]

They stayed with Mr. Golightly at the Bridge End Inn in Ebbw Vale for six months, their repertoire, arranged to last four months, being prolonged by playing the better productions for two nights running, instead of the usual one night. From Ebbw Vale, they moved to Tredegar, where, once again, business was terrific. It was in Tredegar that, in March 1891, Walter recalled that before the end of the play, William had to go on stage and address the audience: 'Ladies and Gentlemen, if any of you have any distance to go, please leave immediately, there are nine inches of snow on the ground.' By the next morning, only the roofs of houses could be seen emerging from the snow: it had been the greatest snowstorm of the nineteenth century.[38] It was in Tredegar, too, that Fred Haggar signalled his independence: in March 1891 he was in lodgings on his own; next year, in March 1892, although he was only 19, he married Catherine Waldron, also 19, the daughter of an Abertillery writer. Fred and Catherine then went off on their own,[39] and it was to be ten years before the Haggars saw much of them again.

Lily May, the Haggars' youngest child, was born in Brynmawr on 2 June 1891, the family's next venue after Tredegar: the living vans were parked in the Coal Yard, and ever afterwards Lily was jokingly referred to as 'Coalyard Lil'![40] It was just a year after Nell's death, and Lily liked to think that she had helped to heal her father's heartbreak over Nell: 'indeed, I think I did take her place in his affections to some extent', Lily wrote.[41] During these years the earliest surviving family photographs were taken. First comes one from 1889, of William with 2-year-old Violet, looking curiously elderly in a cap or beret, and at the same time the image of her father. Next there is a picture of the three youngest boys, Walter, Archie and Henry, taken in 1892 against a background of a castle amid mountains and a lake, either scenery for a play, or a standard background in William's 'Castle Theatre',[42] beside which William had put up his photographic studio as another money-making sideline. Sadly, in 1895, when still only twelve, Archie was to contract tuberculosis: he died during one of the theatre's stays in Tonypandy. Lastly from these years, there is a photo of Lily, aged about two (she claimed), sitting on a chair with her feet barely touching the ground, holding a bunch of flowers, grasses and ferns. The picture is edged with the caption, W. Haggar, Photographer, Castle Theatre Studio: Lily well remembered posing for it.[43] She took after her mother in looks, although, in old age, in a photo taken in the 1960s, she and Violet look like twins.

Things were now going so well that William decided to run a second portable theatre, which the company constructed. It was sent out under the direction of Will Haggar Junior, who, in January

1893, at Tonypandy, married Jane Emily Silverton, aged 19 and already an experienced actress, always known as Jenny from her stage name Jenny Lindon.[44] From then on they had their own theatre for much of the time, although they kept in close touch with William and were to co-operate in the making of many films. William and Sarah stayed in Tonypandy for eighteen months during 1893/4, their repertoire once again being prolonged, this time by the employment of a different cast every six months. From Tonypandy in 1895 they went to Llanelly for the whole of the winter, but, Walter reports, they did not even cover their expenses. So they returned to the coal district in the Rhondda Valley and Treorchy, where business immediately revived and cash was plentiful once more. Meanwhile, the second theatre had visited Pontypool, Cwmbran, Blaenavon, and Tonpentre, where it was sold. Will Junior joined forces again with William at Aberavon, which then had a population of only about 5,000, but was about to expand greatly, due to the construction of the new Margam Docks. The town was full of labourers anxious to spend their wages: the theatre did so well there that William packed up the portable theatre on its trucks and took the actors on a thirteen week tour to the various halls in the mountain valleys, two nights here and three nights there, throughout a vast area and even as far as Pembrokeshire.[45]

Back in Aberavon for the winter, they had a great success with the pantomime **Cinderella**. Lily remembered that her father had painted the scenery with silver and gold leaf, which could then be bought in booklets similar to books of stamps. The transformation scene was particularly memorable. Huge silver and gilt fans, made in two halves, were held together by a girl behind each one. The girls, dressed in different national costumes, at a certain cue would drop the fans and emerge from behind them, to perform a dance. The company also had an orchestra, usually a violin, piano, cornet and drums. Walter, who learnt to play the violin,was also a very fine actor, and, wrote Lily, 'had the best brain in the family. In spite of Father's knowledge of acting and photography, I do not think he would have got as far as he did in the world of moving pictures without Walter's help.'[46]

For the new season of 1897, William built a new 'Castle Theatre'. It played at Aberavon, Treorchy, Ferndale, and back in Aberavon again.[47] That summer, just before Lily was sent to her grandmother Elizabeth for schooling, her father had become interested in the new moving pictures:

> He had heard that they had been shown in Cardiff as a novelty in the 'Panopticon' in St. Mary's Street, advertised as a new invention by the late Sir Oswald Stoll in 1895. Father became more and more interested in them, and was running around to London, Birmingham, and anywhere else where he hoped he could see these new moving films, and he decided to launch into it himself. But machines, as they were called in those days, were very scarce, and the moving pictures themselves were very few indeed. There were only half a dozen films available at the most, and the running time of these was only about ten minutes. All Father's friends advised him against changing over to moving pictures, saying that it was a mere flash in the pan and would not last; but he was an actor and photographer and could see the possibilities of this new medium of entertainment, and would not be dissuaded.[48]

Now Walter's account takes over, with a graphic description of his family's first acquaintance with a cinematograph:

> It was September 1897, at the Market Place in Aberavon. My father was a subscriber to a photographic periodical called 'Focus'.[49] In this there were several technical articles dealing with animated photography, and its use and application for various purposes including entertainment. One day while reading this publication, Mr. Haggar saw an advertisement for the sale of a Cinematograph and Triunial Lantern,[50] including the gas cylinders, regulators, gauges, lantern slides, films, etc., the whole for £80. Away went Mr. Haggar to Exeter, and came back with the outfit, all agog with excitement and very nearly broke, because £80 in those days was a lot of money - and it was a cash transaction paid in gold. The most important thing in this equipment was the instruction book. I would like to point out that my father was an actor with a portable theatre, who had never seen or handled a gas cylinder. The light used to project films in those days

was limelight. This comprised two gases, oxygen and hydrogen, under pressure in their cylinders, impinging on the lime (the lime being a cone about the size of a cotton reel), the result being a brilliant white light known as limelight. This of course went out of fashion years ago.[51]

My father arrived from Exeter with the new equipment, and with the aid of my brother, Mr. James Haggar, erected it on the stage behind the backdrop. They patted it and fondled it, and then had to take it down and put it back in its cases as it was time for opening the theatre. Repeat process next day, having another look at it. On the third or fourth day, with the aid of the very important instruction book, they pursued a little further. 'What did the instruction book say?' (Father). 'First turn on the hydrogen - the red tab.' 'Have you got the cylinder key?' 'Here it is, Dad.' 'Right, turn on the hydrogen - red cylinder. Have you got the instruction book, what is next?' 'Light the hydrogen on a low gas.' 'Got a match?' 'No, Dad.' Out went Jim for a match. All this time the lantern which houses the limelight is filling with that highly combustible gas, hydrogen. When Jim finally arrived back with the matches, they applied one to this miniature bomb, result 'bang' and panic. Shouts of 'Shut off the cylinders'. Palpitating hearts, utter darkness, then, 'What did you do?' 'Nothing, I only struck a match!' said Jim.[52]

They tried again, only to cause another explosion, not realising that the gas in the cylinders was at very high pressure.

However, they were not daunted by their two panics, although they were getting very much afraid by now; but like good troupers (and having paid £80 for the outfit) there was nothing left but to get on with it. So rehearsal number 3 took place. This time they took the precaution of warming the gas pipes to ensure that they did not blow under pressure: it was getting obvious that these gases were under pressure and had to be controlled. Very well, out came the inevitable instruction book at the same page. They turned on the hydrogen gently, lit it, let it warm up the lime, and then gently lit the oxygen. After various attempts, they got the right mixture of the two gases, got a good light, and projected it onto a screen.

This took them nearly a fortnight. They were quite elated to get a good light, even going so far as to turn the cinematograph handle to see the thing flicker. After weeks of experimenting with the aid of the instruction book, and a great deal of perseverance, they were able to run a film. Included in the outfit from Exeter were 13 or 14 films of varying lengths - 50 ft., 75 ft., and the longest being 100 feet. There were no spools, no reels, just a naked film, running at one foot per second. We had **The turn-out of the London Fire Brigade**,[53] **A Boxing Match, Lõie Fuller dancing**,[54] **Train emerging from a tunnel**, etc.[55] I remember one gentleman saying to my father, 'All you need to complete your collection of films is a rough sea.'[56] Try to visualise, whoever reads this, that in those days acted films were never thought of: one had an animated picture camera, and anything that was animated was the subject of a film.

We were progressing, getting more experience, and we were now confident enough to invite the local doctor, the vicar, and one or two friends to a private exhibition of our latest acquisition of the entertainment world, the cinematograph.[57] I operated the projector and showed **All Hell!**[58] - and was at once reprimanded and told to use a better one, the Vicar was present. A first class show was given, and compliments from all were received.[59]

This success persuaded William to leave his theatrical career, and pin his hopes on the cinema. Turning over the Castle Theatre to Will Junior, he made himself a small portable show, painted to resemble Windsor Castle, and called 'The Windsor Castle Biograph'. On the morning of 5 April 1898 William and his sons pushed this show on two light trolleys onto Harry Studt's fairground in Aberavon.[60] His debut as a film exhibitor was at hand.

Before proceeding with the story of that debut, however, it will be appropriate, in the next chapter, to consider the context in which he was now to operate, by describing the early British cinema, and the part in it played by the fairground bioscope shows.

4. The early cinema and the fairground

IT WOULD DOUBTLESS SEEM strange if upon a screen a portrait of a person were projected, and this picture slowly became of an animated character, opened its mouth and began to talk, accompanied by an ever-changing countenance, including the formation of the mouth as each peculiar sound is uttered; or if instead of one head, two were produced, and an argument gone through with all the turns and twists of the head incidental to each.

It would also appear curious to have a street scene depicted upon the screen, and for the spectators to witness the various horses and vehicles running past in all directions, persons walking to and fro, and dogs running along, all at varying speeds and with life-like motion. Imagine the sensation that would be produced if the whole of the recent Lord Mayor's Show were to be presented upon a screen exactly as seen by a person stationed at one particular point looking across the street. The houses on the opposite side would remain stationary, and the procession would pass along, each minute movement as if it actually took place at this given point being represented.

The name of Friese-Greene, the eminent photographer of Brook Street, W, will become familiar throughout the land in connection with an invention by which all these effects can be produced.[1]

Friese-Greene had taken his first film on celluloid of the scene at Hyde Park Corner. A year later, having photographed the traffic in Kings Road, Chelsea, on a hundred-foot strip of celluloid, he showed the film at the British Photographic Convention, on 26 June 1890. But, although he is credited with the invention of the movie-camera, Friese-Greene was not the inventor of the cinema.

William Friese-Greene was born in Bristol on 7 September 1855, and attended Queen Elizabeth's Hospital, the Bluecoat School founded in 1586 on the model of Christ's Hospital at Horsham in Sussex. He wore the school boarders' uniform of long blue 'gown', white bands, leather girdle, knee-breeches, long yellow stockings and stout black shoes. He left school on his fourteenth birthday, to be apprenticed to a Bath photographer. Moving to London, he initiated advances in photographic techniques, culminating in his moving pictures taken in the years 1888-90. He remained well-known: Esme Collings, a Brighton photographer who made films in 1896-7, advertised on his shop front that he was 'formerly in partnership with Mr. Friese-Greene'. Yet Greene advanced no further, and was overtaken by the later pioneers. He then fell on hard times. In 1916, an appeal to the film industry was made on his behalf: it raised only £136 0s. 2d. On 5 May 1921, he attended a meeting about the future of the British film industry, which was at that time, as so often since, in dire straits. Rising from his seat in the body of the hall, he made an impassioned plea for the continuance of film-making in this country. The audience is said to have been deeply swayed. He sat down. Presently, his neighbour leant forward to speak to him, and discovered to his horror that Friese-Greene was dead. It was found that he had 1s. 10d. on him - all the money he had in the world.[2]

Not unnaturally, Americans regard the American citizen, Thomas Alva Edison, as the inventor of the cinema - and as there have been more American histories of the cinema than British versions, this has come to be widely accepted. Edison was a prolific inventor: at one time he had over 1000 patents for inventions of all kinds, including the phonograph and the electric light bulb, and he did develop moving pictures. His Kinetoscope was introduced in 1894, with the help of W.K.L. Dickson, who also took the photographs for it. It was an individual film-viewing machine: a kind of 'what the butler saw' movie machine for one viewer, the show taking about a minute. Animated pictures were mounted on an endless belt; the customer put a coin in a slot and looked through an eyepiece onto the film as it revolved. Film subjects varied from spectaculars (Buffalo Bill and his troupe) to made-up films such as **The Kiss**. Initially there was an enormous demand for them, but they could not withstand the challenge of the cinema, and ultimately they and their cousins, the 'Mutoscopes' survived only at the end of the seaside pier. Edison went in for individual viewing because he had not been able to solve the problem of jerkiness when trying to project pictures from a moving film onto a screen. He never did solve this problem, and, although he later made and commissioned films, it was not until others had made the necessary discoveries.[3]

It was, in fact, the Lumières in France, and R. W. Paul in England who solved that problem. Antoine Lumière had a factory for manufacturing photographic plates; his sons Auguste and Louis assisted him. On 28 December 1895 they unveiled, to a large audience, their Cinématographe. A box on a tripod, it worked by turning a handle to project. Motion picture projection and the cinema was born, although their method of projection was not to achieve long-term success. Their associate Felicien Trewey brought the Cinématographe to London, showing films commercially for the first time at the Regent Street Polytechnic on 20 February 1896. The show included **The Biter Bit, Arrival of a Train in a Country Station, Fall of a Wall**, and **Bathing in the Mediterranean**. After that, it transferred to the Empire Music Hall, Leicester Square, where it ran for eighteen months.[4]

Meanwhile, Robert Paul, an optician and manufacturer of scientific instruments, having bought one of Edison's Kinetoscopes in 1894, had begun making and selling them. Edison's inventions were not patented in England. Paul realised that Edison's continuous reel could not show true moving pictures. In seeing movement, the eye is, so to speak, deceived. When we look at a film, what we see is a succession of separate pictures ('frames', nowadays 18 of them to a foot length of 35mm film), projected so rapidly, in those early days at about 1 foot per second, that we perceive them to be continuous and moving: this phenomenon is called 'persistence of vision'.[5] Paul needed a device to hold each frame for a fraction of a second, to make the film clearer, and prevent the blurring caused by continuous movement; coupled with a shutter to cut off the light between each frame, to prevent flicker. His solution was to build in to the projector a small wheel cut in the shape of a Maltese cross. As it revolved, a pinion fell into the cut-out portions of the wheel, and held the strip of film motionless for the fraction of a second which was all that was necessary. By coincidence, Paul first publicly demonstrated his film projection on the very same day, 20 February 1896, that Trewey showed the Lumières'

Cinématographe: and it is his Maltese cross method, rather than the Lumières' claw jerking the film forward, which has been used ever since.[6]

The world beat a path to Paul's door to buy his projector. Cecil Hepworth[7] joked that to get up the stairs to Paul's office, you had to go 'stumbling over the bodies of dozens of Poles and Armenians who had been sleeping there for days awaiting delivery of projection machines'.[8] Edison, however, intervened. Realising that Paul had used his invention, he sought to block it; but when that move failed, he cut off the supply of his films. This forced Paul to make his own - at first in 40 foot lengths for the Kinetoscopes, and then films of the same length and double it for cinema projection. Later, these sizes were rationalised to 50 and 100 feet. Paul took some of his own films, but was also reliant on Birt Acres, an experienced photographer. Acres shot the first moving pictures throughout England and Wales - two trawlers, for example, captured from the end of Gorleston pier in 1896,[9] and the Industrial Exhibition in Cardiff, also in 1896. Paul filmed street scenes in Cardiff in the same year. At about the same time, the American Charles Urban[10] arrived in London to sell Edison products. Paul and Urban between them set up the first distribution systems for selling both films and equipment - at first the original Edison and Lumière models, and then their own developments and improvements. They were soon joined by the French firm Gaumont, set up in this country by A.C. Bromhead and T.A. Welsh.[11]

Word of the new inventions was spread through trade magazines and trade fairs: the World's Fair in Brussels in 1897, and later in Islington, and the Great Exhibition in Paris in 1900. Soon, everyone was making films, particularly professional photographers and dealers in photographic equipment, who made films to demonstrate their products. In the words of Tom Lehrer 60 years later, 'You just stand there looking cute, and when something moves, you shoot!' If it moved, they shot it. Rough seas, and trains emerging from tunnels were particularly popular, as were sports (the Derby was filmed every year from 1895), fire engines, and anything to do with the Royal Family: no less than 64 films have been traced of parts of Queen Victoria's Diamond Jubilee procession in 1897.[12]

The first cinema tragedy happened in 1897, when a projector caught fire at the Bazaar de la Chariété in Paris. The fire became an inferno: 73 people were burnt to death, many of them French nobility or people holding high places in society at that time. The operator, using limelight with an ether saturator, had attempted to recharge the saturator; it exploded, setting fire to the films which were loose in a basket. 'This sad event caused a widespread fear of such disasters', recalled Paul later.[13] Reports of smaller fires became commonplace: it was after one such, which destroyed his stock, that William Haggar first met Charles Urban. Eventually this hazard was to lead to the passing, in 1909, of the Cinematograph Act, enforcing safety measures.

The first 'made-up' fiction films began to appear: Paul photographed **The Soldier's Courtship**, the first comedy film, and Collings[14] made **The Broken Melody**, the first film of a London stage actor. Films were made of stage and music-hall personalities: **Miss Ellen Terry taking tea** and Mr. Dan Leno's music-hall turns. Many short slapstick comedies were made, lasting only a minute or two, about contests between millers and sweeps, for instance, and about eating macaroni or spaghetti. Films about bathers and their misfortunes or pranks were legion. Early film-makers found that their audiences had an unbounded appetite for comedy. Charlie Chaplin, in 1922, gave an insight into his practice, which is also applicable to the earlier silent comedies:

> The mere fact of a hat being blown away isn't funny in itself. What is, is to see its owner running after it, with his hair blown about and his coat tails flying. A man is walking along the street - that doesn't lend itself to laughter. But placed in a ridiculous and embarrassing position, the human being becomes a cause of laughter to his fellow-creatures. Every comic situation is based on that. And comic films had immediate success because most of them showed policemen falling down drain-holes, stumbling into whitewash pails, falling out of carts, and put to all kinds of botheration. Here are people who stand for the dignity of power being made ridiculous and getting laughed at, and the sight of their mishaps makes the public want to laugh

twice as much as if it were only ordinary citizens undergoing the same transformation. And still funnier is the person in a ludicrous position who, in spite of it all, refuses to admit that anything out of the ordinary is happening, and is obstinate in preserving his dignity. That is why all my films rest on the idea of getting myself into awkward situations, so as to give me the chance of being desperately serious in my attempts to look like a very normal little gentleman.[15]

Chaplin was inheriting a tradition reaching back to the earliest films: William Haggar, for instance, made **Whitewashing the Policeman** in 1903.

The early cinema was a litigious business, as inventors and entrepreneurs fought to protect their rights. William Haggar was a key witness in a High Court case in 1904, testifying that the term 'Bioscope' was in common use, when the Warwick Trading Co. would have prevented Charles Urban, setting up on his own, from using this name.[16] From 1903 to 1908, the United States was so involved in litigation, as Edison fought to protect his patents, that it could produce very few films. The US Congress under President McKinley even passed protectionist legislation imposing import duty on foreign films and equipment. Although this handicapped British exports, it did result in British film-makers being protected from American competition during these formative years.

After the first flush of enthusiasm - by 1899 some 30 people or firms had made films for exhibition in this country[17] - many early producers concluded that filming was not for them. During the next six or seven years, the stage was left to the real pioneers, a mere ten individuals or partnerships[18] who, alongside the entrepreneurs Urban and Bromhead, constituted the British film industry until much more money was attracted by the realisation that profits were to be made, and film-making became a big business, carried on by companies rather than by individuals. Building on the foundations laid by 1900, and, gradually developing their own techniques and acquiring the first studios, these pioneers produced more and more topical films, newsreels, films on scientific subjects, comedies, thrillers and trick films, at first mostly lasting only one or two minutes, but gradually lengthening as equipment to handle them was invented and improved. Travelling showmen up and down the country were also producing their own films, William Haggar being noted by historians of the period because his films achieved wide circulation through Gaumont, which included his name in later catalogues.[19] Although other showmen made short topical films, Haggar was the only pioneer to make fiction films primarily to exhibit direct to the public in his own show, rather than to sell on to someone else to exhibit.

Thirty years later, in 1936, three of these pioneers entertained the British Kinematograph Society with anecdotes of the early days.[20] Robert Paul recalled that customers for his first projectors

> came from nearly every country and beset the office with their interpreters, while each insisted on waiting until a projector could be finished. Four Turks, speaking little English, came daily for weeks, put on their slippers, and practised. Finally, they found that the attractiveness of night life in London had led to the complete exhaustion of their financial resources. A gentleman from Spain, anxious to return quickly, proved too impatient to learn how to centre the arc light, and left with his projector, unboxed, in a cab. Arriving in Barcelona, his first attempt at projection failed, so the disappointed audience threw knives at the screen and wrecked the theatre. He himself retired to serve a term in a Spanish prison.

Cecil Hepworth remembered difficulties showing the first films in church halls.

> I had a difficult experience in a large hall built underneath a church, where the parson had at the last moment asked to see my programme. Now I had just acquired the then topical film of the big Corbett and Fitzsimmons fight, and put it, of course, in the place of honour near the end of the first reel, and it was to this film that the reverend gentleman took exception. I was at my wits' end to know what to do, but at last, in sheer desperation, I did the only thing I could think of. I never thought I should get away with it, but I did! I called it 'The Historic Combat between

David and Goliath!' Believe me, or believe me not, everyone was completely pleased and satisfied, especially the parson, who said in his speech afterwards that he had no idea that the cinematograph had been invented so long.

Hepworth later told the same story, but of the film of Löie Fuller dancing her serpentine dance: this time, he told the parson that it was Salome dancing before Herod.[21]

Will Barker[22] emphasized the importance of getting topical films to the public as quickly as possible. He remembered developing film of the Grand National in the luggage van of the train back to London, and another film maker tearing along Holborn at eight miles per hour in a hansom cab, with the film flying out of the window to dry in the wind, before reaching the theatre where it was to be shown. A film of the entire Boat Race was on show a mere 90 minutes after the end of the race.[23] Speedy production techniques also produced economies when funds were low:

Here's how we prepared **Hamlet** in 22 scenes, and, with the exception of Ophelia floating down the river on a raft of flowers, we did the whole job in one day in one reel. For about three weeks beforehand the scenic artists had been painting the scenery, and all being ready to take, and having arranged with a man - who knew the part - to play Hamlet, we turn up the 'rogues gallery' of photos of all the artists who applied to us for work. Any who wanted more than 10s. per day was NOT written to. Well, we got the artists into the studio at 8.30 in the morning. I stand on a chair and look the lot over. 'Here', I say, 'you're nice and tall: you can play the Ghost. Can any lady swim?' A hand goes up. 'You will play Ophelia, Miss', and that's how Polonius, the Queen and all the other characters were chosen. Now a rush to the dressing-rooms, and we are shooting our first scenes before 10 o'clock. We stop for coffee and bread and cheese for 20 minutes about one, and before four in the afternoon all have been paid and are on their way home. So confident were we of our lighting - daylight - that we made no provision for retakes!

From the first, films had been exhibited in places of working-class entertainment: the Lumières' show running at the Leicester Square Empire and Paul's at the Alhambra opposite. For the first ten years, Music Halls, the fairgrounds and the 'penny gaff' were almost the only places where films could be seen, the films made, therefore, reflecting this. By 1906 filming in Britain had, after its early exuberance, reached a plateau, where it had become stuck in a rut. Numbers of non-fiction films had declined from a peak of 450 per year in 1899 and 1900, to an average of 250 or so by 1905. The number of fiction films made had reached 250 a year by 1905, but stayed at about that level until 1907. Compilations and accumulations of very short films apart, the longest films had reached 700 feet by 1905, but the great majority remained much shorter, lasting five minutes at most.[24] Now that the novelty had worn off, there came a time when the popularity of the cinematograph as a music-hall turn was on the wane: it seemed that films were good only for 'chasers', to be turned on as the audience was filing out. As A.C. Bromhead recalled in 1908, 'How many of us remember the time, which after all is but a few years since, when it was the custom, even with those actively engaged in some department of the cinematograph or entertaining business, to imagine that this fascinating form of amusement was of an ephemeral nature, and would very quickly live out its little life and pass into the realms of extreme minor importance.'[25] It is to the fairground showmen that the film owes its ultimate success, for the new toy, a passing fancy in the music-halls, became a firmly established feature of the fairgrounds. It was those showmen who, demonstrating that money was to be made from exhibiting films, and providing regular custom for the film-makers, kept the industry afloat until, from 1907 onwards, more capital was put into building the first permanent cinemas, where audiences could watch longer films in comfort.[26]

In the early nineteenth century, showfolk often lived in tented homes, travelling either on foot or by horse or donkey. By the 1830s, improvements in lifestyle took place with the move to horse drawn living wagons. Their style evolved by cooperation between showmen and construction firms. Designs derived from farm wagons predated, in this country, similar adaptations by travelling gypsies. The typical living wagon was built on a four wheel trailer chassis and would contain three rooms, a parlour, a bedroom, and a second bedroom or kitchen.[27]

As the century wore on, the pace of invention increased, more of the population lived in towns and cities, and trading methods changed. This greatly affected the traditional fairs, mostly established in the Middle Ages: many of them faded away, or were terminated as nuisances. The 1871 Fairs Act condemned fairs as unnecessary and 'the cause of grievous immorality': it enabled local authorities and landowners to take steps to close fairs, and many did. In the county of Somerset, there were 180 fairs in 1729, and more later: only 34 remained in the 1930s. But the popularity of the entertainment provided by the fairs grew as their trading activities decreased: hiring labour at the Mops all but ceased, but many survived to become purely pleasure fairs. In Yorkshire the so-called 'Feasts' had been in imminent danger of extinction by the middle of the nineteenth century, but fifty years later, they were thriving again, the popularity of the travelling shows and roundabouts having saved them. With shops closed and pubs open, the 'Feasts' provided for many a welcome light relief in an otherwise drab existence.

By 1900 the fair was accompanied by roundabouts and helter-skelters, boxing booths, travelling theatres and ghost shows, shooting galleries and menageries. Sideshows of all kinds exhibited freaks, midgets and bearded ladies, and held coconut shies, puppet shows, performing dogs and monkeys, hurdy-gurdy men and fortune tellers. A big change came about when showmen began to buy their own traction engines. Before that, if they wanted electricity, they used a portable lighting set, such sets being built by Savages of Kings Lynn. At first their traction engines were not fitted with dynamo brackets, because of the weight: instead they would set a dynamo, weighing nearly a ton, on a flat truck and couple the steam engine up to it with a belt, as the farmers did when threshing. Later, the engines were fitted with brackets at the front, to carry the dynamo on the engine. This led to the development of the showman's engine's canopy, to protect the dynamo from rain and prevent the belt from slipping. Once these engines were established, far more power was available, and rides could become ever more spectacular.

Visitors to the fair nowadays may be only subconsciously aware of the role of decorated showfronts. The importance of eye-catching size, style and content in attracting custom is well recognised by the showmen themselves. The grandest era for large carved and painted fronts at the fair came with the advent of the first moving picture shows, from the 1890s until the outbreak of war in 1914. These colourful fronts with their associated fair organs drew the customers in crowds, and acted as the introduction to the entertainment conducted in the darkened interior of the show. Music formed an accompaniment to the roundabout right from the start. In the mid-1800s, this would be provided by a small group of musicians, but the demand for mechanical fair organs had increased by the 1890s. European organ manufacturers were the dominant suppliers for the UK, the most prolific of these being the Gavioli and Marenghi companies, from Paris. Charles Marenghi had been Ludovico Gavioli's foreman, but in 1903 he broke away to found his own firm.

The Victorians were fond of displaying their learning, christening new inventions with made-up words taken from Ancient Greek. Many such words are so familiar that we do not stop to consider them: for example, 'photograph', from 'phos' meaning 'light' and 'graphe' meaning 'picture', and 'telescope' from 'tele' meaning 'distant' and 'scopeo' meaning 'to see'. When moving pictures were invented, the Greek words for 'moving object' ('kinema'), 'living' ('bio'), and the Latin for 'changing' ('muto') were added to these combinations, thus producing 'kinetoscope' and 'kinematograph', 'biograph' and 'bioscope', and 'mutoscope', in addition to more unusual combinations such as Paul's 'Theatrograph', or 'picture-show'. On the fairground, 'bioscope' or 'living-picture' caught on, and became common parlance for the fairground cinema shows, no matter what grandiose names were used by individual showmen.

Although some travelling theatres gave performances at the larger fairs (William Haggar was supposed to have visited Neath Fair with his portable theatre in the 1890s), the main fairground precursor of the bioscope was the ghost show. John Henry Pepper had patented his 'apparatus for exhibiting dramatic and other performances' in 1863, and soon displays of 'phantasmagoria' and the like became very popular. Biddall's

Ghost Show called itself a 'Phantomspectre and Ghostodrama' show. Illusions were created by positioning a large sheet of plate glass on a stage, fixed at an angle of 45° to the audience. Behind it, backlit actors, hidden from the audience, created ghostly apparitions, reflected in the glass: an old showman remembered that 'my big thing was ghost business. People cottoned on to ghosts done in a slap-up manner, with low lights and creepy music and red fire, when the goblins came climbing up gilt poles and sliding down 'em, and appearing and disappearing with a fiendish smile. Why, I got almost to believe in ghosts myself, such was the cleverness with which they were done.'[28]

Throughout the 1880s and into the 1890s the ghost shows continued to expand, until they were the most spectacular of all the fairground shows. Randall Williams, called 'the King of Showmen' by the Rev. Thomas Horne, the showmen's chaplain, had a famous ghost show, including conjuring acts, illusion shows and dancing girls, as well as the ghosts and goblins of the grand finale. He did so well with this that by 1890 he became the first showman to use a traction engine: a new Fowler engine which he bought in 1895 cost £712 8s. 0d.[29] But by the middle of the 1890s, ghost shows were proving less popular; the public wanted novelty, and Randall Williams wanted to give it to them. At Hull Fair in October 1896 he advertised 'living pictures and tableaux vivants', and at the Agricultural Hall that Christmas, Randall was showing 'animated pictures' which included **Lõie Fuller's serpentine dance**, and **The Czar of Russia in Paris**. He presented these same films at Kings Lynn in February 1897, later that year showing films of the Queen's Diamond Jubilee. At Hull Fair in October 1898, he advertised his 'New Improved American Bioscope', possibly the Maguire & Baucus projector marketed by Charles Urban. The fairground bioscope show was well and truly launched. Randall Williams himself died in November 1898, but his son-in-law Richard Monte continued his show under the same name.[30]

Many other showmen now came in on the act. At first, travelling bioscope shows were simple affairs called 'ground booths', in which the audience stood to watch the show; but later as seating was provided and the back rows were raised, entrances tended to be up a central flight of steps, occasioning the cry, 'walk up, walk up!' to see the show. Then came the years of the large organ-fronted shows. More than 150 bioscope shows, ranging from the minute to the magnificent, have been documented from those years.[31] Showmen gave themselves grandiloquent titles: Captain Payne, Colonel Clark, Senator Leo, and President Kemp among them: 'Professors' were ten a penny. Shows had names such as 'Wonderland', 'Dreamland', 'New Palace of Varieties and Living Pictures', 'Palace of Light', 'Royal Coliseum' and 'Theatre Unique'. Charles Thurston produced 'England's Greatest Show', with a huge, 104 key Marenghi organ.

A few showmen took their own films. Harry Scard of Wadbrook's filmed a Welsh soccer international in 1900/01, and later secured the sole rights to film soccer in Wales. He also filmed the Stratford Mop. Harry Crecraft filmed a railway disaster at Llanelly, and the funeral of the Ton Pentre murder victim. Edward Danter filmed the Tredegar Whitsun Procession. James Crighton took his own show on the road, and Richard Chipperfield took Shakespeare's Birthday Procession at Stratford.[32]

The travelling bioscope shows were at their peak from 1906 to 1912, but after that, decline set in. The canniest showmen sold up and bought into the new and more powerful rides instead. The age of the permanent cinema was at hand. The Cinematograph Act 1909, which came into force in 1910, made life more difficult for portable shows by insisting upon projectors and film being separated from the audience by means of a fireproof enclosure: a canvas screen was no longer enough. Restrictions on travelling during wartime, and requisition of traction engines for the war effort further reduced the number of shows, and almost none re-opened after the war in 1919.

Fifteen years later, A.C. Bromhead, who had completed his war service with the rank of lieutenant-colonel, shared his reminiscences with the British Kinematograph Society.[33] He particularly recalled the old fairground showmen, who were very much a race unto themselves. There were many fine, if quaint, characters among them, John Proctor, George Green, George Kemp, Scard, Wadbrook and Colonel Clark, with his enormous gold watch chain spread over a very ample bow window, and the one and only Sophie Hancock. Bromhead likened her sunburnt and weatherbeaten face to a railway map printed on leather, 'and her voice was the most powerful and raucous one I have ever heard in a woman, strong enough to be heard above the din of the West Country fairs she frequented: when she visited the office, her fair ground voice could be heard coming down the Charing Cross Road to herald her approach.'

Another visitor to Bromhead's office was a Mrs. Scott, whose progenitors had travelled the fairgrounds for generations, and who, as a result of a family conclave, had decided to embark on a picture show. She gave a liberal order for outfit and films. When it came to payment she produced from under her skirt a stocking full of threepenny bits; other members of the family also produced quantities of coppers and sixpences, but the great bulk of the total of £200 was in Mrs. Scott's threepences. Bromhead always wondered how she could have secreted the weight of the threepenny bits she was carrying about her person, and how the stocking stood the strain!

These showmen's customs were rough and ready - either they kept no accounts at all, or what they did keep were of an extremely primitive character. There were often difficulties in collecting bills due. A representative meeting a showman who was behind with his account was immediately invited to come and collect it himself. He then spent a couple of days on the roundabouts, collecting the amount due, in tuppences. Selling films on the fairground could also be bad for the waistline. A film traveller would arrive early in the morning. His first client invited him to a breakfast consisting of a huge steak with many trimmings. Leaving a parcel of films, after breakfasting the traveller strolled on to the next customer, and was again pressed to a hearty meal. Not wishing to turn down the chance of business, he did his best, but finally, after a third such encounter, he had to retire with severe indigestion.

Bromhead concluded this part of his lecture by paying a personal tribute:

> To one of these who stands out in my memory I owe a personal debt of gratitude. I refer to dear old William Haggar, who took many very successful films which he

sent to me for development and printing. The agreement on which we traded was verbal and simply to the effect that in return for a free print the negative was mine to issue. I think we also supplied him free with the negative stock upon which to make his exposures. It was on terms such as these that films, of which some in their day were classics, were made. I will give you an instance - a film 220 ft. in length called **The Poachers,** the first of the chase films - it was beautifully photographed and very cleverly acted by Haggar's sons and some of his assistants. That film not only sold in large quantities in England, but it went all over the world. The total issue was, I believe, 480 original prints,[34] of which over 100 went to the Continent of Europe. There were no doubt a great many dupes[35] as well. I could recall many other films taken by Mr. Haggar, but will mention only **The Sign of the Cross**, total length of this being sensational at the time, namely 600 ft.[36] There was no question of copyright to be considered either as to the exhibition or production of that picture and, so far as I remember, the only special condition attached by Mr. Haggar to the rights of selling films he made was that no copy should be sold to other travelling showmen in his immediate vicinity. This was moderate enough! Mr. Haggar travelled generally in South Wales, and I remember too a very pleasant habit of his whenever he reached Milford Haven, of sending me a fine basket of fresh fish from the dock.

If it were not for this mention, in a formal lecture which was afterwards printed and published, William Haggar's name would not appear in the annals of the British cinema.[37]

5. 'I knew there was money in it!'

ON THE MORNING OF 5 April 1898, the Haggars pushed their bioscope show on two trolleys onto Harry Studt's ground in Aberavon, and into the world of film shows on fairgrounds. Then they had to wait all day for the sun to set: only then would their tent be dark enough.

We put it upon our allotted site [Walter wrote later] and had a busy time erecting this wonderful cinematograph. The lighting of this tent, or auditorium, was by acetylene gas, produced from a mixture of carbide and water, the generator for which was in the operating box. While the lights in the auditorium were on, the gas generator functioned very well, but when the lights were extinguished at the start of the show, the damn thing kept making gas, no provision having been thought of for this contingency. My father and brother Jim, who were operating, were in a canvas operating box with the acetylene gas generator giving off its superfluous fumes, the two high powered hydrogen and oxygen cylinders for the limelight, and a linen bag full of inflammable film - and they escaped unhurt! Needless to say, the acetylene generator was hastily discarded in favour of the old fashioned naphtha lamps which were so very essential on the fairground in those days.

At the first public performance the little show was packed with between 250 and 300 people. Naturally, my father, being the chief operator, was extremely nervous, and anxious that it should go well. We had a lecturer to describe the seven short films, on subjects such as the turn-out of a fire brigade, and so on; and there would be an interval between each to fit up the next one. Unfortunately, after a short time, so hot, so anxious was Father, as he bent over and peered at his machine, to make sure the film was threaded correctly, that the perspiration from his manly brow steamed the lenses fore and aft, and he could not get even a glimmer of light on the screen. In despair, he spoke to the lecturer: 'For God's sake say something!' The lecturer looked at the blank screen and said, 'Ladies and Gentlemen, if you could see this picture, it would be a train emerging from a tunnel!' This unhappy state of affairs continued for the first two performances, by which time the heat from the projecting light overcame the mist on the lenses - so the last three performances were quite good.[1]

Walter never forgot the excitement of that first day's show. He was responsible for the sound effects, beating the kettle drum and bass drum for **Train Emerging From A Tunnel**, and playing in the four-piece brass band which formed their main means of advertisement. The bandsmen wore frock coats, but Walter had deferred putting on his top hat until the last moment. When the call came to play, he removed his cap,[2] and for safety put it in the bell of one of the largest brass instruments, thus putting that instrument out of action. For sheer nervousness, inefficiency and lack of practice, he rated that brass band second to none! But despite this catastrophe, they drew five full houses that day, taking the huge sum of £15, at admission prices of 2d. and 3d. When they counted the total, William said to his sons, with a gasp of satisfaction, 'I knew there was money in it!'

On the second day, however, they took only 15 shillings. The public were evidently not impressed by the blackout fiasco of the first day. Now in the fairground business, they pulled down the show, and moved to another of the Studt family's grounds, at Pontypridd, where the Rhondda meets the Taff, at the centre of the Welsh coalfield: but the bank holiday weather turned against them, Easter Monday being a washout, on which they took nothing. This petty misfortune, however, was nothing to that which now loomed: the coal strike in South Wales, which was to last for the next six months.

Trade Unionism was pressing ahead through the eighteen-nineties with a new emphasis. In 1892, its membership total in the United Kingdom was 1,576,000: by 1900 it was 2,022,000, an increase of almost a third. There were many more industrial stoppages: some 30 million days' work was lost in 1893, and the figures for 1897 and 1898 were comparable. In 1893, the most famous dispute was the miners' lockout, caused by the coal owners' demand for a cut in wages of 10%: it lasted fifteen weeks. The Miners' Federation, whose writ did not officially run in the South Wales area, sought, in opposition to the local unions, to close the South Wales pits. It did so by fomenting a hauliers' strike. This was run violently, the hauliers forming 'marching gangs' which went from pit to pit stopping work and handling miners brutally. The end came when the miners of Ebbw Vale, who had been forewarned and forearmed, emerged from their pits 2000 strong, fought a pitched battle on the mountainside with a great army of the gangs, and utterly defeated them. Many were injured: it was a marvel no one was killed. The hauliers' strike then collapsed, and South Wales seceded from the strike. Elsewhere troops were called out, and two miners were shot during riots in Doncaster. The Prime Minister, Gladstone, and Asquith, as the Minister responsible, were denounced as 'murderers' on labour platforms. Legacies of bitterness were left for the future. In South Wales these welled up in 1898, when the owners there demanded a reduction in the minimum wage. The resultant strike dragged on for six months, ending in the men's defeat. The building of the South Wales Miners' Federation resulted from it.[3]

When the strike began, the Haggars moved away from the coalfields to Ross, and what was known as 'private business'. On the fairgrounds, all the different attractions, boxing booths, hoop-las, shooting galleries and so on, surrounded the big roundabouts with their horses and gondolas. The roundabout owners, such as the Studts and Danters, would rent the whole of the ground and then sub-let it to the smaller businesses. The cinematographs did not always have to stand on the fairground: but when a show was opened anywhere else, it was 'private business'. The Haggars never did so well in private business, and, true to form, they did not do well at Ross. Nobody had heard of a cinematograph, so people did not know what they were being offered. On one occasion when William was touting for an audience, a rather supercilious 'toff' came up to him and said, 'Here's 2d., old boy, I don't want to see your show - go and get a shave.' William replied, 'Thank you, sir; if you give me another 2d., I can have a glass of beer as well!'[4]

Moving on from Ross to Hereford, they met, for the first time, Wadbrook's Travelling Cinema, whose manager, Harry Scard, was to become a great friend of William's. Wadbrook's was a fine show; they had recently changed from a ghost show to the cinema, and, knowing the business, they were experienced in making their appeal to the customers. The sight of the crowds drawn to their show confirmed William's hunch that the business would eventually be lucrative, even if, for the Haggars, it was not yet so. The optimism which had stood him in good stead all his life did not falter: he had burned his boats now. Journeying on by train to Builth, at first the show did well, but then, on Fair Night, the cinematograph machine broke down. William had to improvise. With the triunial projector had come hundreds of lantern slides, one fine set being entitled 'Victoria's Glorious Reign', which, accordingly, he showed. Few knew the difference: everyone was pleased, except one old gentleman who had seen a cinema show before. This performance was repeated several times the same evening until the close of the fair. Then the cinematograph had to be repaired. William took it to London next day: travelling expenses were £4, and the cost of the repair, 6d. One tiny screw had shaken out, which anyone with a screwdriver could have replaced had they been able to find it![5]

On moving to Hay-on-Wye, the Haggars came up against determined opposition from another cinematograph show on the same ground. Walter gleefully described the contest.

Bill Samuels of Swansea,[6] the one time celebrated Welsh pugilist, had a very fine boxing show and a small cinematograph show, and was very jealous of our intrusion in what might be called his own domain. Bill Samuels, God rest his soul, a good man in his own line, used to refer to Father as 'the old mummer', referring to his play acting days. On this occasion, we were standing next to Mr. Samuels' Boxing Show, and when opening time came for us the night before the fair at about 7 o'clock, we turned out our little brass band to play some music to attract the crowd (we had by this time engaged a professional cornet player), but Mr. Samuels thought differently. Every time we turned out our band, Bill Samuels turned out his boxers, their raucous voices touting their own show. This rather took the wind out of our sails: we could not get the people to hear what we had to say, and in the end we retired into our own show in ignominy. But Father's persistence would not be suppressed. 'Time to organise things', he said to the cornet player. 'You have been in the army, haven't you?' 'Yes, governor.' 'When I say 'go', you go out and blow bugle calls towards Bill Samuels' show until I tell you to stop.' Another man was told to bang the big drum until told to stop. Father was directing the battle: he waited until Mr. Samuels had finished springing his lines and had a nice crowd of people round him to listen to what he had to say, then he gave the word. With drum and bugle we surged forth and would not desist. 'Bang, bang, bang', we repeated until poor Bill Samuels was almost demented. He turned towards Father saying, 'Stop that ruddy drum!' But we did not stop, and Bill Samuels and his boxers in their turn retired into their show in ignominy. The crowds were enjoying this rivalry, and Father, ever ready to seize an opportunity, invited the public into his show free. We had a packed house and this proved to be an excellent advertisement: we did very well on the two following days.[7]

From Hay Fair in May 1898, they returned to Mountain Ash Fair on Whit Sunday, being persuaded to do so by 'that stout old trooper' Harry Studt senior. The Welsh strike had been on for six weeks. William spoke to the crowds, 'Ladies and Gentlemen, we are amongst you once more, and, in consultation with my worthy friend, Harry Studt, we do not see fit that you should be deprived of your annual fair although you have been on strike a considerable time. We know you have not much money, so, to enable you to see what we have to offer in the form of entertainment, we have decided to show our films for the humble sum of one penny.' He intended to say a lot more, but he had no time. The people crowded in at every available entrance with their pennies in their hands, and the Haggars were busy all day taking more money at a penny a time than they had taken during the previous month. One old lady who seemed impressed by the frock coats and top hats of the little brass band asked whether they were in mourning! Soon afterwards, William, feeling that something must be done to create a better impression, exchanged this somewhat funereal uniform for some second-hand cherry pickers' uniforms with brass buttons, gold braid, and peaked caps. This effect, when backed by the Windsor Castle front of the show inspired another old lady to say, 'I was in your barracks last night!'

After that, the Haggars had no alternative but to keep moving on: their problem being that, at that time, the cinema was what showmen would call a 'oncer'. The public would not pay to see it more than once, or at most twice, so it was not possible to make an extended stay anywhere (as it had been with the theatre). They visited Treorchy, Builth again, Chepstow and Lydney, the result being near starvation. This state of affairs prevailed for the whole summer of 1898. They were reduced to dispensing with their two living vans and proceeding as best they could with the two trailers which carried the show itself: they slept where they could, and ate when they could afford it. It was a bad time - people in the agricultural areas of Wiltshire and Gloucestershire had never heard of the cinematograph, and had little money to spend on it, and in Wales the strike was still on. At last, however, at the end of the summer, hearing that the strike was over, they returned to Wales. William decided on a tour of the halls with the pantomime **Cinderella,** a gamble risking the loss of all his remaining financial resources. But it was an immense success: there had been no entertainment of this kind during the whole six months of the strike, and it seemed that everywhere they were the first entertainers to return, and could not go wrong. They showed seven days a week at three towns a week, a pantomime on weekdays, and what was billed as a 'sacred concert' on Sundays.[8] On one occasion, the cinematograph machine was fixed in a balcony at a Sunday Concert. During the running of the programme, the shutter blade came loose from its shaft, and spun down among the audience, striking an old gentleman on his bald head. It left a very handsome scar on his forehead which curved around to the back of his neck; but he just sat beaming all over his face - the programme had so delighted him, and there were no complaints. The theatrical tour ended where it had begun, at Cwmbran, William being anxious to get back on the road with his bioscope show again. He was still convinced there was money in it.

For the summer season of 1899, following a fire which destroyed their old show, they made a new show-front using the two living vans, which they could now afford again, and adopting Maguire & Baucus' bioscope, sold to them by Charles Urban, who described his first meeting with William, in his memoirs.[9] Urban had placed in his office window new posters advertising his bioscope, which attracted William as he was passing by. 'One day', wrote Urban, 'Rosie' (his stock keeper, sales lady and cashier) 'called me into the General Office to meet a Mr. W. Haggar, as he introduced himself. His head was bandaged and he looked otherwise knocked about. He explained that he had had an accident to his show tent and elaborate front, which were entirely consumed by fire.' William was in London hoping to persuade John Wrench and Son to let him have a replacement for their triunial projector on credit. Urban, sensing a sales opportunity, took William into his theatre and demonstrated his bioscope projector and films. 'He had established a regular circuit throughout North (sic) Wales, and was very well known by all the regular showmen. I proposed to fit him up with the very best our firm could procure, so as to enable him to give a better show than any of his many competitors. His eyes fairly bulged from his head with excitement, and he promised to pay by instalments out of his first profits. It was a risk, but the man struck me as being honest. I was not mistaken: within three months he had paid back his account in full, besides buying lots of new films and posters.' Thus began a friendship between William and Charles Urban, which lasted for many years.

With the new show, William, Jim and Walter visited the April Fairs at Aberavon and Aberdare, Will Junior proceeding independently with his theatre show. Then, despite the bad experience of the previous year, they left Wales again, hoping for the best: but they had another bad summer, and at last, at Gloucester in August, they packed up the four vans of the show on railway trucks, and wondered which way to go. William's greatest friend on the fairgrounds in this part of the country was 'Milky' Symonds,[10] who was doing his best to persuade the Haggars to take the show to Trowbridge Flower Show, but Jim argued strongly in favour of Wales. Common sense prevailed. They returned to Wales, pitching at Ebbw Vale Market Place. From then on they 'stuck to the coal' and could not go wrong.[11]

William had the impression that a travelling cinematograph show was not a good proposition in the winter months, so he laid up the show at Mountain Ash, and again went on tour with the theatre. He and Jim went into partnership as 'W. & J. Haggar's Dramatic Company', in recognition of Jim's impending marriage to actress Kate Silverton, Jenny Lindon's sister. During this winter tour, Lily recalled their singing a song called 'The Little Crossing Sweeper', behind a gauze screen, showing a little ragged urchin sweeping the snow and then, the song ended, 'in the snow he died': a real tear-jerker. It would take the younger children days and days to cut up old newspapers for snow, and they used to fight each other for the privilege of playing the part of the crossing-sweeper, because they loved to see the audience cry. People would be so moved by this performance that they would throw pennies on to the stage.[12] This winter's tour took them as far as Pembrokeshire and a typical programme included the play, **The Penalty of Crime**, a bioscope display and the inevitable Sunday concert, which, Walter claimed, paid the rent. The tour finished at Brynaman.[13]

During the summer of 1900, the Haggars took their travelling cinema show on the road again, opening at Aberdare in April, continuing to Pembrokeshire, and returning to Aberavon and Neath Fairs and Llanelly during the autumn. While in Pembrokeshire, they personally contacted the Pembrokeshire Imperial Yeomanry, who invariably occupied the best seats wherever they went. They took their stand in Pembroke Town itself for the annual October Fair for the first of nineteen successive years, with good business every visit. They also visited Pembroke Dock, Haverfordwest and Milford Haven, where, years later, William presented the church with a peal of bells. They wintered at Aberdare Market Yard for the first time: it was to become their winter headquarters every year.[14]

The family had already encountered Wadbrook's show: at this time it was a fine electrically lit show, which took the cream of the money everywhere, according to Walter. This had inspired William, during their tour of Pembrokeshire, to order a 'portable' steam-powered electricity generating engine, costing £600. He had had enough of the eccentricities of limelight, deciding that electric light was a business necessity. The engine arrived while they were at Treorchy in the autumn. Adding greatly to the appearance of the front of the show, and decidedly improving the showing of the films, it attracted more people than ever. From now on, he had no need to revert to the theatre in the winter. The only drawback was that the engine was 'portable' in name only: it was in fact a heavy and cumbersome affair, and gave its owners a great deal of trouble and anxiety by sinking into the mud whenever the fairgrounds were soft or muddy. But it provided electricity to enhance the show for the next four years.[15]

They opened at Aberdare in March 1901 with a new double-wagon show,[16] 'Haggar's Royal Electric Bioscope': a photograph taken at Pontypool Park in 1902 shows it standing by a set of partly erected swinging boats. It has a central entrance, at the back of which can be seen the double doors, painted with portraits of the heroes of the Boer War, Generals Roberts and Kitchener. An 87-key organ manufactured by Gavioli of Paris, stands on the left of the entrance, and the engine, with its extended funnel to keep the smoke away from the customers, is on the right. Presumably there were sacks of coal around the back.[17] The census at the end of the month found William, Sarah and Walter in their living van at the Navigation Ground in Mountain Ash.[18]

It had been during the winter of 1900/01 that Harry Scard, the manager of Wadbrook's, had sprung a march on the opposition by having the Welsh soccer internationals at Cardiff filmed and shown exclusively in his show. This decided William to venture into the business of topical film-making, so in June he bought a camera and tripod, with a roll of film, 350 feet, in those days costing a shilling a foot. At Burry Port, near Llanelly, looking for a suitable subject, they decided to film a train entering Burry Port station. 'This was our first filming effort, the first of many great successes and a few failures', comments Walter.[19] 'With added zest we took many topical items, including football matches which were very popular. Eventually we acted small plays, one of our most successful being **A phantom ride through Swansea**, which was taken from the front of a tram.' They showed films of local views at the Swansea Gala in August that year, and soon afterwards **The Dumb Man of Manchester**, William's first attempt at filmed drama, using Will Junior's acting company and props.[20]

Walter told three anecdotes of William's early film-making:

During the following year, [1902] my brother Will was showing his theatre at Maesteg, and the weather was fine (the weather being the deciding factor in the making of films in those days), so we took the train to Maesteg where we induced Will's threatrical company to act something for us to film. What film should we take, we wondered. We had no scenery, and there was not much time for rehearsing. Will wanted to put on 'The Dumb Man of Manchester', but eventually I insisted on the taking of a Welsh local story entitled **The Maid of Cefn Ydfa**. We shot that film in an hour and a half, there being seven scenes, and the total length of the film being approximately 450 feet. This film was to bring in hundreds and hundreds of pounds. It was despatched to the photographer's and returned to Treorchy by the following Wednesday, when, at the admission price of 2d. and 3d., we took £40 - and for years afterwards this film did similar business throughout the whole of South Wales, and was the despair of our rival shows.

Each summer when the weather was fine, especially when in Pembrokeshire, we would take our own films. It was probably in the year 1904 when we returned to Maesteg and one afternoon we set out with some dogs, a coconut-shy net, a live rabbit, a camera and the actors from my brother's portable theatre - as usual, with no script - asking nobody's permission: we went up into the hills and arranged, rehearsed and took a film called **The Poachers**. Did you ever see a rabbit caught in a coconut-shy net? This film was a huge success.[21]

At this time we had a very fine half-plate camera and two quarter-plate snapshot cameras, and at every available opportunity we were either taking films or taking snapshots of local scenes, events and personalities. For instance, on the day following the erection of our portable cinema, Father would take his camera charged with half a dozen quarter-plates, and wander round the town seeking local colour - old ladies, children, groups of boys, anything of interest. On returning home, he would develop the plates himself, making lantern slides from them, and they were washed, dried and on the screen the same night. This was an advantage not shared by any other touring cinema show. Father was an expert photographer: when we took films, he snipped off 4-6 inches of the film and developed it himself, scrutinizing the quality and exposure, always trying to improve his work. Many amusing incidents occurred over the snapshot-cum-slide part of the entertainment. If Father saw an interesting old lady, he would say, 'Just a minute, Ma', and a close-up photograph of her would appear on our screen the same night. We have had requests from relations: 'Please, Mr. Haggar, don't put Mother on the show tonight.'[22]

A newly discovered scrap of film, **Outside the Works**, illustrates this last anecdote. A mere 45 seconds long, it shows men walking past a large Works, from which clouds of smoke are issuing, then a street scene with women and children in their Sunday best. Finally William himself appears, carrying a large board, advertising 'Haggar's Bioscope Camera'.[23]

Their lantern accommodated the dual use of films and slides. At that time, they could buy slides made to match almost any popular song, the slides being shown while one of the three Haggar girls sang the song standing at the side of the screen.[24] A photograph of the time shows Violet dressed in scouting costume to sing a song about the Boer War, and she, Rose and Lily are said to have appeared in front of the show dressed as soldiers and nurses. The Haggars made their own, successful 'newsreel' films of the Boer War,[25] taking most of them on the hills above the Rhondda Valley. A few years later, they repeated the process, taking fake newsreels of the Russo-Japanese War on the snow-clad tops of the hills above the Rhymney Valley. In the spring of 1903, when they were at Port Talbot, on a very fine windy Sunday, Mumbles lifeboat sailed across Swansea Bay, lost its rudder, and was dashed to pieces on the breakwater of Aberavon Docks, in view of hundreds of people. Six men were drowned, the onlookers being helpless to assist. There was a mass funeral at Mumbles the following week, which the Haggars filmed, supplying their friend Harry Scard with a copy, which was also shown at Moss Empires, Cardiff, Newport and Swansea.[26]

With the travelling cinema, it was not unusual to have 16 or 20 performances, or 'Bioscope Exhibitions' as they were termed, on a Fair day, with an average length of 20 minutes each, made up of five subjects, always finishing with a comedy: if the audience went away laughing, they would be sure to return. A typical programme would consist of:

1. Exciting drama: **The Last Cartridge**.
2. Local interest: **Phantom Ride through Swansea High Street.**
3. Exciting drama: **The Poachers**.
4. Interesting subject: **Löie Fuller's Serpentine Dance** (in colour).
5. Comedy: **Weary Willie and Tired Tim at the Races**.

Then it would be, 'Side doors out, kindly recommend the entertainment to your friends'; the organ would strike up outside, and they would proceed to entice and usher in another house.[27]

On the English fairgrounds, an anonymous bard hymned an occasion at Hull, when:

Of all the sights I ever saw, I mean that's worth recalling,
Was seven Cinnys all in a row, and all the showmen bawling,
At Hull's Great Fair, the Cinnys there, numbered seven.[28]

Walter gives a Welsh counterpart to this:

I call to mind one visit to Treorchy, when there were seven cinematograph shows in a circle: Chipperfield's circus and pictures in one corner, Cedric's menagerie and pictures, Dooner's, Relph and Pedley, Anderton & Rowland's, Wadbrook's and Haggar's. It was a very fine fair - there was enough entertainment on the outside of these shows without anyone paying a penny to go inside! All were electrically lit, and all had attractive showfronts and parading girls and jugglers to attract the crowds. They did attract the crowds - so did we. They attracted the crowds for one or two nights - we attracted them every night. Why? We always had a change of programme and always found time, on the busiest of fair days, even doing 20 performances, to show on the screen the forthcoming attractions. Where we were able to give a fresh programme every night for a fortnight, the other shows had very few films, and could only show the same ones night after night, relying more on their outside attractions to draw the crowds. Even at the absurdly low admission prices, takings on a Fair day, with no entertainment tax, might work out at anything between £40 and £70, all in silver, copper, or a sprinkling of gold. It often happened that we were in such a hurry to reach the next town that these takings were just thrown under the bed in one of the living vans and counted at our leisure - our motto being, 'get it - and count it when you can!'[29]

William had been sure that there was money in it - and he had been right.

6. 'In one leap, we went right to the top'

IN MARCH 1904, *THE Era* announced that 'Mr. William Haggar has just bought a splendid new traction and electric engine, which he has appropriately christened *The Maid of Cefn Ydfa*'.[1] The Haggars had had enough of what Walter described as the 'turmoil' of getting the show about by rail (horses being too much trouble), and of the heavy old 'portable' sinking in the mud - it went to light Will Junior's show at New Tredegar. Walter recalled the meeting which his father had had with Fowlers' travelling salesman, a Mr. Robinson. After the virtues of the engine had been extolled, 'Do I get anything off if I pay cash?' asked William. 'Can you pay cash?' 'Do I get anything off if I pay cash?' 'Why, yes,' was the reply: 'You get 10% and 2½%.' 'That makes 12½%' said William. 'No' said Mr. Robinson, '10% first and 2½% for the balance.' 'Do it up' said William: 'I will pay cash.' He learned that he would save £90. Mr. Robinson closed his book, looked over his glasses, and said, 'You are the only showman who has ever paid cash for an engine!'[2]

Lily recalled that her father never used banks until he settled in Aberdare. He used to take all his money about with him in strong boxes and under mattresses; but she could only remember one robbery, in the days of the portable theatre, when they had stayed as long as six months in one place. Her mother had employed a daily help, and one day William missed ten gold sovereigns from under one of the mattresses. After questioning the family, he asked the maid. Of course she denied all knowledge, but Sarah searched her and found five sovereigns in each of her shoes.[3] So Mr. Robinson was paid in sovereigns from under the bed. The engine eased their transport problems immensely: instead of paying rail charges, they purchased half a ton of coal and were able to cover a larger field of operations.

The coming of electric light had enhanced William's show enormously, and the traction engine improved the means of supplying it. Now William improved his projection facilities, by changing from Urban's Bioscope (which had replaced the Wrench triunial machine) to Gaumont's 'Chrono'. William issued a ringing endorsement of this 'Chrono', in a letter to Gaumont from his Royal Electric Bioscope Exhibition at Aberavon Fairground, N. Wales (sic), dated Oct. 8th 1904:

> Gentlemen, I have pleasure in informing you that the Chrono machine you recently sold me has proved a big success. I have had seven years on this same circuit, and I am happy to tell you our 'bis' is better than ever using the Chrono, and our patrons are simply delighted with the beautiful clear and steady pictures on the screen. I myself, as an exhibitor, consider the Chrono machine perfect. I beg to remain, Yours faithfully, W. Haggar.[4]

Next, William had to consider his show-front, at that time a 1903 update of the 'Royal Electric Bioscope' from 1901. His first priority was always a clean screen, a good light, and good pictures, but now that these had been amply dealt with, he was wondering whether to buy a double wagon carved and gilded front which was being offered for sale by Orton & Sons of Burton-on-Trent, when one evening at tea-time, with no appointment, in walked Jim Wentworth, agent for Charles Marenghi et Cie., Organ Builders of Paris, with a large scale drawing of a 44ft. organ and show-front combined with a double entrance. This was such a fine piece of work that William placed an order within the hour, on the proviso that the suppliers kept the organ in tune for twelve months.[5] Walter described the organ in glowing terms:

> This organ was such a great step forward from the general run of organs. All travelling shows in those days had one central entrance. The engine generating the electric light would be on one side, and the old barrel organ on the other side. This Charles Marenghi organ had two entrances, one right and one left. The organ and show front with its workmanship and gilded figures was a marvellous piece of work. It could play paper music, songs, overtures, anything you wanted - and the crowds used to stand enthralled by its grandeur. Incorporated in the front were 840 miniature incandescent lamps of various colours. Each lamp had to be in its own particular place: the gold leaf of a flower would warrant an amber

lamp, a spray of violets a curving of violet lamps, red costumes on the paintings called for red lamps, and so on. There were three separate electrical circuits embracing the whole of the front of this organ. When these three circuits were illuminated simultaneously, the whole of this 44ft. organ resembled a large church window. No wonder the crowds stayed for hours to watch this display, it was wonderful. All the main lighting was extinguished whilst the display was in progress. These circuits worked mechanically but were not timed to the music, so we worked them by hand, keeping in time with the various tempos as the music was playing.[6]

It must indeed have been quite a sight - family tradition has it that the organ cost £1000, a vast sum in those days - and Walter in this recollection manages to preserve something of the sense of the enormous improvement over the old organ. The Marenghi was delivered to the Haggars in time for the Llanelly Fair in May 1906.[7] William kept the arrival of the new organ a secret from the other showmen, and even from the younger members of his own family. When it arrived, he prowled around the trucks containing it all night, so afraid was he that something would happen to it if he did not keep watch. When it was erected the next day, everyone realised what a wonderful piece of work it was: for Lily, 'it was the most wonderful organ I have ever heard'.[8] Henry Haggar remembered that the organ, taking up the entire front of their building, attracted such a large crowd that it was impossible for them to find the time to play it. However, the crowd kept shouting to them to play it, so they put on the ever-popular song, 'The Village Blacksmith'. The crowd simply stormed the various stalls and riding machines in the fair, and they too were stopped so that people might see and hear the wonder of the age.[9] Walter's conclusion was unequivocal: 'In one leap we went right to the top in the cinematograph business in South Wales!'[10] All the other travelling cinema shows were forced to follow suit and alter their fronts, to keep up with the 'old'un,' as William was increasingly called in the fairground press.

As if this was not enough, within a year, William had bought an even larger organ. For, in November 1906, Walter married Ada Roberts at St. Elvan's, the parish church in Aberdare, and from then on, he travelled separately with the Marenghi showfront, whilst William bought a 110-key Gavioli organ showfront, christening it 'Haggar's Electric Coliseum', with a new traction engine, *Cymru am byth* (Wales for ever!).[11] Father Greville, the fairground historian, remembered Haggar's 'Electric Coliseum': 'this show, new in 1907, had a most beautiful and elaborate front, a mass of gold work and beautiful figures, with lovely panelling at the sides and roofing the stage. The organ was one of the new 110-key Gaviolis, which had just begun to arrive here. The troupe of dancers was led by Miss Violet Haggar, and the doorsman and lecturer was a friend of mine, Cyril Yorke.' The 'doorsman' was the fairground barker, whose job it was to invite the crowds to walk up the steps of the show and tell them what they would find inside. Cyril Yorke had the voice for this, and for the films inside,[12] an attribute which he was to pass on to his son and grandson.

The big free feature of Haggar's show was the troupe of dancing girls on the walkup platform.[13] Parading in front of the show to attract the customers was a device borrowed from the travelling theatres, when the actors put on a show outside the theatre. The custom of advertising shows by short-skirted girls drew accusations of 'suggestiveness', which the showmen sought to counter by employing family members: Wadbrook's paraders included Flo Scard, Nellie Wadbrook, and Mary Davies, who married Harry Scard Junior, and who had also paraded for the Haggars. Lily recalled intense competition between the parading girls: all their marvellous dresses would be kept secret, in case someone should copy them and steal their thunder. 'Haggar's dancing girls and beautiful cinematograph show' were a major attraction at Pembroke Fair in 1909, and that August a reporter for *World's Fair* was very taken with Haggar's 'bevy of beauties in short skirts gracefully throwing their nether limbs about'.[14] But they were not always girls. Walter's grandson Roy Haggar had met an old man, 'Scissors' Thomas (a tailor), who told him that he had once taken one of the Haggar paraders to The Commons in Pembroke for a cuddle: but found to his disgust that he was proposing to cuddle a man! Roy's grandma, Ada, reluctantly confirmed this story.[15] What Roy did not know was that the parader might have been Henry Haggar, who in 1936 confided to an audience of Rotarians in Merthyr, where he was managing the Castle Cinema, that he himself had danced with his sisters before the show![16]

Henry took his audience back to those first days in 1898, when, he said, they used to travel from town to town with the portable cinema, which had to be built up and pulled down at every stop, the building and apparatus then being transported by rail to the next stop. These first cinemas were built almost entirely of wood, and a crude affair they were compared with the modern super-cinema and talkies projector. Henry remembered the incident, related by Walter, when the projector had broken down, and lantern slides were shown instead. Everything had gone all right until one patron, who had seen the living pictures before, and knew what they were like, came out shouting, 'not one living picture!', and the further away he got, the louder he shouted. Their first traction engine had frightened the family by its huge size, Henry revealed. It had its drawbacks, as was proved on one occasion when it ran away on Treharris Hill, smashing the glass fronts of two shops next to the corner where - in 1936 - the chemist's shop stood. Henry continued:

Our record in those days - and for the number of performances it is still the record - was at Mountain Ash on Easter Monday. We opened at 9 am, and continued until 11 pm, giving 24 performances. The price of admission was 3d., and I believe we took £100 on that day alone. This meant, of course, 8,000 admittances, which is more than we can do today. I started in the business at the age of 12, and my job was in the operating box, where I would wind the films up as they came through the machine. I was later left behind at Carmarthen for my schooling. We showed pictures in Merthyr on the Iron Bridge in the year that Mafeking was relieved, and we did so well that my parents were quite glad of a rest when the time came for us to leave. We settled at Aberdare for our winter quarters, and just before Easter of each year, we used to start our spring and summer tour, visiting Pontardulais, Milford Haven, Haverfordwest to Fishguard, and then back again through Carmarthen and Llanelly to Aberdare for the next winter. During this period the family used to take hundreds of short films - all, of course, during the summer when the light was good. The only pictures that Pembrokeshire and

Carmarthenshire saw were the ones we showed when we visited these places once each year. It was quite the regular thing for us to take big 'jumps' from one town to another. I remember at Llanelly Fair our last performance came out at 12 midnight, but we would immediately afterwards start to pull down the building, load the four vans on the railway trucks, come back from the station, have a wash and supper, and then load our three remaining vans behind the traction engine, which had most likely been going full steam since first thing in the morning generating electricity. It would then be about 3.30 am when we were ready to start, and off we would go without any sleep, arriving at Haverfordwest about 6 pm on Sunday, the day following. We would then get to work, put the large organ wagon into position ready for the Monday morning's work, and finally call it a day. Up again the following morning, to build up the show and open by 10 am, do about 15 to 20 more performances, and then close down at midnight with another typical day gone. Our journey from Llanelly to Haverfordwest was generally done in the pouring rain, and I can remember changing my clothes on one journey no less than four times, finally arriving at Haverfordwest in a suit of Father's.[17]

The postman found the Haggars at 'The Bioscope' - Jenny wrote a card to her mother-in-law, Sarah, catching the 8.15pm collection at Bargoed on 30 July 1906, addressed to Mrs. W. Haggar, The Bioscope, Market Place, Milford Haven. 'Dear Mother, I hope you are quite well. Love from all, Jenny', was the message, the card being a photograph of Will and Jenny's theatre company. Similarly, Lily sent a card-photo of herself to Ada, 'Mrs. Walter Haggar, Bioscope, Haverfordwest, Wales', from Aberdare at 6.15pm on 22 July 1910. Edward VII's portrait is on the halfpenny green stamps.[18]

Lily also remembered the long journey to Pembrokeshire, taking a day and a half to reach Carmarthen and two whole days to reach Pembroke from Aberdare or Mountain Ash. They always had to travel on secondary roads because the engine needed to be re-filled with water, which they managed by using small roads with bridge-covered streams. The girls used to have great fun on those journeys:

> In the summer we would start at daybreak, and my two sisters and myself would be fast asleep in bed, only to wake up as soon as we started moving. We had to stop and eat, and our eating places had to coincide with the engine taking water. To save time, the engineer would warn us that we would be stopping at a certain place in half an hour, so we would begin to prepare a meal of sandwiches and cups of tea. It was quite difficult to cut sandwiches and hold the kettle on the range that we had in the caravan while we were still on the move. We had to plug bits of clean cloth around the lid and spout of the kettle because the roads were very bumpy. There was an old lady living at a farm called 'The Roses', at the top of a long hill, and we always sent her a postcard to tell her that we would be passing on a certain day. She would then make a lot of pancakes and sell them to us at 2d. each, and during the summer we would make pigs of ourselves eating strawberries at 3d. per pound.[19]

As well as being bumpy, the roads were also very dusty. William made several comedy films about a tramp named 'Dusty Rhodes': although 'Dusty' was sometimes a nickname for Rhodeses (as well as for Millers), was it also a pun? The *Monmouthshire Beacon* printed an editorial in June 1905, headed, 'Dustproof roads wanted'. 'Although automobilism has been the means of stirring up the dust problem to an extent not at all disproportionate to its importance', the leader-writer claimed, 'we seem very little nearer to the solution to the difficulty than when the question first presented itself.' He went on to state that, although various experiments had been tried, none had succeeded. The full danger, not to mention the extreme unpleasantness of the dust nuisance created by motor traffic, was not realised as it should be. The medical profession was not making enough of an outcry against the spread of germs, perhaps because they were themselves adopting these 'dust distributors' as their preferred means of travel. The writer could not deny the utility of the horseless carriage: all that was required was that the roads should be adapted to a means of locomotion for which they were at present wholly unsuited. The problem had also arisen in France where, the editorial revealed, everything pointed to tar being selected as the remedy.[20]

As the decade wore on, the Haggars continued with their summers in West Wales, where many of their films were made. 1908 in particular was a busy year, with longer remakes of some of the first films, including the ever popular **Maid of Cefn Ydfa**. Most of the family were involved: Will Junior and Jenny in **The Maid** and **The Dumb Man of Manchester**, Walter and Violet in **The Red Barn Crime**, and Jim and Kate in **The Sheep Stealer**. Lily had been partnered by her brothers in **Desperate Footpads**, the year before. Both the Haggar shows were together at Neath's Great Fair that autumn: they were unique in putting on two such large organ-fronted shows at the same fair. Father Greville wrote an eye-witness account of them, for publication in *World's Fair*.[21] Winters were spent in Aberdare, in the Market Yard: in 1908 William filled the Market Hall with a great variety show.[22] He filmed an incident in Aberdare when Lewis Thomas, a solicitor and brother of the President of the Welsh Rugby Union, saved a boy from drowning.[23]

By now, thoughts were turning to what to do next. Walter and Lily make it clear that the family was only conversant with the affairs of the South Wales area. For news from the English fairgrounds, they relied on Henry Studt,[24] whose brother Jacob travelled mainly in England, but would visit South Wales twice a year, to meet his brothers John and Henry, who each owned two or more roundabouts. Henry Studt was a great friend of William's, Lily recollecting the two of them sitting talking on the steps of the cinema for hours on Sundays. Walter remembered his father being given conflicting advice. Cricks & Martin,[25] who supplied him with a camera, tried to induce William to abandon showing films, in order to concentrate on making them; but Leon Vint of Abertillery[26] said, 'Haggar, you're on the wrong track - all this labour and moving the show from place to place: why don't you get a series of halls for continuous showing? I have already got Neath. You, with your boys, should establish a circuit at once, while you have the opportunity, and while the going is good.' But it was to be several years before William took this advice and built his first picture houses, in Merthyr and Mountain Ash.

During the summer of 1909, the Haggars' tours with their two shows were going as usual, when Sarah fell ill. 'She was taken ill several times with heavy haemorrhages, but the doctors did not seem to know the exact nature of her illness', writes Lily. 'On reflection, I think she must have suffered from gastric ulcers, but the treatment prescribed was very strange. She was put on a diet of champagne and grapes and, though she rallied for a time, she soon began to fail in health.'[27]

Sarah died on 13 August 1909, at the fairground at Carmarthen, from pneumonia and heart failure, according to her death certificate. Lily nursed her mother until her death, Violet, the only other unmarried daughter, being busy with her parader-leading duties. Family sources[28] have suggested that alcohol was a factor in Sarah's death, not as a failed diet, but because her ambitious husband had neglected her, and she felt left alone. But she had a wonderful funeral, attended by showpeople from all over England and Wales. William had to hire extra landaus to carry all the flowers.[29] As *The Era* reported:

Quite a gloom was cast over the town of Carmarthen on Friday of last week, when the sad news became known that Mrs. Sarah Haggar, the beloved wife of Mr. William Haggar, the proprietor of Haggar's Bioscope Exhibition, had passed away at the fair ground, and the feeling of regret was of the most genuine character, as Mr. Haggar and his family - especially the deceased lady - had endeared themselves, by their kindness and sympathy in assisting any deserving cause, to the townspeople. The same feeling was manifest among their fellow showmen on the Welsh round, and expressions of sympathy and letters of condolence poured in to the sorrowing husband and family. The deceased lady had been ailing since about Christmas, but was not confined to her room until a fortnight ago, and the end was not anticipated. She, however, succumbed on Friday afternoon, the cause of death being paralysis of the nerves. She was fifty-eight years of age, and leaves, besides her sorrowing husband, a family of eight children - five sons and three daughters - to mourn their irreparable loss.[30]

Sarah had had a hard life. She had never had a permanent home. Brought up in the travelling theatre, she had roamed the country with her husband for all 38 years of their married life. She had had eleven children in twenty years, and had suffered the deaths of three of them. She had endured near-starvation, and times when her family didn't possess even a single living van. The family's prosperity of her last few years had not brought any let-up in the touring routine. She did not live to settle down on the proceeds of her hard work.

She is an elusive figure. Only three photographs of her survive, all taken during her last ten years, one, the most commonly published, showing the marks of her illness. The best of these was taken at Jim and Kate's wedding in 1900: it portrays Sarah, in a jaunty hat but unsmiling, and shows that her likeness lives on amongst her great-grandchildren. Beyond that, little description of her personality has survived. Her son Walter, in his recollections of the theatre and cinema days, fails to mention her: his history was that of the men. Her daughter Lily praises Sarah as an actress, a seamstress, and an economical housewife, but, in writing the biography of her father, does not allow her mother to speak: all she says by way of an epitaph is: 'She was sadly missed by us all and by all the showpeople who loved her dearly. She had had an extremely hard life, but would help anyone who was in trouble, and nurse anyone who was sick.'[31] Perhaps the best epitaph came from her grandson, Cyril Haggar Yorke, who, speaking 80 years later of the grandmother he had never known (Sarah died three years before he was born), said: 'the girls' (Rose, Violet and Lily) 'had a great love for their mother, as it was she who had kept the family together.'[32]

The show had to go on. The No. 1 Show continued its summer tour, making a great hit at Brynmawr Fair in September, showing a film recently made of the Welsh National Pageant.[33] It wintered as usual in Aberdare. There, 'the old'un' was at last planning to settle down.

7. William turns film-maker, 1901-05

AT THAT TIME, ANYONE with the ingenuity to devise the elementary apparatus needed, and film a few hundred feet of 'phantom ride', comic scene or news event, could set themselves up as a film producer.[1] So it was for William: when he took the decision to make his own films, all he had to do was to assemble the necessary tools and equipment. A camera, supplies of film, and the means of processing it, he would get from his friends Urban or Bromhead. But never having a studio, he had to film in the open air when the sun shone. He loved filming in Pembrokeshire, missing no opportunity: given a sunny day he would be off in his pony and trap with the camera and a couple of members of the family, and they would shoot a scene. One such afternoon involved young Walter cycling down the road at the Pill on the Neyland side of Milford and into the water. He had to do this time and again until his father was satisfied he had a satisfactory shot. 'He'd brood over it in his mind,' Lily said, 'and talk it over with my brothers, Jim and Walter, and when they were pretty sure the weather was going to be fine, he'd tell my mother, 'drop everything, we're going a couple of miles out.' He'd have his spot previously, and take his film from beginning to end. There were no scripts: we'd be told what to do.'[2] The Haggars even made an attempt at colour films: selecting a 'short' of an actress undressing, they hand-coloured her first petticoat red and her second petticoat blue, but when the film was shown in private, the colours clashed, due to the varying density of the dyes employed for the colouring. The film was greeted with roars of laughter, so the experiment was abandoned.[3]

William's films include topicals and actualities (of which he made hundreds[4] including **Outside the Works**), short comedies, chase films and dramas. It is fortunate that, although most films are lost, examples of all of these types survive. In **The Stepney Wedding**, filmed in 1911 in Llanelly at the wedding of local notables, Sir Edward Stafford Howard and Lady Catherine Meriel Stepney, two cameras are used to show the wedding processions head on and sideways on. **The Bathers' Revenge** from 1904 is a good example of the kind of short comedy films made in vast numbers by all the

No version of **The Maid** appears to have been marketed nationally. But four other play scenes were: **Thrilling Scene from 'The Maniac's Guillotine', The Duel Scene from 'The Two Orphans', The Wild Man of Borneo**,[18] and **True as Steel**, each lasting about two minutes, were marketed, at a price of about 6d per foot length, by Charles Urban's Warwick Trading Company.[19] William had gone into film-making to provide for his show a secure source of films which would attract his audiences, and outdo his competitors. He had not thought of making money by selling his films to other people. Now, unexpectedly as it must have seemed, Charles Urban had offered to pay William to market his films. This was a bonus for William: an extra £10 or £20 per film, or whatever it was, which otherwise he would not have made. It explains why only certain Haggar films were distributed nationally: Urban may well have decided that he could not make a profit by selling a film with a Welsh title such as **The Maid of Cefn Ydfa**: the market for it, and other Haggar films of purely local interest, would be too limited. But for films of scenes from well-known plays, and for comedies, there would be a market.[20] Once Charles Urban had bought them, they became his, and William was not credited with them in catalogues or adverts: so it is possible that other films in Urban catalogues are also William's: films with titles such as **The Weary Willies and the Policeman, Weary Willie and his pal on the rampage,** and **Unfair exchange is robbery**, whose maker is now unknown, might have been his.[21] These may have been the forerunners of the many such films which William made during the next few years.

1903

More topical films were made this year, including perhaps **Outside the Works**, and that of the funeral of the men of the Mumbles lifeboat.[22] William now turned his hand to comedy in earnest, making several **Weary Willie and Tired Tim** comedies, marketed by both Urban and Gaumont, with Jim Haggar, being tall, playing Tired Tim, and Walter, who was shorter, as Weary Willie. The two tramps tried their hand at barbering, with hilarious results, but came to grief when expecting beer to flow from a barrel of gunpowder.[23]

William had for some time been friendly with Gaumont's A.C. Bromhead, and now he did a deal with him: Gaumont would sell Haggar films (except in William's South Wales area), in return for keeping William supplied with film, and developing it for him free of charge. As it turned out, Gaumont was to get a huge bargain. Years later, the family had forgotten that Urban had once bought William's films. Henry and Lily remembered only the special deal with Gaumont - and lamented the apparent loss of profit. But William, who did not have time or facilities for selling films, had been happy with his deal: as Walter wrote, 'anything good was marketed.'[24]

Bromhead was able to sell **Weary Willie and Tired Tim turned barbers, The Tramp and the Washerwoman** and other slapstick comedies, and also the first in a series of Mirthful Mary comedies. His film of the year, out of which he made over £2000 in sales, was **Desperate Poaching Affray**.[25] This film was, in its time, seen by more people than any other yet made. It sold 480 copies @ £5 10s. each : no film was ever said to have sold more.[26] **The Poachers** (as it was retitled for selling abroad) was seen all over Europe and in the United States: American film historians view it as 'the film that helped set the pattern for chase sequences in the movies.'[27]

The cast includes Will Haggar Junior and Sid Griffiths as the two poachers, with Walter and Fred Haggar as two of the gamekeepers. Policemen and the chasing crowd are played by other actors in Will Junior's company.[28] The synopsis of the film in the Gaumont catalogues is lyrical and extensive:

> Taken amid beautiful natural scenery, this film is of a highly exciting and sensational order, and may be briefly described and epitomised as follows. The snare - a low net is set across some bushes, and several hares and other game are struggling in it. The poachers arrive to secure their prey, and are surprised by gamekeepers; hurriedly hiding until the gamekeepers, accompanied by police, enter the bushes in search, they make a dash directly the latter are out of sight. Keepers and police give chase - over the gate, through the bracken, across the fields. The poachers turn and fire upon their pursuers, who return the fire, and one poacher is wounded in the arm. They are off again, but hard pressed, and turning in a narrow country lane, the poachers succeed this time with two hasty shots in dropping a couple of their pursuers. Another short run and poachers, pursuers and police are

mixed up in a desperate hand-to-hand struggle, in which the butt ends of their guns are freely used. They break away and make a run for it, but are headed off into a broad but shallow stream, into which one leaps in his efforts to escape. A policeman follows, and the struggle is resumed in the water. The policeman gets the worst of it, and once again the poacher gets away. His mate also gets flung into the water during a struggle on the bank. They are driven back into the water again from one side, and captured in an effort to escape from the other. Being brought close past the camera, their desperate and exhausted condition are plainly discernible.[29]

The film includes what is perhaps William's first panning shot, when the camera is moved to survey the way open to the poachers' escape. In those days re-takes were unknown, and someone walks across in front of the camera during the shot at the ford, where everyone gets the customary wetting. A whole pack of dogs joins in the chase. The catalogues list the film as 220 feet long, the surviving version lasting just three minutes: the earlier Haggar films run at about 70 feet per minute. Ada Haggar remembered many more people joining in the chase: eventually about 30, she thought, including a mother wheeling a pram.[30] Presumably William produced his own longer version afterwards, joining some new chase sequences onto the original film.

William also this year produced **A Dash For Liberty**, another chase movie of 300 feet, in five scenes, which he allowed Urban to sell. It appears that Urban, mindful of the success for Gaumont of **The Poachers**, hoped that he had as great a success on his hands - for he advertised **A Dash For Liberty, or, The Convict's Escape and Capture** as 'A splendid Sequel to our Film no. 1034, **A Daring Daylight Burglary.**'[31] What success he actually had is not known - but this time his catalogue does credit it to Haggar, an indication that William's fame as a film-maker was spreading.

1904

During this year, William produced, apart from several short comedies, the film for which he was later remembered by his friend Bromhead, **The Sign of the Cross**. Regrettably, the Gaumont catalogue containing its synopsis has not survived, but

Gaumont advertised it in *The Era* for six weeks, with the words, 'Great new serious picture: a powerful production of the religious drama. Seven Scenes: price £17 10s.'[32] The story was based on the play by Wilson Barrett, which during 1896/7 had had a run of 348 performances at the Lyric Theatre. It was a 'toga drama' of Christian persecution set in the Roman Empire, in which the hero, Marcus Superbus, falls in love with and is converted by the virtuous Christian maiden, Mercia (a role which the actress Lillah McCarthy had made her own). They die together in the Arena.[33]

It was in this year that the young evangelist and spiritual author of the Welsh Revival, Evan Roberts, visited Trecynon and Aberdare, producing a great sensation. David Matthews, who lived in Aberdare and described these events, says that one result was that 'Aberdare theatre-going dropped markedly.'[34] Did William choose to film **The Sign of the Cross** in the light of the news of the burgeoning Revival? Its story of Christian faith and martyrdom could hardly fail to appeal to the Revivalists, and might therefore be especially good for business.[35]

The Haggars made the film at Rhymney, with Will Junior as Marcus, Jenny Lindon as Mercia, and Jim Haggar as the Emperor Nero. Will Desmond, later to star in Hollywood Westerns, was also in the cast. As Bromhead recalled, it was a sensation for its length of 700 feet (lasting about ten minutes), and was pirated in the United States.[36] It was later remarked that there were no lions in the picture, Will Haggar always maintaining that lions were only introduced by the Americans, to give colour to the Yankee versions.[37]

Two more comic films featuring the actress 'Mog'[38] were sold by Gaumont. Mog had made her film debut the previous year in **Mirthful Mary - a case for the Blacklist**, in which she had been drunk and disorderly. Now she came to court in **Mirthful Mary in the dock**. She was evidently a large lady: 'With as much of a spring as her ponderous weight will allow, she gets over the dock rail and stands unsteadily in the centre of the room' - but her bulk made her easily able to fight off policemen ('Coppers fall like skittles'), lay waste the magistrate's court, and generally cause comic mayhem. When she falls, 'one can see at a glance she is still wearing the same conspicuous costume as when arrested.'[39]

Sold by Biograph in the U.S.A., the synopsis is Americanised: 'A husky fishwife is on trial for drunkenness and not liking the way her trial is conducted she proceeds to make a rough house of it. After she has finished off the courtroom attendants she throws a bottle of ink at the judge and climbing up on the bench pulls him down and pummels him.'[40] In **Snowballing**, the same actress went by the name of 'Mog the fireman', 'and the picture finishes with her fighting gamely in various and interesting attitudes with astonishing vigour.'[41]

Meanwhile, Urban marketed a number of short slapsticks including **The Bathers' Revenge.** The film is 75 feet long, lasting just over a minute. 'Some youths enjoying a refreshing dip in a stream, having left their wardrobe on a seat on the bank. A spooning couple coming up, toss the bathers' belongings contemptuously aside, and the bathers in revenge pull the seat, and so tumble the interrupters into the water, from which they escape after only the most determined and ludicrous exertions.'[42] At the very end, a large black dog occupies the foreground, watching the unfortunate couple struggle out of the water. Made on the Western Cleddau, in Pembrokeshire, one of William's favourite haunts, it features Walter as the 'female' half of the courting couple in drag: one of the first films in which this was done.[43] It was found in the National Film Archive, under another name: there since 1936, it went unrecognised until 1995. It is a fine specimen of the short comedies made by William and the other film-makers of the time.

In this year, too, as in other years, there are films in the catalogues which, from their plot or the language of their synopsis, may have been by Haggar, although not hitherto attributed to him.[44]

1905
The year's film-making commenced in the winter, when the whole country was extraordinarily interested in the Russo-Japanese War, then at its height, many film cameramen being despatched to the front to send back action pictures. More prudent directors stayed at home, among them the Haggars. As Walter told it:

We took some Russo-Japanese war films on the snow-clad tops of the hills of the Rhymney Valley. In one incident at Quaker's Yard, I acted the part of a little Japanese, and my brother James (a burly fellow) was a Russian. The film was arranged, staged and fought with bayonets and guns, and it was decided that at the conclusion of the fight, the Jap should stab the Russian. When the camera stopped, the burly Russian put his hand to his head and withdrew it covered with blood. In the excitement of the fight, I had stabbed him in reality and he was bleeding profusely. In fact in most of the mêlées of film production, there were wounds, cuts and bruises, but they were never noticed until later.[45]

There could be pitfalls in making fake documentaries, as William found out at Treharris. All the male members of the family and any men working for the Haggars at the time took part in the film. All were heavily made up with beards and uniforms, in order not to be recognised. But, unfortunately, a local lad had somehow managed to get mixed up with the 'soldiers', and when the film was shown, one of the audience shouted out, 'Look bach, there's Dai Jones on the screen.' It took them some time to live this down.[46]

A film of local interest made this year, which was not marketed by Gaumont (Urban having now dropped out, preferring to concentrate on scientific films), was **The Landing of the French**, concerning the French invasion of Wales, at Fishguard in 1797. The film was made at Llangwm in Pembrokeshire: it used the local fisherwomen, who, led by William's daughters, had to pull red flannel petticoats over their heads to appear like redcoats, and march round and round in front of the camera, just as the 400 women of Fishguard had done in fact (dressed in their red Welsh wool, they had marched round and round a hill, to give the appearance of overwhelming force, so terrifying the French that they surrendered to the local militia). The film-making was remembered as a disaster: the weather was bad, the actors and actresses recalcitrant, and the extras were problematical, 'being the ladies of Llangwm' was the family joke.[47]

Gaumont marketed eleven or twelve films this year. Among them were the usual short comedies; a last 'Mirthful Mary' film, **Mary is**

Dry, in which the miscreant wrecked a pub; a trick film, **DTs, or, The Effects of Drink**, in which a toper sees his bed turned into a monster; and another chase film, **The Salmon Poachers,** in which the plot of **Desperate Poaching Affray** is repeated but with more opportunities for wettings offered by the use of a boat.

The principal films this year were longer dramas. **The Squire's Daughter**, filmed at Haverfordwest, featuring Fred and Lily Haggar, was advertised as 'Sensational. Humorous, Pathetic. Splendid Acting. Delightful Scenery, Excellent Photography. A Drama in a Nutshell. Refined and Pleasing. Length 600 ft. Price £15.'[48]

The first scene of **A Message from the Sea** survives: in it, Harry Mainstay, a sailor, played by Will Junior, bids goodbye to his family: he leaves his parents at the gate, and takes his wife and daughter down to the quay. Walter described how it was made:

> Mr. Haggar resolved to produce a big feature picture. He called in his son, Will Haggar, who was travelling the country with his own theatrical company. Will readily agreed to help his father, so the company proceeded to Burry Port sands, where **A Message from the Sea** was filmed. The making of this drama of the sea took two days, and much film was spoiled due to actors wandering out of the picture. There was no scenario and no script, for the performers had to obey the calls of the cameraman, who was also producer. Sometimes the father took charge, then Walter or his brother James had a try at filming. And so the work began to develop. The film might have been a drama, but there were several amusing incidents, one being where the hero and his fellow sailors were supposed to be on a raft in the middle of the Atlantic Ocean. The raft got stuck on a sandbank and the hero had to move it by standing waist high in the 'ocean'![49]

The plot involves Harry's wife receiving a message ('Shipwrecked, alone on a raft, no hope, God bless you, farewell - Harry Mainstay'), which in despair he has committed to the sea in a bottle. In the melodramatic final scene, she is in widow's weeds tending his memorial in a churchyard, when he returns: 'no language could describe such a homecoming. The widow's cap is thrown away, the jolly sailor's 'kerchief adorns the comely head of the mother, who is now a wife once more', ends the synopsis.[50]

But the biggest film of this busy year, a 770 feet blockbuster, the longest yet made, was the surviving drama, **The Life of Charles Peace**. The most famous of William's films, it was purchased by the National Film Archive from Collingridge and Co. in 1937, and stills from it have appeared in film histories ever since.[51] Originally thought to be by Mottershaw, it was recognised as William's in 1948.[52] The surviving version is complete:[53] it lasts for eleven minutes. Charles Peace was a thief who was hanged for murder in 1879.[54] The filmed story is factual and details true to life - for example, the real-life Peace had something of an obsession with violins, and was said to be a master of disguise. Lily explained her part in the film:

> Pembrokeshire was Father's favourite site for making films, and there he made **The Life of Charles Peace**, the notorious burglar and murderer. This film was a classic of its time. All the parts were played by members of the family. My brother Walter took the part of Charles Peace and my 12 year old self played a minor role. I have never been able to understand why - I had a brother 2 years older - why he didn't take the part I took. But I think it was that the brother who took the part of Charles Peace was short, although he must have been 22, and I was shorter than him and the brother next to me was a big fellow, and I think they wanted someone shorter than Charlie Peace as his henchman. I wore my brother's suit and I had long hair, all under my brother's cap. I didn't do much. All I did was stand outside. And then again, what people would do! This woman loaned us her house and they used a window for Charlie Peace to open and climb in and do his burglary act, and I needed to be on the lookout outside and hold his tools and give them to him. Another scene was him making merry, making love to a married woman, she was his mistress. He was playing his violin and everyone else was dancing. My mother was in it - all the family were in it, except my father.[55]

Walter later related that at Pembroke Dock, during the filming of their Charlie Peace story, a railway guard had loaned them his train as well as helping to catch the elusive Charlie - the part he himself had played. Dressed up as a convict, he was put into the train in charge of warders. At an opportune moment, when the little camera was centred upon the carriage, out came Charlie through the window in his attempt to escape. But not the real Charlie, only a dummy. The hanging scene in the film, however, was quite real, and he had a very narrow escape from being choked to death.[56]

The cast list is:

Charles Peace:	Walter Haggar
His accomplice:	Lily Haggar
Dyson:	James Haggar
Mrs. Dyson:	Violet Haggar
Mrs. Peace:	Sarah Haggar
First policeman	Henry Haggar
Second policeman	Fred Haggar
Third policeman	Joe Giddings
Others:	Members of William Haggar's company.[57]

Ernest Lindgren, the Librarian at the British Film Institute, quotes the synopsis of the first three scenes.[58]

1. Peace's First Burglary. (Interior: a room.)
Peace and his accomplice climb in through a window and begin to lever open a chest. While they are at work, the occupants of the house come into the room and surprise them. Peace escapes through the window. His accomplice tries to follow him but he is shot and falls back into the room.
2. Peace at Dyson's House. (Interior: a room in Dyson's house.)
Peace is discovered playing his violin to Mr. and Mrs. Dyson, who beat time to the music. When Peace stops, Dyson suggests a drink and goes out to get the glasses. Peace sits beside Mrs. Dyson and begins to embrace her.[59] Dyson returns suddenly, and realising the situation, grabs hold of Peace and throws him down. Peace gets up and goes out, shaking his fist at Dyson.
3: The murder of Dyson. (Exterior: a corner of a field, close to a hedge.)

Peace enters with a note; he fastens it onto a bush and then hides behind the hedge. Mrs. Dyson enters, sees the note, and takes hold of it to read it. At this moment her husband enters, and although she tries to conceal the note, he snatches it from her and reads. Looking into the hedge, he finds Peace hiding, and drags him out. Peace then draws a revolver and shoots him. Mrs. Dyson throws herself on the body, and Peace walks off in triumph.[60]

Michael Chanan, in *The Dream that Kicks*[61] includes a lengthy account of, and commentary on **The Life of Charles Peace**, including the remainder of the synopsis. The following is a shortened version.[62]

Scene 4: Chas Peace at Home.
This scene consists of two shots, connected by a straight cut. Peace is once again playing the fiddle in a domestic scene with his family. One of them starts gesturing to warn of the arrival of the police and to indicate that Peace should get into bed and pretend to be asleep. He dons a woman's night-cap and shawl, and lies down, covering himself well. The police enter and search around, without realizing that the figure in bed is Peace. As they leave, Peace begins to get up from the bed, but too quickly, and they spot him. A brawl begins, but Peace manages to escape up a ladder standing to one side against the wall opposite the camera, and the picture cuts to the rooftop on to which Peace has climbed. It is not a matching cut. Again this scene is a stage set, but the shot which follows is almost twice as long as any which has yet been seen. It consists of Peace repelling the police, who have followed him, as they struggle on the roof. [63] He shoots two of them in the course of the struggle. One of them falls through a skylight (evidently made of paper) in the roof, and Peace escapes.

Scene 5: Burglary at Blackheath.
Here, for the second time in the film, a real exterior location is used, the frontage of a respectable-looking house, although the camera is nonetheless placed almost directly opposite just as if it were a stage set. Peace enters with an accomplice and forces entry through the

window. The accomplice waits outside. Three policemen enter from behind the accomplice's back and nab him. One of them takes his place and receives the loot which Peace, unsuspecting, hands out to him through the window. Then the police nab Peace as he too climbs out after it. He manages to fight them off and escapes, running out of frame on the left towards the camera. We cut to a second shot, of another exterior location. Here, for the first time, the camera position seems to have been chosen to benefit from depth of field, since it allows, with considerable economy, for three distinct 'areas' of action. First, Peace climbs over the section of the wall facing the camera. Then a fight with the policeman takes place in front of the wall, but again Peace manages to escape, fleeing up the side lane away from the camera. As he disappears in the distance, we cut to the third shot of the sequence - we speak of 'sequence' here for the first time - the continuation of the chase across a mound of rubble, another real exterior location. The cut reverses the direction, for in this shot Peace is running towards camera. The shot lasts only a few seconds, and suggests that here the film maker is beginning to sense the need to pace the action through cutting. Is it an accident that this occurs at a point which does not advance the narrative, but rather, by delaying the passage to the next scene, provides a moment of emotive effect which increases its tension? And is it a coincidence that in these shots is made real use of picture depth, with movement away from and towards the camera, instead of simply from side to side? Only the first shot in the sequence really conforms to a stage-bound *mise-en-scène*, although the whole sequence could have been played on stage with characters chasing each other across the proscenium and back again. But it wouldn't have had as much tension and fluidity that way.

Scene 6: Peace, the Parson and the Police.

Again a real exterior location, a country lane. Peace enters from the rear and proceeds to disguise himself as a parson. Trick photography - stop-frame or 'interrupted camera' action - is used to allow him to complete his transformation as if by magic. Then three policemen enter, one by one, searching for their man, and Peace sends them off in different directions. The scene provides an opportunity for a kind of comic play which firmly roots the appeal of the film within working-class culture, since it takes two forms of authority, police and parson, as the butts of its humour. As Peace the Parson directs the policemen in their pursuit, he offers them a tract. The first two policemen accept politely, but the third knocks the tracts out of Peace's hand impatiently. Peace cocks a snook at him,[64] then turns tail and runs.

Scene 7: Peace captured by P.C. Robinson.

This runs for just over a minute, the longest shot in the film, as if, although we know the outcome in advance, the film maker is trying to spin out the suspense as long as possible. Again an exterior location, on a heath. Peace is captured only after a fight in which he twice shoots at his pursuers. One of the policemen, repulsed by Peace, rushes away from the action, which takes place in the middle distance, towards the camera, exiting very close to it on the left of frame. Again, in other words, the use of picture depth for effect at a moment which doesn't directly advance the narrative. It must have been a very startling moment.

Scene 8: Peace being taken to Sheffield for trial.

This scene lasts about a quarter of a minute, and continues the use of real locations, taking place on a railway station platform. Peace is wearing gaolbird dress, and cowers before his captors, but he still has enough insolence left to make a couple of half-hearted attempts to escape them.

Scene 9: Struggle in the railway carriage.

We are now approaching the film's central tour de force, a portrayal of the episode which made Peace particularly famous - his attempt to escape the police by jumping through the window of a moving train. We can well imagine the audience being on tenterhooks as they wondered how the film was going to manage to portray the incident. It was one of the cinema's first real stunts, a moment when the screen reached beyond all known limitations of art and entertainment by conquering the need for the suspension of disbelief, so that each member of the audience could come out afterwards and say, 'I saw it with my own eyes'.

The sequence consists of three shots. The first is taken with the camera outside the railway carriage facing it, and shows Peace sticking his body out of the window trying to escape. Faint wisps of steam crossing the bottom of the frame give a slight impression that the train is in motion, though we cannot see any scenery, and the shot was obviously (to our more analytic eyes) taken with the train stationary. [65] We then cut to another angle of the same action - for the first time a shot in strict continuity with the preceding one, an intended matching cut. This shot looks as if it was taken by holding the camera outside the window of the train as it rounded a bend, which emphasizes the movement in the shot. Peace is seen struggling with his body half out of the window. He gets pulled back in, and then you see his figure shooting out of the window and completely out of shot to the right of frame. Close examination of the film reveals that the figure which shoots through the window is a dummy, but the action is too fast for it to be clearly spotted. We immediately cut to a chase along the railway line towards the camera. Peace stumbles (perhaps he's sprained his ankle) and the police catch up, and finally exit with him towards camera right.

Scene 10: Chas Peace in prison.

This shows an identity parade in a real exterior location, with Mrs. Dyson making the identification. As she does so Peace jumps at her and attempts to throttle her - an unexpected and dramatic way of emphasizing his despair.

Scene 11: The Execution.

Finally comes one of the most controversial scenes. A procession of Peace, a parson, and warders mount a platform, the rope and hood are placed over Peace's head, and he disappears through the floor. Mottershaw's version of 'Charles Peace', made in the same year, does not include the execution; the catalogue description states: 'It has been decided not to reproduce the Execution scene, as we believe it is too ghastly and repulsive.'[66]

'If Haggar's film stands as a paradigm of early cinema at the end of its first decade,' concludes Chanan, 'it is not because its aesthetics are out of the ordinary but rather because they are entirely symptomatic. What is remarkable about it is the indicative, almost didactic way in which it combines so many facets of the filmographic objective of the time.' By this, Chanan explains, he means that the ending is known, but still the audience is kept in suspense as to how it is to be shown. The film combines the use of stage sets with the real exterior locations. It uses trick photography and stunts, and discovers, in the use of depth of action, the plasticity of screen space as it expands into the scenic distance of the chase, and contracts to the stage-set of the gallows.

8. William's longer films, 1906-14

1906 and 1907

THIS SECOND PHASE OF William's film-making, concluding as it does with his greatest effort, the three-reel epic last remake of **The Maid of Cefn Ydfa**, begins with something of a pause, in contrast with the busy year 1905. The whole family may have been more occupied with show business, on the arrival of the two big new showfronts; or William may have found more topical films to make, or (since not all William's fiction films are known) the 'pause' may be more apparent than real. At all events, during 1906/7 there are only two definite entries in the national catalogues, **Pongo the Man Monkey**, a fantasy embodying slapstick and a chase, and **Desperate Footpads** - although **The Two Orphans** may be a longer remake of his 1902 venture. **Pongo** seems to have been the last of William's films which Bromhead sold, and Charles Urban had also dropped out, preferring to concentrate on educational films and those of scientific interest. When Haggar films re-appear in *The British Film Catalogue*, they are being sold by other dealers - the well established Walturdaw, and Walter Tyler, new to film sales, but with a large and successful concern hiring out lantern slides.[1] At the same time, thriving businesses had sprung up to deal in second-hand films: many Haggar films, including **Poaching Affray** from 1903 and various comedies from 1904/5 were being advertised for sale in the press.[2]

Lily Richards had special cause to remember **Desperate Footpads:**[3]

One of the best films that Father took was called **The Farmer's Daughter and the Desperate Footpads**. It was taken in Haverfordwest in 1907. I took the part of the farmer's daughter, and two of my brothers played the footpads. I had to struggle with them on a bridge over a river[4] and was eventually thrown in. I could not swim, but the river was not very deep, and I was rescued and brought back up onto the bridge. I hated that film because I looked such a mess when they fished me out of the water. Well, I had long hair, and you can just imagine

91

what I looked like. I felt terrible! There were no scripts. 'You come across the bridge, the footpads will attack you, and throw you into the river. You'll be quite safe, the river is shallow, and a couple of your brothers will be there and rescue you.'[5]

Lily also remembered dramas and comedies which may have been made in the same year. **East Lynne** and **Uncle Tom's Cabin**, which she described as among the most famous of her father's films,[6] were staples of the Haggars' theatrical repertoire, to which William turned in these years for film subjects alongside topicals and comedies.[7] **Wanted - a Wife** was filmed at Maesteg, on a set which William created on the back of a flat truck. Walter, playing a bachelor advertising for a wife, interviewed a string of girls who, entering up a set of steps, knocked at the door and went in. At the end of the film, the chosen beauty proceeded to divest herself of her wig, false teeth, wooden leg and various similar attractions. It may have been inspired by a Gaumont comedy of 1905 entitled, **Wanted - a Husband**, in which a man places that false advert in the press, with comic results. Similarly, William's **Spaghetti Eating** may have been an answer to Hepworth's **Macaroni Feast**: it involved Walter and Violet in close-up, sitting on the ground eating spaghetti.[8]

Topical films recalled from those years included **The wreck of the schooner** *Amazon* on Margam sands, **A Walking Match at Treorchy**, and a film about **Deep-sea Fishing**, for which a trawler was hired.[9]

1908
William now turned his hand to lengthened remakes. **A Dash for Liberty, The Dumb Man of Manchester, The Maid of Cefn Ydfa** and **A Message from the Sea** all received longer treatment, Will Junior and Jenny Lindon and members of their theatrical company supplying the cast. None of these survive. With Walter, Violet and Jim, who had formed the nucleus of his theatrical company after Will Junior had gone his own way, William made new films, including the popular stock drama, **The Red Barn Crime - Maria Martin**,[10] and two chase films, **Dick the Kisser** and **The Sheep Stealer**.[11] The latter survives in its entirety. Featuring Jim Haggar as the Sheep Stealer, with his wife Kate and children James and

Lily in the opening and closing scenes, it lasts about seven minutes.[12]

The film opens on a bare room in a cottage. A husband, his wife and their two children have no food. A title comes up on the screen: 'My wife and children shall not starve'. The husband goes out, and encounters a farmer and his shepherd driving sheep through the village. He begs the farmer for employment, but in vain. As the shepherd follows the sheep, the husband enters from the front and grabs one. The shepherd runs off to fetch the farmer, and the chase begins. A crowd follows. The husband gets away, and is seen in comic close-up with the sheep on his shoulders: it is a large and heavy sheep, and it struggles. He puts it down, the crowd catch him up, and the sheep escapes. A dog joins in the fun, then more. The sheep stealer gets away from the police, who have now been summoned, and the chase continues, through rolling countryside and across a weir, where everyone gets a wetting. At last the husband reaches his cottage, limping. Inside, he flops down on the floor. He has had it. The farmer, the shepherd and the police enter. The wife appeals to them - we have nothing, she gestures. The second title appears: 'the farmer forgives him'. The farmer gives money to the children while the husband and wife embrace. 'A conclusion which should have a good effect on most audiences, shows the family once more prosperous and happy.'[13]

As in previous years, other films in the catalogue may be William's: a comedy, two dramas, and another surviving chase film, **The Plumber and the Lunatics**. Neither the actors nor the location are recognisable, but the action is Haggarish. It is quite short: about five minutes. A plumber is sent to a lunatic asylum to mend a broken window. He mounts a ladder, but drops his knife in surprise when two inmates appear below. They pick up the knife and gesticulate with it, frightening him. He runs away, and they give chase, with the Warden after them, hurdling the empty pens of a cattle market, into a house, over its roof, and through road works. Eventually the lunatics corner the plumber, but hand him back the knife with a fulsome salute. The Warden takes them away. 'All that fuss just to give a fellow a knife' is the closing title.

No Haggar films appear in *The British Film Catalogue* for these years. But topicals continued to be made: 'A year or two later we received some assistance and co-operation from Moss Empires, Cardiff, in taking a film of the **Welsh National Pageant** there. A copy of this film is today [1953] in the Welsh National Museum in Cardiff in a sealed metal container', wrote Walter; the film made a hit at Brynmawr Fair in September 1909. Unfortunately, enquiry of the Welsh National Museum about the film has produced no result.[14]

But the Llanelli museum has been able to find a Haggar topical, a film of a grand society wedding, **The Stepney Wedding**, which took place in the town in 1911, when Jim Haggar was there managing the Royalty Theatre which his father had bought the previous year. The film was taken by two cameramen, Jim and his father, in different positions outside the church, and so views the arrival of the guests, the vicar and his choir, the bride on the arm of her father, and the departure of the whole procession, from the front and from the side. Right at the end, one cameraman photographs the other: only the second surviving view of William on film.

Jim made several other films that year, when Llanelly was in the news. Strikes by seamen and firemen had precipitated a national rail strike in support, and the railwaymen had grievances of their own. The Prime Minister, H. H. Asquith, communicated with them and a meeting was held at the Board of Trade. He offered a Royal Commission, but got on his high horse and said the country could not allow a general paralysis of the railway system. Probably, says a historian of the times, his reason was that the country then stood in almost hourly danger of a war with Germany: but the railway leaders knew nothing of it, and received the worst impression. The first general railway strike was called, on 16 August 1911, amid the hottest and driest summer since 1868, and much of industry was paralysed.[15] Troops were freely used to overawe disorder; in London they camped in the parks. The worst rioting was at Llanelly, where shops and a train were looted: soldiers fired, killing two men, and five more men perished by an explosion among the freight. It was this riot which Jim filmed.

1912-14

William now had no need to make films for a living. Plenty were available to buy, and later to hire: during these years, the family was spending £1000 a year on stocks of films.[16] The industry in the United States got over its patent litigation and swung into action. In 1911, two-thirds of all U.S. films were Westerns, and in January 1913 William was advertising Vitagraphs, Kalems, A.B. and Essanays: all the main American producers. This was what his audience wanted to see, and he would give it to them. Charlie Chaplin and Broncho Billy would pack his cinemas now.

However, William had not entirely forgotten his film-making. Topicals helped to advertise the weekly programme: it was always a draw for audiences to go to the pictures hoping to see themselves amongst the crowds at the Aberdare Carnival or the Pembroke Fair. During the summer of 1911, he decided to make a film of the story of a lifeboat disaster at the Mumbles, near Swansea. To be called, **The Women of Mumbles Head**, it related an incident in January 1883, when the German barque, *Admiral Prinz Albert* of Danzig was driven onto the rocks off the Mumbles light. The lifeboat *Wolverhampton* went alongside and took off the crew, but then capsized. The Lighthouse keeper and his daughters Jessie and Maggie Wright went down to the shore and managed to pull two crew members to safety. All the rest were lost.

William started with actual footage, taken eight years before. In February 1903, the lifeboat *Jenny Stevens* had attended the schooner *Christine*, but was not required. The gale blowing at the time increased in severity, and the lifeboat sought shelter in the mouth of the river Afan. The cox'n laid out a sea anchor, which failed: like the *Wolverhampton* twenty years before, the *Jenny Stevens* too capsized, and all hands were lost in sight of shore. A week later, the whole of Port Talbot had turned out for the funeral, which Walter had filmed: all the halls had carried this early piece of newsreel.[17] In addition, more recently, Jim had filmed a schooner breaking up on Cefn Sidon sands at Burry Port. So, armed with this handy material, William went to Fishguard, with the actors from Will Junior's company, and once more enlisted local fisherwomen to help as 'extras'. It rained incessantly, and the actors were in a bad temper - they would keep walking in and out of the shot. Jenny Lindon was hoity-toity, complaining about her dress. Her sister Kate, Jim's wife, was there too, with her daughter, Lily. Fishing boats were hired, and filled with actors. The day was rough: the actors, having little experience with boats, got into trouble, and the fictitious rescue had to be carried out in reality. This added spice to their performance in the film.[18]

It took William, busy with his new cinemas and his second marriage, two years to prepare the film for its release in 1913 (during his honeymoon in New York in April 1912, Walter and Jim rushed out the shipwreck and rescue footage as 'newsreel' of the sinking of the *Titanic*).[19] At the same time, he was faced with another challenge: Will Junior asked his help to film a second remake of **The Maid of Cefn Ydfa.**

The old mansion named Cefn Ydfa[20] was situated in the parish of Llangynwyd, near Maesteg. It was said to have been the home of Ann Thomas (1704-27), around whose name a romantic and sad legend grew up - although historians have doubted whether there was any truth in it. Ann's true love was Will Hopkins, a local slater, plasterer, and poet, but she was forced by her parents to marry, against her will, Anthony Maddox, a wealthy solicitor. Will, grieving, left the district. He later returned in response to Ann's earnest entreaty. She became very ill, and died in his arms. Her body is buried in Llangynwyd churchyard, where Will, too, lies - he died in 1741 at the age of 47. A play was written on the subject, and, in 1881 it was turned into a popular novel and much embroidered by Isaac Craigfryn Hughes.[21] Will Haggar's company put on the play with great success: so much so, that it was a natural choice for a subject when, in 1902, William Haggar needed more films to make. The story of that first film version of **The Maid** has already been told. It was remembered later by correspondents in the *World's Fair* and the *South Wales Echo* as a sensational triumph for the family: everywhere it was shown, the 'full house' notices appeared with amazing regularity. When the first film had worn out, in 1908, William made a longer version.[22]

By 1912, the 1908 version of **The Maid** may also have become unshowable. The film industry and techniques had moved on. Will Junior decided that he would like to try to repeat his earlier success, in a bigger way. He discussed the project with his father, but William, having recently remarried, and now planning his next ventures in Aberdare and elsewhere, was reluctant to become as fully involved as before. Lengthy shoots with the cumbersome cameras of those days he could leave to someone else: Will could hire an experienced film cameraman from London. But he and Jim would agree with Will a scenario, to decide what parts of the stage play they would omit, and what advantages to take of the exterior locations. They may have agreed to shoot all the interior scenes together, leaving the exteriors to be done later, in order to economise on the amount of time for which the London cameraman would be required: in the film as we have it, there are only three interiors, in which fourteen scenes are played, but some fifteen exteriors: logistically it is far more complicated than any previous surviving Haggar film, and, indeed, than most contemporary films of which we have record.

So William put up the money, Will hired the cameraman, and, during that summer of 1912, this cameraman and Will's company produced at least the interior scenes, outdoors of course, when the sun shone, with the scenery set up on the cabbage patch at Pontardulais. These shots were then handed over to William to edit, and complete the shooting at the exterior locations.[23] William was horrified with what was handed over to him: he spent long hours editing, but realised that he would have to re-shoot scenes to make the film work.[24] This he did during the next summer, when the exterior scenes were also shot, and the result was put together during the earlier part of 1914, having been delayed by William's illness in the winter of 1913. Making one coherent film out of this disparate material must indeed have been a major enterprise for William: in the film it is easy to distinguish his more vividly directed action from the static theatrical scenes directed by Will and shot by the London cameraman.

William never considered that he had got it right: he was not satisfied with the final result. If he had directed it all, it would have been a different film. But that might be a pity: much of the value of **The Maid** now rests in the fact that it is a visual record of an Edwardian touring company in action. Their style, akin to that developed universally for acting in silent films, is pure 'Commedia del Arte': the gestures and movement are traditional, studied and conventional.[25] But despite the awkwardness of the combination of two very different styles of action, the film works as a coherent narrative unity: for that, William was responsible, and in that respect it is certainly a 'William Haggar film'.[26]

The film was trailed in the *World's Fair* in August 1914, advertised in the *Aberdare Leader* for eight weeks from 17 October 1914, and shown for the first time on Monday, Tuesday and Wednesday, 14, 15 and 16 December 1914, in Aberdare, and on the Thursday, Friday and Saturday of the same week in Mountain Ash.[27] The audience in the Shanty Cinema at Aberdare on that 14th of December will have settled into their seats - not over comfortable, those benches, this being still a temporary structure in the Market Yard. They will have watched some short topical films - **The Looters of Liège, Sons of the Sea**, or **Wireless from the War**. Then Haggar's Quartette strikes up, and Cyril Yorke calls for their attention. He assures them that the film has been passed for showing by the new British Board of Film Censors. At last, the titles, 'The love story of Ann Thomas, the Maid of Cefn Ydfa, produced by Mr. and Mrs. Will Haggar Jnr and their Dramatic Company' come up on the screen.[28] There is an excited hum, then a hush as the cast appears, parading past Will Hopkins and his harp. During festivities at Cefn Ydfa, Ann (played by Jenny Lindon) meets and falls in love with Will (Will Junior). But at her home, Anthony Maddox, instructed by his father, proposes to Ann. She rejects him. At Bridgend Fair, the drunken Maddox insults Ann, and Will thrashes him. In revenge, Maddox hires two ruffians to kill Will, although he himself strikes the blow - after which the ruffians throw Will into the river. He is rescued by Morgan the Seer, and helped back to Morgan's hut by Lewis Bach (played by Will Fyffe) and Gwenny, Ann's maid (Jennie Haggar), who are first seen together as Gwenny is wheeling the drunken Lewis Bach home in a wheelbarrow. Ann is told by Maddox that Will is dead, but Will sends her a note to say that he is alive. Ann, having accused Maddox of Will's murder, and by now a prisoner of her mother in her own home, escapes to meet Will in Morgan's hut, but is followed and recaptured. Maddox has forged a will: he tells Ann that she will be disinherited if she does not marry him - but Morgan steals the real will, which gives Ann the inheritance, from under Maddox' nose. Will serenades Ann from outside her window, and she replies, writing on a leaf, using blood for ink:

'Will, Will, I am a prisoner here, save me!'

Will is persuaded by the guileless Morgan to sign an agreement to go abroad for two years to prove his love for Ann, but Maddox, by a clever trick (the agreement has been specially drafted so that, when torn in two, one half can seem to mean that Will has accepted a bribe to leave for ever) demonstrates to Ann that Will has renounced her. Ann gives in, and agrees to marry him. There is a dramatic scene at the church when Will arrives too late to expose the trick and prevent the marriage. He then does go abroad. Some years pass. Lewis Bach, Ann's faithful retainer, now married to Gwenny, waves goodbye to her and their three children, and sets off to find Will. 'Farewell England, farewell Wales, here's off to the Rhondda Valley!' proclaims the title. Morgan the seer is murdered by the villainous Maddox to regain the real will. Ann is beset by troubles - her drunken husband and the death of her child drive her to madness. Crooning over the body of her dead baby in the cemetery, she takes off her wedding ring and hurls it away. 'It hurts like the sting of a snake', she cries out: 'Will, Will, why don't you come to me?'

At this point, our surviving version fails. It would have continued to show Will's return, only for Ann to die in his arms, and his subsequent death. It was a powerful and affecting drama. The audience, having felt pity and terror, will have emerged uplifted, as by all good tragedies. They will also have marvelled at the film's scope and length - at 50 minutes, it was by far the longest film that most of them had ever seen.[29]

It is a film of contrasts - partly a filmed play, and partly a filmed version of the story, now modified by the different possibilities of the new medium. It has its static acting scenes, in the interiors and in some distant shots outside: but also it possesses lively movement, close-ups, changes of angle, and cuts from exterior to interior and back again. If a little of it is difficult to interpret, that is only due to an unsuccessful attempt to transfer to silent film the subtleties of the spoken play. In all this, it is fully a child of its time. From 1913, film adaptations of plays and novels were all the rage. Famous actors were filmed, silently speaking their lines. **The Maid's** theme of a disputed inheritance was the subject of large numbers of films at that time. Contemporary reviewers praised the films, but criticized comprehensibility and 'grouping' - the visual staging of the films. **Richard III, East Lynne** and **David Copperfield** are surviving contemporary British films with which **The Maid of Cefn Ydfa** can be compared.[30]

At the time, most films were made in studios, cameras remaining fixed to survey the stage.[31] **The Maid** is a considerable advance on such studio-bound films, in its use of its different outside locations, and in the moving of its camera within scenes. It is extremely well edited, with sophisticated cutting between interiors and exteriors, as for example when Ann, in her chamber, receives Will's note, and writes to him her message in blood: William's tour de force in this respect. The film also shows what an experienced dramatic company could do with a traditional and well-known theme. In point of fact, **The Maid** is positively Shakespearian: it has a balcony scene out of **Romeo and Juliet** when Will serenades Ann, on his Welsh harp; a counterpart of Friar Lawrence in Morgan the Seer; and a comic sub-plot to relieve the dramatic tension, worthy of **Macbeth's** drunken porter, or the two grave-diggers in **Hamlet**, when the drunken Lewis Bach and Gwenny change places in their wheelbarrow.

 In making it when he did, Will Junior hoped to repeat the success of the earlier versions. In this he succeeded locally.[32] But although the film was popular in Wales, being shown in Aberdare and Mountain Ash, in Walter's travelling bioscope and at Will's cinema in Pontardulais, it did not make any other mark. It was too parochial, and was released too late: it could not compete with the war topicals and the increasingly sophisticated product from America. It was at once the culmination of the Haggars' film-making, and its termination.

It is difficult to do justice, in prose, to the Haggar films. Even seeing the survivors on video or dvd, in silence as they are,[33] is insufficient, though charming. In their time they were new, bold, brash, thrilling. They were made for crowds of excited people, full of the fun of the fair, dressed up in their best, to giggle and squeal at. These viewers had been deafened by their favourite tunes on the huge organ, had goggled at the saucy paraders' legs, had passed in through the doors in the gaudily lit showfront, and were now, two or three hundred of them, crammed onto the wooden benches of the auditorium. There is a roll on the drums, a flourish on the piano. The lights go down. 'Ladies and Gentlemen', says Cyril Yorke, the Lecturer, 'You are about to see, for the very first time, the 'orrible burglar Charlie Peace meet 'is fate.' No wonder they 'oohed' and 'ahhed', booed and cheered, hooted and laughed! Present-day viewers cannot participate in that way, but they can still laugh at the chase, hope that the poachers get away, and that the Sheep Stealer can feed his family, because these are universal themes which arouse in everyone their sympathy for the underdog. And they can still be touched by the plight of the hapless Maid, as, like the heroine in a Jane Austen novel, both her love and her inheritance are threatened. These films, made a century ago, possess an enduring appeal.

9. Old Haggar settles down

THE SHOW MUST GO on: after Sarah's death in August 1909, William had continued on tour with the bioscope show for the rest of the season. Then he returned to his winter base in the Market Yard at Aberdare, to live in the family vans at the back of the show with his youngest son, Henry, and his two unmarried daughters, Violet and Lily.

The touring show now came to rest, being transformed into 'Haggar's Shanty Cinema', in the Market Yard.[1] During 1910 William started building up a chain of cinemas, buying the Royalty Theatre in Market Street, Llanelly, where he installed his son Jim as manager, in charge of a programme combining stage shows and music hall turns with films. He bought the skating rink at Pontardulais to convert into a theatre/cinema, and began building the Palace Cinema in Mountain Ash, and the Castle Cinema in Merthyr. He also negotiated for the Old Post Office buildings in Llanelly, although this bid for a second theatre there came to nothing. Meanwhile he looked for suitable premises for a permanent cinema in Aberdare, but not until 1913 was he able to buy the Drill Hall opposite the Market Yard, where, after demolishing the old hall, he would build his new luxury cinema, the Kosy.[2]

In January 1912, at St. Elvan's Church, Violet married Cyril Sydney Yorke, William's Bioscope lecturer and manager of the 'Shanty'. The local press called it a 'pretty wedding'. At the end of August, it was Lily's turn to have a 'pretty wedding' at St. Elvan's, the parish church in the centre of Aberdare.[3] Her husband was Bert Richards, manager of William's new cinema, the Palace in Mountain Ash. William kept a tight rein on the management of the Palace, placing the adverts for its programme side by side with his on the front page of the *Aberdare Leader*. Bert and Lily's cinema became known, simply, as 'Haggar's'.[4]

It is possible that both of these weddings were at William's suggestion: for neither marriage was to succeed. He had his own fish to fry: he had decided to marry again, and unmarried daughters at home would have been inconvenient. The bride of his choice was May Davies, the daughter of Jenkin Davies, landlord of the Bird in Hand Inn, in Monk Street, Aberdare. At eight o'-clock in the morning on 19 March 1912, they were married at Bryn Seion Chapel, Cwmbach, Aberdare, the paper deeming this an 'interesting wedding'. He was then just 61: May was 28. None of William's children attended the wedding breakfast: perhaps that portrays their attitude to this turn of events.[5] William and May left by the 10.37 Taff Vale Railway train en route for London, and thence to New York - they had tried in vain to obtain a passage on the new super-liner, the *Titanic*.[6] Most of their time in the USA was spent in New York sightseeing, visiting May's brother, and William's old friend Charles Urban, who was running his English firm, now called Kineto, from across the Atlantic. One day, while crossing Fifth Avenue, William suddenly lost his sight. May was panic-stricken, but fortunately a passer-by came to help and, discovering that William, like himself, was a freemason, immediately took him to an eye specialist who supplied him with dark glasses - and he recovered.[7]

The family now scattered. Will Junior and Jenny combined touring the South Wales halls with operating the Castle Theatre at their winter yard at Pontlottyn. Fred had returned to Wales after Catharine's death in 1907: he was a member of Will's theatrical company until his own death in 1913. Jim and Kate were busy managing the theatre at Llanelly, while Walter and Ada toured with the 'Electric Coliseum', from Abergavenny and Brecon out to Pembroke. Only Rose took no part in show business: after her marriage to Sid Moses in 1908, she went to live in Rhymney where he was a miner. Violet and Cyril remained in Aberdare, where Cyril managed the 'Shanty', and their son, Cyril Haggar Yorke, was born in the living van in January 1913. Henry was sent to manage the cinema in Pontardulais. Lily and Bert lived near the cinema in Mountain Ash.

Just at this time, William's name was dragged into a local controversy about the influence of the cinema on the impressionable population of Trecynon, a village just outside Aberdare. Already by 1910 'the influence of the film' had become a popular phrase, pundits discovering a large variety of real and imaginary effects of films, including both the emptying of churches and new ways of filling them. One beneficent influence appeared during the coal strikes of 1912. Strikes the year before had led to riots in Llanelly, in which two strikers died. In 1912 there were more strikes, over the minimum wage, serious enough for parliament to intervene. These failed to lead to the usual violence because the strikers spent their temporary freedom at the pictures. The high-principled criticised them: they should have been manning the picket lines and fighting blacklegs.[8]

The controversy was played out in the columns of the *Aberdare Leader*.[9] Following the great Welsh Revival of chapel-going inspired by evangelist Evan Roberts in 1904, the voice of the Nonconformist ministers was still powerful, although they did not have things all their own way. Early in 1912 the Glynneath Free Church Council had passed a strong resolution against the growing practices of opening picture halls on Sundays, all night dancing, and Sunday trading in the district. A deputation of ministers had addressed Aberdare Council, to no effect. This was small beer compared with the row stirred up by Rev. W. Cynog Williams, the Minister of the Baptist Chapel at Heolyfelin. On 2 March 1912 he wrote to the paper to protest about a proposal by the Trecynon Public Hall Committee to let the hall for use as a cinema. He followed this by getting his Church Meeting to pass a resolution of protest, on the grounds that such entertainment would be harmful to the moral, religious and industrial welfare of the locality, and that the miners would be without a place to hold public meetings. The next Sunday, he preached a powerful sermon, commencing with the stirring, but non-scriptural words, 'Assur also is joined with them; they have helped the children of Lot.'[10] This was fully reported in the *Leader*. After blasting overcrowded housing for its tendency to incite to immorality, he fulminated against bookmakers and 'loose women' being admitted to public houses.

> Wheresoever the carcass is, there will the eagles be gathered together. The streets of Trecynon teemed with moral consumptives. All admitted that cinematograph shows were detrimental to morals. A man, who was not a religious man, had testified to him that the picture shows at Aberdare were indecent. He opposed the granting of the Trecynon hall to such a company, because that

company in catering pictures would have to compete with Aberdare, and in doing so would have to descend as low as they could possibly go. It was held that such an exhibition would be a counter attraction to the public house. No, it would be a counter attraction to the churches. He had once expressed his belief that Trecynon chapels would become cinematograph shows, and it appeared as if his prophecy was being fulfilled. Because Mr. Haggar gave an occasional benefit concert, some people in Aberdare closed their eyes to certain things. A benefit concert was a sop to many a conscience. Not only was he opposed to a strange syndicate running such a show in the Hall, but he would oppose the granting of it for such a purpose even to a local company of Bwllfa men.

Such a declaration of war put the cat among the pigeons. The *Leader* printed angry and scathing replies. 'Trecynonite' complained that it was a disgrace for a man in Cynog's position to bring such grave accusations of immorality against nearly all classes of the inhabitants of Trecynon, based merely on hearsay evidence. If he had evidence of law-breaking, he should inform the police. If the streets teemed with moral consumptives, what had Cynog been doing all these years? 'Another Williams' asked if Cynog would allow a film of himself, delivering his dreadful anathema, to be shown, accompanied by his great sermon on a gramophone, in order to smash Haggar and Poole? 'Old Pal' took William's part:

It does not require anyone to champion Mr. Haggar. It is well known that he has been the means of collecting and has given hundreds of pounds to various causes in Aberdare during the last 10 or 15 years. The entertainment for the benefit of the Dyllas strikers realised over £70. May I ask Cynog, did he give a helping hand in this matter? Take next the Railwaymen's Widows and Orphans' Fund. Mr. Haggar has given three or four benefit concerts towards this, besides dozens of other such concerts. Let me take the year 1912, which is about 10 or 11 weeks old. Mr. Haggar has already given 4 or 5 charity concerts, one of which was for the benefit of the parents of the Robertstown flood victims. The money, which realised between £50 and £60, is in the hands of a committee, at the head of which is our highly-respected High Constable, Mr. F.Hodges. Rev. Cynog, I ask you - did you do anything to help this very worthy and deserving cause?

Cynog made no reply to these darts. Instead, on the platform in the Trecynon Public Hall at a 'Lively Meeting' of the Nonconformist League, he moved a proposition to take over the hall from the present committee and guarantors, dealing 'at great length' with the work of the hall committee. His supporters howled down the hall committee members, who would have given their version of events, and soon the audience was in an uproar. Cynog's motion carried, he need take little notice of public obloquy. He got himself elected chairman of the new hall committee; and next year, his thunderbolts were directed against breakers of the Sabbath and a predicted invasion of 'the sweepings of English cities being planted here in our town with their low habits and infidel ideas.' Neither did William take any notice: at Christmas 1912, he advertised, 'We still draw the crowds in spite of Swank and Oppositions: Old Haggar wishes his Patrons a Prosperous New Year.'[11]

On their return from New York, William and May moved into their new house, Kinema House in Abernant Road, Aberdare.[12] William took up gardening, growing his own vegetables, and cooking and serving them. His travelling days were done: he had plans to become a local worthy, capitalising on the fact that he was now so well known in the town, that, during the 1910 General Election, a cartoon could make a comic play on his name: a canvasser is shown saying to Mrs. Jones, 'And you tell Mr. Jones from me that if Fox-Davies isn't in, it will be the ruin and downfall of the Empire!!' Mrs. Jones replies: 'It don't trouble us 'cos me an' my 'usband always goes to HAGGARS!' Among other reasons for his popularity was his generosity, as Cynog's detractors had pointed out: another cartoon had depicted him as Father Christmas.[13] The proceeds of William's Sunday concerts, held on special staging when the cinema was not open, were always given to charity. Some of these proceeds went towards the building of the first hospital in Aberdare, others to strike funds and the Railwaymen's Widows and Orphans Fund.[14] William played up to his popularity:

No word could better describe Old Haggar's Picture House in Aberdare than the word 'popular'. There are many reasons for this, and one great one is, always please your public. Old Haggar knows the game, and knows it from both ends of the cricket pitch. Among the numerous successes he has brought to Aberdare, scarcely one will stand out with more prominence than the picture, **Passions of Men** for this weekend, Thursday, Friday and Saturday. It has been engaged at enormous expense and by the kind favours of the Moss Empire Co., Ltd. It is absolutely exclusive to Old Haggar's House. The story is a thrilling one of love and war, and will impress everyone who sees it. It is well written and magnificently staged, and cannot fail to create an impression rarely seen in picture theatres. Those who have looked up Haggar in the past are continually looking him up now.[15]

But film business was not all straightforward. In the middle of bringing out **The Women of Mumbles Head**, and shooting and re-shooting scenes for **The Maid of Cefn Ydfa**, William got into trouble in Mountain Ash, where he had instructed his architect to widen the new cinema, without bothering that it thus encroached on the next plot of land. He was sued for compensation by W. H. Brown, a Temperance Hotel Proprietor, of Swansea, at the Glamorgan Assizes in July 1913, who claimed that he would have to charge a reduced rent for one of the four shops he was building next door. William offered Brown £350 compensation, but this was rejected. In court, William told the judge that he knew nothing of architecture or business: he was only a humble entertainer. The judge believed him and dismissed the case, so, as the *Leader* concluded, 'Not only has Mr. Haggar nothing to pay, but he has not to pull down any part of his building, and the plaintiff has to pay Mr. Haggar's as well as his own costs.'[16]

In October 1913, William put his name forward as a candidate for election as a Poor Law Guardian. His election address, reported in the *Leader*, assured the townspeople that he valued their appreciation, goodwill and patronage. Knowing, from his own experience, what the poor had to undergo, he had been anxious and willing to help suffering humanity by rendering all the assistance he could extend to charitable and deserving causes, considering himself to be a friend of the working man. It was his ardent desire that nothing vulgar, objectionable, or indecent should be shown in his picture show. If elected, he was favourably placed to attend meetings, as his work had to be carried on during the evenings; thus he could help to check any wasteful or unnecessary expenditure on the part of any particular district, and, consequently, more effectually watch the interests of their own town to the best advantage. His only regret was that he could not speak the Welsh language: but he understood that all Meetings of the Guardians were conducted in English. He took no part in Politics. His long and varied experience of the world, and its ways, and its hardships, in all parts of the country, enabled him to say that he thoroughly knew the needs of the aged poor and the deserving; his desire being to look upon the Workhouse (or the Union) not as a cold and awful place, in which poor and old men and women were cast aside like starving dogs, but as a pleasant home in which they could end their days in comfort, in peace and in cleanliness.

In contrast to this somewhat vague programme, his opponent, Mr.D.P.Jones, emphasized the need for the strictest economy: the other districts had been profligate and had sent their 'professional tramps' to Aberdare. This must be stopped, and the ratepayers relieved of their heavy burden. He had several swipes at Haggar - he could attend Standing Committees which were invariably held in the evening; whilst the ability to speak Welsh was of vital importance in all meetings of the Board.

Despite this, William was decisively elected. He wrote to the paper to thank the electors, but could not resist complaining of dirty tricks by his opponent, at whose campaign meeting speakers 'thought it necessary to elect Christian men to public bodies'. William was not going to ask who were Christians, and what Christianity meant, but he would forgive the 'Christians' who so hurt him, and could assure them and the 849 ladies and gentlemen who kindly thought better of him that his best services would always be at their disposal.[17]

That winter William fell very ill, and could not engage in his new public duties for a time: but after he recovered, next summer he stood for the Aberdare Urban District Council, in the Town Ward.

The *Leader* noted that it promised to be an interesting contest, as Mrs. Maria Richards, the sitting candidate with 20 years' experience as a Poor Law Guardian and six years on the Education Committee behind her, was defending her seat, while Mr. Haggar was determined to stand, and Mr. J. H. Bruton, treasurer of the Trades Council, would be the Labour nominee. In the event, Mr. Richard Morgan also stood, as a 'Stop Haggar' candidate, thus ensuring an exciting four-sided election.

William's election address was again long on appeals for support and short on proposals for action. He began by complaining that his opponents accused him of not pulling his weight as a Guardian, although most people knew that his doctor had forbidden him to leave his house, so severely ill had he been. Many of his friends were nonconformists, and he took no part in politics. He would at all times promote the education of children, but he did not believe in making rash promises, as candidates too often did. He was proud that it had always been his pleasure to help any charitable or deserving cause and, if he was deemed worthy of election, he would always have the best interests of the electorate uppermost in his thoughts.

Richard Morgan criticised the waste of the ratepayers' money on ill-considered schemes. He went on to propose housing on modern Garden City principles, wider thoroughfares generally and Municipal Baths for the benefit of the community, 'the bath being quite a rarity in the cheaper rented cottages.' In defiance of the South Wales climate, he also advocated 'the open-air type of school of certain English towns, believing that such schools are healthier for the children and cheaper to the ratepayers.'[18]

There was great interest in the contest for the Town Ward. The *World's Fair* was so exercised by William's candidature that it sent its own reporter to cover the election. Under the headline, 'Mr. William Haggar elected to Aberdare Council by substantial majority', it reported:

> Mr. William Haggar, the popular South Wales showman has been elected by a substantial majority to the Aberdare District Council. Four candidates contested the election for one seat, and excitement, as may be expected, was very

great. Unfortunately, personalities were indulged in by some of the candidates, and the following remarks could be heard whilst the polling was taking place: 'He is too old. What does he know about business, etc.' One of the candidates thought it a great shame and a disgrace that they should have to sit at the same table as an old showman. Mr. Haggar refused to be drawn, and when spoken to, remarked 'I am leaving this election to my agent, committee, and above all, to the goodwill of the electors if they want me. I know I shall head the poll.'[19]

Such confidence was well-placed: William topped the poll, with 438 votes, a majority of 74 over Mr. Morgan, with the Labour candidate third, and Mrs. Richards, the sitting candidate, last. He duly took his seat, and from now on called himself 'Councillor Haggar' in his adverts. But he was not a great success either as a councillor or as a guardian. He served until 1919, but after his death the Leader's gossip columnist, 'Chatterbox' recorded that the work of guardian did not appeal to him, and on the District Council he was out of his element, and he never attempted to master the details of the subjects under discussion. 'Mr. Haggar was a showman first and last.'[20]

Under the banner headline, 'Britain at war with Germany' the Leader on 8 August 1914 reported that 'Great Britain on Tuesday presented an ultimatum to Germany, expiring at midnight, demanding a satisfactory reply on the question of the neutrality of Belgium. Long before the ultimatum had expired, however, reports were received of the invasion of Belgian territory by German troops at three points. Germany then declared war against Belgium. Great Britain and Germany are now in a state of war.' The film industry responded with alacrity, rushing out topical films and war dramas. Even before the outbreak of war, in July, Haggar's was showing **The Curse of War** ('see the great battle of aeroplanes in mid-air'). All the adverts for war topicals or dramas became larger and more dramatic when, from 19 September, Haggar's for the first time topped the front page of the Leader, with programmes at Aberdare and Mountain Ash side by side. 'War Pictures with the Belgian Army: capture of Louvain. It's Haggar's - Nuff Sed.'[21]

William was also helping the war effort in other ways. On 8 October

1914, he held 'under the auspices of the Aberdare Chamber of Trade, in conjunction with Councillor W. Haggar' a Benefit Concert in aid of the Prince of Wales' National Fund. Billed as a 'Monster Entertainment', the programme included solos by local singers, items by a boys' choir, and 'Mr. Haggar's specially selected pictures (Mr. Haggar has kindly consented to close his own place of entertainment for this evening). Stage Manager: Mr. W. Haggar. Reserved seats 2/-, Front seats 1/-, Gallery 6d.'[22] A few days later, Aberdare Chamber of Trade was discussing whether businesses should close for a dinner hour. After a lengthy debate, it was agreed not to proceed with the matter, but not before Councillor Haggar had suggested 'getting the Kaiser here to tell us how they do it in Germany.'[23]

Meanwhile, William was busy preparing for the first screening of the family's Welsh epic. 'Coming shortly, The great Welsh Story, **The Maid of Cefn Ydfa'** first appeared at the head of the front page of the *Leader* on Saturday, 17 October, 1914, in the company of **Adventures of a Midshipmite, Sons of the Sea**, and **Wireless from the war**. It was advertised each week until its showing on 14, 15 and 16 December in Aberdare, and the next three days in Mountain Ash. Such a large advertising effort must have generated much interest in the film, but there was no review, and no family tradition of numbers of showings or audience sizes. William immediately reverted to advertising his next American films and Christmas Holiday programme.[24] It was as if **The Maid** had never existed: the film had to wait another 24 years for 'The Prompter's' independent review.

Next summer, William opened his grand Kosy Kinema.

> Opposite the Market Yard in those days stood the Drill Hall. This was acquired by Haggar in 1914 and was transformed by him into the magnificent Kosy Kinema, balconied, ornate and grandiose. The 'talking apparatus' gave way to a six-piece orchestra, throbbing out a soulful accompaniment to the wonderful 'silents' of those days. The Kosy was truly a splendid cinema, and Haggar, always a man of vision, installed two-seaters in the back rows of the balcony. Many are they who occupied them and never saw the film! Memories return, too, of the

uniformed commissionaire shouting to the passing crowds, 'Seats at 3, 6 and 9' - pence, of course![25]

William, as usual, mounted a sustained campaign of adverts at the head of the *Leader,* culminating in the proud announcement on Saturday 21 August 1915, that Haggar's New Kinema, Aberdare, would open next Monday with **The Morals of Marcus, For the King, Aberdare Civic Sunday Parade** ('Come and see yourselves on the screen'), and Humorous subjects including **Charles Chaplin**. 'Popular prices of Admission to the Prettiest and Best Equipped Hall in South Wales - 3d, 4d and Balcony (Upholstered Armchairs) 6d. No Higher Prices.'[26] A photograph shows the crowd gathered outside the 700-seat cinema for its opening. 'Haggars' is in lights above the building, and the first film, **For the King**, a patriotic account of the King's Armed Forces in wartime, is billed. Walter Haggar stands at the top of the steps up to the entrance doors, looking out over the crowd. The cinema front is designed to match, in general style, but slightly overtop the Court House next to it, built the year before: together, they would have looked a handsome pair.[27]

William could now rest on his laurels. When peacetime conditions returned, he relinquished his seats on the Board of Guardians and the Urban District Council, claiming pressure of business, but, in reality, he was slowing down; perhaps the hardships of his earlier years were taking their toll on his constitution. He bought a farm at Castlemartin in his beloved Pembrokeshire - it was later expropriated by the government as part of the army range there, with minimal compensation. His family, although scattered, were off his hands, and for the most part managing cinemas - only Rose had never entered the business. She and her husband and family were to emigrate to Australia in 1928, as Jim and Kate had done a few years before: Jim and Kate's marriage had become unhappy, and they had decided on a fresh start. Violet and Cyril Yorke had parted: Violet went into service with an elderly gentleman at Coleford, in the Forest of Dean, paying only occasional visits to her father, with her son, Cyril.[28] Lily and Bert Richards continued to manage the Palace at Mountain Ash, which William settled on Lily. They had five children, but money was always tight: Bert was not a good manager, and over-fond of a flutter on the horses.

In the early 1920s, some changes in the business came about. Henry, having left Pontardulais in 1916 to make way for Will Junior, and after a spell in uniform, moved to Llanelly after Jim's emigration, and then on to Merthyr, where his father settled the Castle Cinema on him. Walter took over the management of the Kosy, and also of the Hippodrome in Llanelly. Will Junior and Jenny, after a fire at Pontlottyn on Boxing Day 1916 destroyed their Castle Theatre Picture House, moved to the former skating rink in Pontardulais, until it too was destroyed by fire in 1923, bankrupting Will in the process. Haydn Thomas, later to become conductor of the world-famous Pontardulais Male Voice Choir, watched the fire: the cinema went up like a matchbox, and Will Junior had to be restrained by friends from plunging into it in an attempt to rescue his beloved scripts and props.[29] This was a serious blow to the family, since Will Junior had stored there the entire family collection of theatrical necessities: scripts, scenery and costumes. Walter's daughter Madge was sent to tell William the bad news: his reaction was histrionic, and his distress intense.[30]

In the summer of 1924, the *Leader* ran a series on the public figures of Aberdare, entitled, 'Men at the Wheel'. On 9 August, the man at the wheel was William, the article praising him as a pioneer of the 'pictures' in Wales. William told the reporter his life story, from his birth in Dedham to his settling in Aberdare, where he had now retired after nearly sixty years as a public entertainer. The article concluded:

> During his residence at Aberdare he has proved very popular with the townspeople and has become noted for his generous disposition. In 1913 he was elected as a member of the Aberdare Urban District Council, and also of the Merthyr Board of Guardians. On both bodies he served with distinction until pressure of business compelled his resignation in 1919. He is also a Governor of the General Hospital. Mr. Haggar has had 11 children, and he has 40 grandchildren and three great-grandchildren. He is now in his 74th year and presents an appearance of bluff heartiness and joviality which seems to make him certain of reaching his century.[31]

But despite the optimism with which this article ended, his 'century' was not to be. Only six months later, William was dead. His beloved wife, May, on whom he had doted,[32] had died suddenly, on 29 August: she was only 40, but had been anaemic for two years. He was heart-broken, and his health, too, failed. He went to live with Walter and Ada at their home nearby, and there, on 4 February, 1925, he died of a coronary thrombosis at the age of 73. There was then, evidently, a rift within the family, or at least a change of plan. William's first death notice in the *Leader* stated that he was to be buried beside Sarah at Carmarthen; but the following week, the paper reported that he had in fact been buried with May in Aberdare cemetary.[33] There, a polished granite obelisk some six feet high, mounted on a rectangular vault chamber, is inscribed HAGGAR in large capital letters. It records that it is erected 'In memory of Arthur William Haggar, Born March 23 1851[34] Died February 4 1925. Also Mary Jane Haggar, Born April 28 1884, Died August 29 1924. At rest.' As befitting the old showman, this imposing memorial overtops William's father-in-law, Jenkin Davies' tomb, and all the other monuments in this section of the cemetery.

His estate was valued at £16,912.13. 5d. In his carefully worded will, made in December 1924, he left the Hippodrome cinema to Walter, with the proviso that £1 a week each from it should be paid to Rose and to Violet. The Kosy was given to Walter and his children, share and share alike. Henry received a special gift of £250, presumably instead of the wedding present which he had never had, but to be paid to him 'in such instalments as in the absolute discretion of my trustees shall be deemed wise'. All the residue was to be divided into five equal shares to be given to 'the wife and children of my son Willie' (Will being bankrupt), Walter, Rose, Violet, and to Henry and Lily - half each as they had each had a cinema as well. Each of these shares amounted to about £1000.[35]

In the *Leader,* the writer of 'Men at the Wheel' continued his account as an obituary. William would be sorely missed in Aberdare. In his prime, he had been a splendid actor and first-class comic. He knew by heart 50 or 60 plays, and could repeat not only his own, but all the other parts as well. When the speaking stage of the theatre was replaced by the silent stage of the cinema, Old Haggar had not lamented, like Desdemona, that his business was gone: instead he took up his place in the film world, and became one of the pioneers of living pictures in Wales. A week later, the paper reported William's funeral, and printed a personal appreciation, extolling his cheery manner, kindness and generosity of spirit. There ever emanated from his spirit that 'something' which impelled him to do good. His memory would be cherished and held in love and reverence by all.[36]

Nowadays, in the twenty-first century, a sizeable proportion of the population is born out of wedlock. To be a partner, rather than a spouse, is commonplace, and attracts no comment. It was far otherwise in 1851. William Haggar was born a disgrace. He was a reproach to his mother, the sign of her incontinence. His father, whoever he was, didn't want to know.

At least William wasn't the only one. Three of his cousins were illegitimate, too. That may or may not have been any help in the village. Were the Haggars taunted with their mothers' propensity for doing what comes naturally? Few of them stayed put. William went away, across the county boundary where he wasn't known, and started to construct the myth of his 'parents', his father Taylor Haggar, and the uncle who owned a sawmill, replacing his grandfather wheelwright who had actually taught him carpentry. He needed to come up in the world. His mother was becoming respectable: he would do the same.

Forty-six years later, he had not much to show for his efforts. A wife and eight children, the first two married and off his hands, but the others still at home - wherever home was: after marrying his actress wife, they had exchanged the partial respectability of a life in digs for the cheaper but rougher life in a living wagon. True, in 1891/2, after Nell's death, business had been so good that the non-family actors had been almost permanently drunk: as a result, they were given their notice, and re-employed on salaries, instead of the old share system. William was now the boss. Despite this, by the summer of 1897 his savings under the bed amounted to only just over £80. Then he took the bold decision which made his fortune. Seeing his opportunity, he grasped it with both hands. Now at last he had the means of making real money. Walter could never forget the excitement of the first opening of the bioscope show. 'I knew there was money in it', William had said: he was right. After only three seasons, he could afford to dispense with the old limelight, and buy a steam-powered mobile electricity generator costing £600. He acquired better projection equipment, and a cine-camera to make his own films. In 1904 he bought his Fowler traction engine, costing another £630. Later he bought two more. In 1906 another £1000 went on the giant Marenghi organ, and next year he bought the even bigger Gavioli. In one leap he went right to the top in the cinematograph business.

Lily Richards, looking back, regretted her father's lack of courage. 'Father bought all his lengths of film from Gaumonts, and had his films developed free. He allowed Gaumonts to keep the negative of every film made, and they could make as many copies as they wished and sell them to any buyer. If Father could have kept the copyright he could have become world-famous and very wealthy.'[37] This was to overlook the capital required to buy film, develop it, store it and retail it. What the economics of the alternatives were, it is impossible to assess now. Lily also wondered why he did not build cinemas in Cardiff: as early as 1905, Walter had advised a timber merchant from Abertillery, a Mr. Tilney, on the wiring techniques needed for his new cinema (later the Capitol) in Cardiff. 'Why didn't he build a cinema in Cardiff?' Lily asked the question in her interview. She answered: 'He was so taken up with everything, the rush and bustle of life. He liked photography, he liked a showman's life, he just couldn't be bothered.' He was more interested in saving for his retirement: not until Sarah's death did he make any move to relinquish the life of a travelling film exhibitor, and set up his own chain of cinemas in the Valleys.

Then at last he settled down in Aberdare to become a local celebrity. He was still a showman – 'the well-known amusement caterer' as the report of Violet's wedding has it.[38] In his advertisements, he was 'Old Haggar', wishing his patrons 'a Prosperous New Year'. He was elected to the Board of Guardians and the Council, becoming 'Councillor Haggar' in his own publicity. He had arrived. By 1924, he was one of the 'Men at the Wheel'. When he died the next year, his estate was valued at £16,912. Seventy-five years later, measured by inflation in house prices during that time, it would have been worth £1.5 million.

That, and the fact that the tale of his career is still enthralling, is a measure of his success.

To what extent, however, was that success achieved at the expense of his family? There are hints that he was domineering. 'Everyone was in awe of him: he ruled the family with a rod of iron' reported his grandson.[39] Sarah was said to have felt neglected;[40] Jim and Kate were unhappy, Violet's and Lily's marriages, perhaps contracted at William's urging, broke down. William had had to be tough to survive his early troubles: later, opportunities had had to be taken, family members used in supporting roles. Yet William was popular in public for his charity, and well-liked: described as 'bluff, hearty and jovial' in his later years, he had many friends, and no enemies. 'K's' tribute celebrated his generosity of spirit, and 'glorious and lovable simplicity.'[41] Walter and Lily, in their family histories, make no criticism. Walter celebrates a job well done. Lily sees William as her hero.

Neither William's 'Men at the Wheel' interview, nor his obituary so much as mentioned his film-making. At that time, the British film industry was all but extinct, and Hollywood ruled the film-making world, as far as most people were concerned. Perhaps it was thought that the first years of the cinema were merely quaint. In the words of the documentary film-maker, Paul Rotha, writing in 1930, 'Except historically and technically, the birth and early years of the cinema are neither interesting nor particularly brilliant in aesthetic achievement.' Nowadays a different view prevails: William's film-making can be assessed in the words of later writers.

Desperate Poaching Affray had been a best-seller worldwide. It had 'helped set the pattern for chase sequences in the movies.' **The Sign of the Cross** was sensational in 1904 for its length: it was pirated in the United States, a sure sign of its popularity. **The Life of Charles Peace** is described as 'the first British fiction film in the proper meaning of the word',[42] and as 'a paradigm of the early cinema at the end of its first decade.'[43] Haggar's comedies, especially the **Mirthful Mary** series of four slapstick films, would have appealed even to the critical Rotha, for 'slapstick', he wrote, 'is the most interesting (of early film types), for it utilised the fantasy capabilities of the cinema';[44] and, in their debunking of figures of authority, they conformed to one of Chaplin's three types of film comedy, ten years before his screen début. In the last version of **The Maid of Cefn Ydfa**, William and Will Junior had produced the longest film yet made without the benefit of a studio: a film which, although it looks back to Victorian theatricality, also looks forward to a more naturalistic and free-flowing use of the camera on location, which other British film-makers had yet to discover.

Well might Cricks and Martin, another of the pioneering firms, praise William's films. He was no D.W. Griffith. His cabbage-patches could not provide the stage for an **Intolerance,** with its cast of thousands. Yet in devising and making films of such calibre and originality, targeted at his own audiences[45] in his Electric Coliseum, William Haggar was unique.

10. Aftermath: rediscovery and recognition

WALTER HAGGAR, THE CHIEF heir to his father's business, did not stay long in Aberdare. Sensing overmuch competition, in June 1927 he sold the Kosy[1] and, moving his family to Bournemouth, bought an old cinema in Fordingbridge, Hampshire, knocked it down, and built his 'new show' in its place. When the new premises came to be licensed, the inspector found all the old films, with William's glass photographic plates, in a garage behind the show. He condemned them as a fire hazard. Walter retained only a select few films, burnt the rest, and smashed the glass.[2]

Will Junior, meanwhile, bankrupted by the fire in 1923, had been forced to return to the theatre for a living. After travelling in west and mid-Wales as far as Aberystwyth,[3] he and Jenny settled in Pembroke, where he leased the cinema in the Assembly Rooms in Main Street, becoming something of a celebrity, and organising the town's silver jubilee pageant in 1935. On his death later that year, Jenny decided not to retain the cinema, so Walter arrived in Pembroke to buy and run 'the show', as the family called Haggar's there. In 1939, his son Len moved from Fordingbridge to take over from him.[4]

Walter was disinclined to let his father's memory die. In 1938, he lent his copy of **The Maid of Cefn Ydfa** to Mr. Key to show once more in Cardiff before the film was donated to the Welsh National Museum.[5] In 1939, he gave a lengthy BBC radio interview to Wynford Vaughan Thomas, which was written up in the *World's Fair*.[6] At the end of his life, in the early 1950s, at the suggestion of his son, Roy Haggar Senior, he wrote his memoirs, publishing the first part in the magazine *Dock Leaves*.[7] But Cardiff was not London, a radio programme was easily forgotten, and the *World's Fair* and *Dock Leaves* were not national newspapers: Walter's efforts made little mark. For the British Film Industry had forgotten its origins. Books written in the 1930s and 1940s accepted the American mythology of the early cinema, barely mentioning the British pioneers. Paul Rotha had dismissed the early years as uninteresting,[8] and F. Maurice Speed, who for decades produced an annual *Film Review*, in his popular history *Movie Cavalcade*, published in 1942, had much to say about the work of Friese-Greene and Paul in developing movie equipment, but devoted just three sentences to Hepworth's films, giving even briefer notices to Paul and Mottershaw.[9] Otherwise, all is Hollywood.

It was Roger Manvell, then Research Officer of the British Film Institute (BFI), who had the idea that there should be some form of publication in 1946 to mark the fiftieth anniversary of the introduction of the cinema to Britain.[10] The BFI adopted this idea, commissioning Rachael Low, daughter of the famous cartoonist David Low[11] to research the history of the British film. Manvell helped her to shape and organise the material into book form.[12] Meanwhile Alberto Cavalcanti, then a prominent film director, made a compilation of such of the first silent films as were in the National Film Archive by that time. This toured the cinemas for the fiftieth anniversary, coming to the cinema at Rhiwbina, Cardiff, where Lily Richards went to see it for old times' sake.[13] She saw herself on screen in **The Life of Charles Peace**, but was annoyed to find it attributed to Frank Mottershaw rather than her father. She wrote to a national newspaper which put her in touch with the National Film Library, as it was called then. Lily's identification of the Haggar film came just in time for it to be included, in a footnote, in Low and Manvell's first volume of *The History of the British Film*, published in 1948.[14]

In that book, despite Bromhead's reference[15] and Lily's intervention, Rachael Low unaccountably miss-named William as Walter throughout.[16] Since her book soon became the prime source for British film history, this mistake has often since been repeated. It misled Lily into thinking that Walter had originated the mistake. In her tape-recorded interview in 1971, she said, 'there are various stories about my brother, Walter. He's dead now. He wrote a short autobiography of his life, and he took to himself all the pioneering fame that belonged to my father. Such is not the case.' It is not, in fact, the case that Walter's *Recollections* take any credit away from William - but because Lily thought it was so, she decided to rectify the position. In the late 1960s, she determined to write a biography of her father, in time for use at the seventy-fifth anniversary of films. But her own memories were dim, including few incidents of the early film-making years, because she had been away in Kilburn with her grandmother. Deciding to pay Walter back for taking credit from William, she borrowed his *Bioscope Recollections* from his son, Len, and proceeded to copy them out, changing tenses and personal pronouns where necessary to disguise the fact that Walter had written them. This gave her material extending from 1896 to 1912, which she supplemented with her own memories. Unaware of Walter's account of the days of the travelling theatre, from 1885 to 1896, Lily did not use it. Instead, she began her father's life with what she could remember having been told in her childhood by her parents and her grandmother, and, where memory failed, she invented. She added an epilogue: her daughter June Bilous typed the whole work out, ironing out errors, and making sense of Lily's many repetitions and inconsistences.[17] Contacting authorities interested in film history, Lily related her memories to Anthony Slide[18] and Denis Gifford.[19] She gave interviews to the *South Wales Echo* in May 1971, for a four-part series on film pioneers,[20] and to Dennis Pope and Frank Sharp of the Canton Film Appreciation Group in Cardiff.[21] At the same time, her granddaughter Caroline Richards, a freelance journalist, wrote a special article in the *Sunday Times* for the seventy-fifth anniversary of moving pictures, using Lily's biography, and interviewing Len Haggar in Pembroke.[22]

Thus, by the early 1970s, Lily's activities had generated a great deal of publicity about William and his films. This was increased by the efforts of Walter's grandson Roy, then teaching drama at the Greenhill School in Tenby. Possessing his grandpa's memoirs, a fund of anecdotes from his grandma Ada, and his own experiences of helping his father Len run Haggar's cinema in Pembroke, he put these together into the form of a lecture, which he gave to interested parties and organisations, many of whom still remembered the earlier Haggars, William more distantly, and Will Junior particularly from his time in Pembroke. As the surviving films became available, Roy added video presentations of them to his lecture.[23]

Publicity was further augmented by the work of David Berry, journalist and film critic of the *South Wales Echo*. Impressed by Lily's interview, and obtaining a copy of her memoirs, he wrote newspaper articles about the early days of films in Wales, mounting a campaign to stir readers to look for half-forgotten film treasures hidden away in cupboards and attics. Later he was to devote to

William and his films almost a whole chapter in his magisterial work, *Wales and Cinema: the first hundred years.*[24]

Academics, too, were becoming interested in William's work. Michael Chanan, then Senior Lecturer in Film and Video at the London College of Printing, published his book on 'the prehistory and early years of cinema in Britain', *The Dream that Kicks* in 1980. Much influenced by the Marxist orthodoxies prevalent at the time, the book's thesis was that cinematography was a product of the forces of nineteenth century capitalism. Yet it accords to William, for the first time, a place as a film-maker on a par with Hepworth, Williamson and the other pioneers, and includes a detailed descriptive analysis of **The Life of Charles Peace**, which Chanan regarded as typical of the best of British fiction films of the time.[25]

Detective work by David Berry and others in the National Film Archive was now rewarded with success. June Bilous was invited to a special film show at the Archive's offices in London in July 1984. Taken there from Folkestone by taxi, she met David Berry and Geoffrey Hill, a respected local historian of the Welsh Valleys, who was later to write a well-researched article about William Haggar for the Cynon Valley History Society.[26] After viewing the two films, June confirmed that the leading actor in **Desperate Poaching Affray** and the surviving fragment of **A Message from the Sea** was her uncle, Will Haggar Junior. For the first time, these were identified as Haggar films.

The interest being generated was picked up by the BBC. In late June 1984, Radio Wales broadcast a documentary entitled *Haggar's Travelling Picture Show*, in which Roy Haggar took part. All these efforts bore fruit when, shortly afterwards, Phyllis Haggar rediscovered **The Maid of Cefn Ydfa**. Since its screening at the Olympia in 1938, the film, a bulky object, its three reels in their tin boxes stored inside a galvanised lined box,[27] had travelled between different members of the Haggar family. First Henry took it, no doubt to show in his Merthyr cinema.[28] On his death in 1945, his nephew Bill Haggar cleared up his effects, and passed it on to Sid Griffiths, manager of the Plaza Cinema in Swansea,[29] Lily trying in vain to recover it from him.[30] After Sid's death, it was returned to Bill's son Peter Haggar: his wife, Phyllis, put it away in a cupboard under the stairs in their home in Swansea. Widowed by 1984, she heard the broadcast, turned out the cupboard and came forward with the film, contacting John Haggar and David Berry, who sent the film to the BFI for conservation: 38 of its fifty minutes' length was saved.[31] Given a special showing in one of the BFI's viewing theatres on 14 December 1984, **The Maid of Cefn Ydfa** lived again.

It was now to feature in **A Penny For Your Dreams**, an hour-long drama-documentary for television, screened on S4C (in Welsh) at Christmas 1987, and on BBC2 on 30 May 1988.[32] Starring Dafydd Hywel and Sue Roderick as William and Sarah, it portrayed William's hard early life, and his road to success through his films, until Sarah's death at Carmarthen, adopting as its central theme the obsession with filming **The Maid** which it claimed William possessed. In 1996, to mark the centenary of the cinema, BBC Radio 4 added its own tribute in the form of a 45 minute play, **The Magic Caravan**.[33]

David Berry has continued his quest for Haggar films, identifying **The Bather's Revenge** in 1995 and **The Sheep Stealer** in 2001. Dafydd Hywel, Roy and John Haggar and David Berry were all present at the Market Hall in Aberdare on a cold, wet day in January 1997, when a plaque marking William's achievement was unveiled by Hywel in the presence of Rhondda Cynon Taff Mayor, Russell Roberts. The plaque, presented by the Cinema 100 Wales Group, bearing a logo in the form of a cine-camera forming the figure 100, records in English and Welsh that 'Arthur William Haggar, 1851-1925, Pioneer Silent-film maker, ran his travelling cinema on this site, c. 1900-1914.'[34]

Thus William attained prosperity and recognition in Aberdare both during his lifetime and after his death; and, although in some cinema histories the old mistake is still made, his place as a pioneer is now fully recognised. In the short-lived Museum of the Moving Image on the South Bank in London in the late 1990s, **The Poachers** was on permanent display alongside Hepworth's **Rescued by Rover** and Williamson's **The Big Swallow**. Stills from **The Poachers** and **The Life of Charles Peace** adorn Patricia Warren's *British Cinema in Pictures*,[35] and Joel W. Finler's *Silent Cinema*,[36] two of the many lavishly illustrated books published to coincide with the centenary of the cinema. The photograph of

Haggar's Royal Electric Bioscope at Pontypool Park in 1902 concludes the first chapter of Richard Gray's *Cinemas in Britain: One Hundred Years of Cinema Architecture*.[37] Yet no such recognition has been accorded to **The Maid**.

The Maid had been a *tour de force*: as long as most films of the time when the rest of the industry was making such films as **Hamlet, Romeo and Juliet** and **East Lynne**[38] in well-equipped film studios with the latest in lighting and staging, it had been made without the benefit of a studio, on a stage set up on a cabbage patch, and on location in Pontardulais and elsewhere. It had employed an experienced cameraman from London, and the even more experienced William had re-shot many scenes to give it more immediacy, moving the camera to follow the action in a manner still ahead of its time. It was well edited, particularly so in the scenes cut and pasted to alternate between indoors in Ann's room, and outdoors below it: the 'balcony scene' where Will serenades Ann could be seen from both viewpoints in a way not possible in the theatre. It contained many close-ups, that of Ann writing her message to Will in her own blood being particularly captivating. The story, told clearly on some forty inter-titles, was easy to follow, at a time when many films were criticized for their unintelligibility. It was the final and greatest achievement of the most independent of the pioneers.

But because histories of film-making in Britain were written from the 1930s to the 1970s, before **The Maid** was rediscovered, only David Berry in his book on the cinema in Wales has noticed it. Treating the film in isolation, because it was an isolated feat in Wales, he characterises the acting as 'crass', and describes the comic sub-plot between Lewis Bach and Gwenny as 'crude'. But when it is remembered that the film was fully a child of its time, in the mainstream of British films when it was made, a different assessment may be attempted. The film is, in fact, a superb record of an Edwardian travelling theatre company acting its *piéce de résistance* in the tradition of the Commedia del' Arte. It deserves re-appraisal and comparison with its few surviving peers. That comparison would not be to its disadvantage: it would result in **The Maid of Cefn Ydfa** taking its rightful place in the history of the British Cinema.

'It's Haggar's - Nuff Sed'.

Stop Press

Since my book was published, I have made three significant discoveries:

The Sign of the Cross (p. 80)
The Gaumont Sales Catalogue had been preserved at the Cinémathèque Française. A 16-page "Special Supplement" (the front is shown overleaf) describes the film in great detail. Of the film's seven scenes, four were illustrated, and Gaumont comment, "The Sign of the Cross is a film the beauty of which has never been surpassed."

The Copyright Photographs (pp. 72ff)
In the 1900s the position of copyright of film was not clear, and for some years film sellers sent images of films to the Stationers' Hall to copyright them. These were rediscovered in the National Archives in Kew in the 1990s. Among them are 13 images of Haggar films sent in by Gaumont during 1904/5. Oddly, Gaumont did not name the films, but using surviving catalogues, I have identified the films as follows:
Already known films:
"A Message from the Sea" (raft scene), "Mirthful Mary in the Dock", "The Sign of the Cross" (two scenes, additional to those in the catalogue), "Snowballing", "Spaghetti Eating", and possibly a (fake) newsreel of the Russo-Japanese War.
Films not previously known to be by William Haggar:
Four short comedies: "Auntie's Cycling Lesson", "Cook's Lovers", Jack's Rival" and "Married Bliss"; and the chase-thriller "Revenge!" (two scenes).

Revenge! (p. xii)
"Revenge!" was imported into the USA by the American Mutoscope & Biograph Co., which sent a paper print of the film, to copyright it, to the US Library of Congress, where it has been preserved. I have a copy on dvd. The film lasts 7 minutes. In it, the hero (Will Haggar Junior) ends the film by strangling the villain with his bare hands!

Peter Yorke, October 2010

Overleaf
The front of the catalogue for "The Sign of the Cross": Marcus (Will Haggar Junior) kneels before Mercia (Jenny Lindon) in the tableau at the end of scene 4.

No. 60. December, 1904.   SPECIAL SUPPLEMENT.

The 'Elgé' List

ELGÉ   ELGÉ

THE SIGN OF THE CROSS.

L. Gaumont & Co.,
LONDON & PARIS.

ELGÉ   ELGÉ

Appendix 1: List of plays put on by the Alexandra Theatre in Monmouth in 1905

KEITH KISSACK, LOCAL HISTORIAN of Monmouth, has unearthed in the pages of the *Monmouthshire Beacon* a fine description of the repertoire of a portable theatre. The Alexandra Theatre Company ('Proprietor and Manager Bert Breamer. Established over 15 years. Well known as one of the best theatres now travelling') performed a ten-week season in Monmouth from 22 June to 26 August 1905, seat prices being 3d., 6d., and a shilling. This was their advertised repertoire:

First and second weeks: **The Fighting Parson, The Poacher's Fate, Firematch Trooper, Jane Shore** and **East Lynne**.

Third week: **Sons of the sea** (Grand Nautical Drama), **The Fighting Parson, The Corsican Brothers, The Stranglers of Paris, Napoleon or, The Divorced Empress, Rip Van Winkle,** and **Diavoletti, or, the Gipsy Queen's Revenge**.

Fourth week: **Turning Queens Evidence, or, The Blind Mother's Devotion, Muldoon's Picnic, Trilby** ('as performed by Beerbohm Tree in London to crammed houses'), **Black-eyed Susan, The Daughter of the Regiment,** and **Gallant Tommy Atkins**.

Fifth week: **Sherlock Holmes, Detective, The Unknown, Charley's Aunt** (a special charity performance of which was given as well), **The Silver King, By the Hand of a Woman, or, Monmouth 200 years ago,** and **The Maniac's Knife,** 'Full of Sensation. Plenty of Fun').

Sixth week: **Uncle Tom's Cabin, or, The Death of Little Eva** ('introducing all the Negro songs and dances - a treat for all'), **Maria Martin, The Private Secretary, The Three Musketeers** ('Magnificent Wardrobe and Effects and special scenery'), **Passion's Slaves,** and **The Dumb Man of Manchester, or, The Felon Hero** ('introducing the famous struggle for life').

Seventh week: **Who's the Man?, The Woman in Red, The Lady of Lyons, British Pluck, Sweeney Todd** and **Cinderella**.

Eigthth week: **Cinderella** (for its second and third nights – 'All new songs, dances, scenery and effects'), **The Maid of Cefn Ydfa, or, The Love Tale of Glamorgan, The Shadow of the Cross, East Lynne, or, The Death of Willie Carlyle** and **The Jack o' Clubs** ('Introducing the Great Sensation: The Crematorium at Woking Cemetary').

Ninth week: **Two Little Drummer Boys, On Shannon's Shore, Napoleon** ('Repeated by special desire'), **Ben Ma Chree, or, Mona the Girl of My Heart, The Octoroon,** and **Charles Peace** ('The modern Ishmael. Full of Sensation. Bound to please').

Final week: **Alone in London City, or, Nan the Flower Girl, The Bugle Call**, a story of the Franco-German War, **Jane Shore** ('Repeated by special desire'), **Paul Kauvar**, a tale of the Reign of Terror, **Leah the Jewish Maiden**, and **Saturday Night in London Town** ('to be followed by a cradle-carrying competition - prize: a silver cruet stand').

These plays were the stuff of Victorian melodrama. Wilson Barrett's **The Sign of the Cross**, an adaptation of Henryk Sienkiewicz' famous novel, *Quo Vadis?,* was one of the three most popular plays of the nineteenth century. Barrett also staged G.R.Sims' crime drama, **The Lights o' London** in 1881, and collaborated with the prolific playwright Henry Arthur Jones to produce, in 1882, his play, **The Silver King**, put on by the Haggars as **The Silver Ring**. Some plays mined wells of sentimentality: **East Lynne**, based on a novel published in 1861 by Mrs. Henry Wood, dwelt on the hardships of Little Willie (whose death was announced by the immortal line: 'Dead! Dead, and never called me Mother!'), whilst in **The Octoroon**, 'a sensational drama' of 1861 by Dion Boucicault, the child post-boy Weenie Paul is murdered by a blow from a Red Indian's tomahawk. But audiences could laugh as well: **Charley's Aunt** by Brandon Thomas, 'took London by storm' in 1892, when it ran for four years, with 1469 performances.

The Haggar family

1. William holding Violet aged 2 (1889)

2. William and Sarah at Walter and Ada's wedding (1906) (Will, Lily and Violet behind them)

3. William as a 'Man at the wheel'
(1924)

4. Walter, Archie and
Henry (1892)

5. Lily aged 2
(1893)

6. Violet in
Boer War
costume
(1902)

7. Rose dressed as a
parader (1907)

8. Henry when manager of
the Castle Cinema, Merthyr
(1930s)

9. Will Junior
and his
theatrical
company
(1906)

The Victorian Theatre

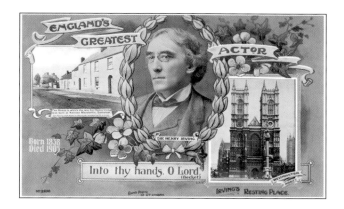

10. Sir Henry Irving

11. Lillah McCarthy as Mercia in **The Sign of the Cross**

12. Dan Leno, comedian: William sang his songs

The early British Cinema

13. Robert Paul, inventor of the 'Maltese Cross' projector (*British Fim Institute*)

14. William's friend Charles Urban (*British Film Institute*)

15. Cecil Hepworth filmed **Rescued by Rover** (*British Film Institute*)

Bioscope Shows

16. Haggar's Royal Electric Bioscope, 1902

17. Haggar's Royal Bioscope, 1908 (the Marenghi organ showfront)

18. Haggar's Electric Coliseum (the Gavioli organ showfront)

19. Walter's traction engine *King George V*

20. Chipperfield's Electric Theatre on the road in 1911 (*Morton's Media Group Archive*)

21. A Bioscope Show from above: Aspland's Pictureland at Boston Fair in 1912 (*Neil Watson*)

Films comparable with The Maid of Cefn Ydfa

22. **Richard III (1911)**: Richard wooing Lady Anne (*British Film Institute*)

23. **East Lynne (1913)**: A dramatic moment shared by Richard, Cornelia, Lady Isabel and a maid (*British Film Institute*)

24. **David Copperfield (1913)**: Peggoty and David in Barkis' cart (*British Film Institute*)

Stills from William Haggar's films

25. **Outside the Works**: Workers in the street (*National Screen and Sound Archive of Wales*)

26. **Outside the Works**: William advertises the show (*National Screen and Sound Archive of Wales*)

27. **Desperate Poaching Affray**: The Poachers (Sid Griffiths and Will Haggar) surprised by the gamekeepers (*National Screen and Sound Archives of Wales*)

28. **Desperate Poaching Affray**: The gamekeepers fire (*National Screen and Sound Archive of Wales*)

29. **Desperate Poaching Affray**: The chase through the pond (*National Screen and Sound Archive of Wales*)

30. **Desperate Poaching Affray**: Dragged away 'desperate and exhausted' past the camera (*National Screen and Sound Archive of Wales*)

31. **The Bathers' Revenge**: "Phew" says Walter, spurning the bathers' clothes (*National Screen and Sound Archive of Wales*)

32. **The Bathers' Revenge**: The spooning couple being tipped into the water (*National Screen and Sound Archive of Wales*)

33. **The Life of Charles Peace**: Peace at Dyson's House (James, Walter and Violet Haggar) (*National Screen and Sound Archive of Wales*)

34. **The Life of Charles Peace**: Peace cocks a snook as the third policeman arrives (*National Screen and Sound Archive of Wales*)

35. **The Life of Charles Peace**: Peace hurling himself from the train (*National Screen and Sound Archive of Wales*)

36. **The Life of Charles Peace**: The execution scene (*National Screen and Sound Archive of Wales*)

37. **The Sheep Stealer**: Title with William's photo (*National Screen and Sound Archive of Wales*)

38. **The Sheep Stealer**: Sheep stealing: the chase begins (*National Screen and Sound Archive of Wales*)

39. **The Sheep Stealer**: Cornered (James and Kate Haggar with Lily Kate and James Junior) (*National Screen and Sound Archive of Wales*)

40. **A Message from the Sea**: Harry Mainstay departs on a voyage (Will Junior, Jenny and Jennie Haggar) (*National Screen and Sound Archive of Wales*)

41. **The Stepney Wedding**: Bride and Groom leave the church (*National Screen and Sound Archive of Wales*)

42. **The Stepney Wedding**: William (in large cap) following the procession (*National Screen and Sound Archive of Wales*)

43. **The Maid of Cefn Ydfa**: Will and Ann fall in love (Will Haggar and Jenny Lindon) (*National Screen and Sound Archive of Wales*)

44. **The Maid of Cefn Ydfa**: Will and Ann betrothed (*National Screen and Sound Archive of Wales*)

45. **The Maid of Cefn Ydfa**: Lewis Bach and Gwenny (Will Fyffe and Jennie Haggar), with Morgan the Seer carrying the injured Will (*National Screen and Sound Archive of Wales*)

46. **The Maid of Cefn Ydfa**: Ann draws blood to write to Will (*National Screen and Sound Archive of Wales*)

47. **The Maid of Cefn Ydfa**: The message on the leaf (*National Screen and Sound Archive of Wales*)

48. **The Maid of Cefn Ydfa**: Will is too late to prevent the wedding (*National Screen and Sound Archive of Wales*)

Appendix 2: The Haggar films

THE FOLLOWING IS A list of the titles of all films known to have been made by William Haggar. Dates and content are as recorded by Denis Gifford, in *The British Film Catalogue, Fiction Films, Third Edition* (BFC), or else inferred from other sources, as noted. The distributors' catalogue nos. and selling prices are given, where available. From the length of a film is derived its running time, @ between 60 and 70 feet to the minute.

BFC No.	Name	Content	Distributor	Length (ft)	Price
	1901				
	Train entering Burry Port Station	"First film" in 1901 [1]			
	Skaters in Aberdare Park	"First film" in 1901 [2]			
	Boer War sequences	"Quickies" filmed in the Rhondda Valley [3]			
	Football and other topicals	"Very popular" items [4]			
	Phantom Ride through Swansea	Views from the front of a tram [5]			
	Patrick Pinches Poultry	Chase film, very popular [6]			
	The Dumb Man of Manchester	Crime drama: a scene from a play [7]			
	1902				
00596	The Maniac's Guillotine	Crime drama: a scene from a play	Warwick Trading Co., 6948	125	£2.12s
00597	The Two Orphans	Period Duel Scene: knife duel between	Warwick Trading Co., 6949	100	£2.2s
	(aka A Duel with Knives (USA))	cripple and marquis, in Paris			
00598	The Wild Man of Borneo	Drama: fight between a knight and a hermit.	Warwick Trading Co., 6950	150	£3.3s
00599	True as steel	Drama: scene from the play of this name.	Warwick Trading Co., 6951	150	£3.3s
	The Maid of Cefn Ydfa	Drama: seven scenes from the play [8]		450	
	Ingomar the Barbarian	Drama: scene from play [9]			
	Twm Shon Catti	Welsh drama [10]			
	The Boer War	Longer film, made in the Rhymney Valley [11]			
	1903				
	Outside the Works/Haggar's Bioscope Camera	Extant actuality in which William Haggar appears			
	Mumbles Funeral	The funeral of six lifeboatmen [12]			

BFC No.	Name	Content	Distributor	Length (ft)	Price
	1903 continued				
	Weary Willie & Tired Tim at the Races	Comedy featuring the two comic strip tramps [13]		150	
00658	Weary Willie & Tired Tim - the Gunpowder Plot	Tramps stick hot poker in barrel labelled beer but containing gunpowder	Warwick Trading Co., 7194	125	£2 12s.
00681	Weary Willie & Tired Tim turned barbers	Tramps take over the shop of an absent barber	Gaumont, 93	118	£2.19s
00714	Weary Willie & Tired Tim - A Dead Shot	"A continuous farce from beginning to end."	Warwick Trading Co., 7299	150	£3 3s
00674	Mirthful Mary - A case for the Blacklist	Comedy: Mary, the worse for drink, beats a policeman with a stick. With the actress Mog.	Gaumont, 82	120	£3.
00694	Desperate Poaching Affray (In USA: The Poachers)	Chase: Police chase poachers and catch them after gun battle in river (in existence)	Gaumont, 114, & in USA Edison & Biograph	220	£5.10s
00758	The Tramp and the Washerwoman	Comedy: tramp steals clothes from washerwoman and flees on bicycle.	Gaumont, 132	100	£2.10s
00759	The Tramp and Baby's Bottle	Comedy: tramp steals milk from baby in park, and is cornered by soldier.	Gaumont, 133	100	£2.10s
00760	A Dash for Liberty	Chase in 5 scenes: convict escapes from quarry, steals cart, but is captured after fight.	Urban Trading Co., 1153	300	£6.6s
00797	Whitewashing the Policeman	Comedy: boys cause fight between tramp and gent in park.	Gaumont, 175	65	£1.12.6d
	1904				
00952	Mirthful Mary in the dock	Comedy: (distributed in USA by Biograph) Mary wreaks havoc in court, attacking policemen, the Clerk, and the Magistrate.	Gaumont, 212	115	£2.17.6d
00953	The Sign of the Cross	Roman Period drama: play by Wilson Barrett: Prefect converted by Christian maid, and they die in the arena. Will Haggar Jnr as Marcus Superbus, Jenny Lindon as Mercia, and James Haggar, Will Desmond & Kate Sylvester.	Gaumont, 253	700	£17 10s
00954	The Bathers' Revenge	Comedy: boy swimmers upset bench and throw lovers into water (in existence)	Urban Trading Co., 1384	75	£1.10.6d
00955	Brutality Rewarded	Comedy: brutal man rebuffs beggar and is chased into stream.	Urban Trading Co., 1385	75	£1.10.6d
00956	The Meddling Policeman	Comedy: an officer is strung with sausages and pelted with eggs by two tramps.	Urban Trading Co., 1386	125	£2.12.6d

BFC No.	Name	Content	Distributor	Length (ft)	Price
	1904 continued				
00957	Flynn's Birthday Celebrations	Comedy: a drunken Irishman throws his wife through the window.	Urban Trading Co., 1414	125	£2.12.6d
00958	The Biter Bitten	Comedy: two tramps attack cyclist who sets dog on them.	Urban Trading Co., 1415	50	£1.1s
00982	Snowballing	Comedy: Mog wins a snowball fight	Gaumont, 288	115	£2.17.6d
	1905				
	Russo-Japanese War The Landing of the French	"Newsreel" : fight between Walter and Jim [14] French invasion of Wales during the Napoleonic Wars: filmed at Fishguard using local fisherwomen, and a dozen men as the French army. [15]			
01138	The Rival Painters	Comedy: a PC rages impotently as he is unable to stop a paint-slapping battle.	Gaumont, 302	90	£2.5s
01149	The Squire's Daughter	Drama, with Fred Haggar, Lily Haggar, and John Freeman.	Gaumont, 329	600	£15.
01150	The Life of Charles Peace	Crime drama, from play based on the life of Charles Peace, who was executed in 1879, in 16 scenes and 11 titles (in existence).	Gaumont, 347	770	£19.5s.
01183	DTs or The Effects of Drink aka The Effects of too much Scotch	Morality with trick photo effects A man returns from his club, sees visions, and reforms. His coat becomes a dog, and his bed a monster.	Gaumont, 331	220	£5.10s
01184	Fun at the Waxworks	Comedy: two men take the place of wax dummies, and strike passers-by.	Gaumont, 334	225	£5.12.6d
01185	Bathing Not Allowed	Comedy: a Bobby and a farmer are dipped in the briny by mischievous boys.	Gaumont, 343	145	£3.12.6
01186	A Boating Accident [16]	Comedy: boating party end up in river.	Gaumont, 344	130	£3.5s
01187	Two's Company, Three's None	Comedy: dude fights rival and they end up in a stream.	Gaumont, 345	75	£1.17.6d
01188	The Salmon Poachers-A Midnight Mêlée	Comedy: miscreants dump two policemen in the river before escaping with their catch. Later they escape from jail and repeat this. Walter Haggar as poacher: a tinted version was made.	Gaumont, 346	274	£6.17s

129

BFC No.	Name	Content	Distributor	Length (ft)	Price
	1905 continued				
01189	Mary is Dry	Comedy: Mary enters a pub and gulps down a customer's beer. On the resultant protest, she lays waste the pub.	Gaumont, 342	94	£2.7s
01190	A Message from the Sea	Drama in 5 scenes, with Will Junior and Henry Haggar. A shipwrecked sailor sends a message in a bottle to his wife, and is saved by a battleship. (a fragment survives).	Gaumont, 349	420	£10.10s
	1906				
	Wreck of "*Amazon*" on Margam Sands	Topical, shown at Newport Empire [17]			
	A Walking Match at Treorchy	Topical [18]			
	A lady disrobing	Hand-coloured Short [19]			
	Wanted - a Wife	Comedy: a line of girls is interviewed [20]			
	Spaghetti Eating	Comic eating by Walter and Violet [21]			
01374	Pongo the Man Monkey	Comedy: a family must mind a wild monkey to please a rich uncle	Gaumont, 489	535	£13.7.6d
	1907				
	Deep-sea Fishing	Topical: a trawler was chartered at Milford [22]			
	East Lynne	Scenes from the famous play [23]			
	Uncle Tom's Cabin	Scenes from the famous play [24]			
01662	The Desperate Footpads	Drama - starring Lily and two of her brothers: she was thrown into a river.	Warwick Trading Co.	360	
	1908				
01775	A Dash for Liberty	Chase: warders chase escaped convicts and shoot them in gun battle	Walturdaw	750	12 10s.
01841	Dick the Kisser	Chase: a flirtatious man is chased into a pond, and tarred and feathered [25]	Walturdaw	355	£3 18.10d
01864	The Red Barn Crime (Maria Martin)	Drama - with Walter Haggar as William Corder and Violet as Maria. 1826: Squire's murder of pregnant mistress revealed by mother's dream. and is caught at a weir. (in existence)	Walter Tyler	685	£11 8.4d

BFC No.	Name	Content	Distributor	Length (ft)	Price
	1908 continued				
01916	The Sheep Stealer	Chase: a starving workman steals a sheep, From play by Barnabas Rayner, with Will Haggar Jnr, Jenny Lindon and Will Desmond.	Walter Tyler	520	£8 13.4d
02045	The Dumb Man of Manchester	Crime drama: lawyer locates locket and witness to save mute from murder charge.	Haggar & Sons	not stated	
02046	The Maid of Cefn Ydfa	Crime. Wales. Lawyer tries to drown thatcher to prevent marriage to heiress. Longer version of 1905 film [26]	Haggar & Sons	not stated	
	A Message from the Sea			745	
	1909				
	Welsh National Pageant	Shown at Brynmawr [27]			
	1911				
	Shipwreck at Burry Port	Topical, made by Jim Haggar [28]			
	Llanelly rail riots	Topical, made by Jim Haggar [29]			
	Labour Demonstration, Llanelly	Topical, made by Jim Haggar [30]			
	The Stepney Wedding in Llanelly	Topical, in existence [31]			
	1913				
	The Women of Mumbles Head	Melded together from previous footage already used as newsreel of the Titanic Disaster in 1912, and new shots using actors in boats off Fishguard, about a real incident when a lighthouse-keeper's daughters rescued men from a shipwreck. [32]			
	1914				
04802	The Maid of Cefn Ydfa (38 minutes survive)	From play by James Haggar; Crime - Wales: Lawyer tries to drown thacher to prevent his marriage to heiress, with Will Haggar Jnr, Jenny Haggar and William Fyffe.	Haggar (distributor)	3000	
	1915				
	Aberdare Civic Sunday Parade	Topical [33]			

ADDENDUM

The following films in the catalogues are, in the main, not attributed to any director, except where noted. Their plots are quite Haggarish.[34]:

BFC No.	Name	Content	Distributor	Length (ft)	Price
	1902				
00604	The Weary Willies and the policeman	Comedy: tramps trick policeman	Warwick Trading Co., 6952	100	£2 2s
00613	Weary Willie and his pal on the rampage	Comedy: two tramps steal things	Warwick Trading Co., 6961	100	£2 2s
00614	Unfair exchange is robbery [35]	Comedy: fair exchange is no robbery, but...	Warwick Trading Co., 6975	100	£2 2s.
	1903				
00643	The Washerwoman, the Tramp and the bike	Comedy: "very funny"	Warwick Trading Co., 7025	125	£2.12.6d
00682	Rivals	Two girls fight over a young man.	Gaumont, 94	70	£1 15s
00715	The Animated Statue	Man poses as statue to fool people	Warwick Trading Co., 7296	200	£4 4s.
00716	Home from the club	Drunkard returns late and dodges wife's missiles	Warwick Trading Co., 7297	100	£2 2s.
00717	The Curate's adventure	Tramp robs curate and is himself robbed	Warwick Trading Co., 7300	75	£1.11.6d.
00742	Putting him on the Blacklist	Prisoner objects to court photo and starts fight	Warwick Trading Co.	200	
	1904				
00990	The Bicycle Thief	Chase: tramp steals bike and police pursue.	Urban Trading Co., 1487	200	£3. 6. 8d
(not listed)	Family Jars	Comedy: A husband kisses a servant and is thrashed by his wife: bobbies join the fun.	Gaumont, 206	65	£1.12.6d
01003	The Three Tramps [36]	The cleverest of all "tramp" pictures	Gaumont, 277	236	£5 18s
	1905				
01067	The Young Ladies' Dormitory [36]	Two tramps invade a girls' dormitory	Gaumont, 304	250	£6 5s
	1906				
01367	The Two Orphans [36]	Drama in six scenes from the French play	Gaumont, 471	560	£14.
	1908				
01890	Bathing Prohibited	Tramps steal bathers clothes, girls and police get a wetting.	Walter Tyler	265	£4 8.4d
01891	The Plumber and the Lunatics [37]	Plumber chased by lunatics who return his knife	Walter Tyler (iin existence)	325	£5 8.4d
01914	Vengeance is Mine	Drama: lightning strikes when blacksmith is about to blind his wife's killer	Walter Tyler	530	£8 16.8d
01915	The Gladiator's Bride	Roman drama: two gladiators fight for girl.	Walter Tyler	410	£6 16.8d

Appendix 3: Synopses of lost Haggar films

DURING THE YEARS 1902-6, William Haggar's films were marketed by his friend Charles Urban, through his Warwick and (subsequently) Charles Urban Trading Companies; and also by the Gaumont Company, headed by another friend, A.C. Bromhead (except in South Wales, which Haggar reserved to himself). Charles Urban and Gaumont issued catalogues with full synopses of the films for sale. Not all catalogues survive, so some synopses are missing. Synopses of films from 1907/8 sold by Walturdaw and Walter Tyler are taken from their advertisements in *The Stage* and *Kinematograph Weekly*. In a few cases, authorship is not certainly that of Haggar (see Appendix 2).

Bathing not allowed
Our picture opens with a quiet rivulet; prominent in the foreground is the notice, "No bathing allowed." What care our boys for this! We see them one after the other, each with their regulation bathing costume, dive into the water; about a score of them are seen. They are thoroughly enjoying their little dip, when up comes Farmer Giles, the owner of the shady spot. "Out you come!" says he: but our boys heed him not. "What, won't come out!" No answer. Giles rushes off and returns with the one and only village policeman, who by his appearance has been dragged out of the "Pig and Whistle." This puts a damper on the appearance of the youths, who one by one come out of the water, only to have their names and addresses taken. The boys, who are now lingering in the background, waiting to hear the verdict, suddenly hit upon an idea. "Charge!" cries their captain. They do so with much vengeance, and our poor policeman with Farmer Giles are hurled headlong into the wetness of the stream. Our boys then quickly decamp with the spoils of war, viz., the officer's notebook, and we are forced to leave the scene, as we have no desire to save the sorry pair, who are clinging to the post which they have placed in the river.

This is a trump card, rattling from start to finish. Quality, photographic and otherwise, excellent.

L. Gaumont & Co., catalogue no. 343, October 1905.   Length   145   ft., Price £3 12s. 6d.

Bathing Prohibited
Two men go bathing - their clothes are stolen by tramps - two girls appear - divest themselves of their outer garments - disport themselves in water - men return and make off with ladies' clothes - police arrive to have a bathe - girls don policemen's clothes - and, finally, all works out amicably after some rollicking fun all round.
Walter Tyler Ltd. - advert in the *Kine Weekly*, 27.8.1908. Length 265 ft., price £6 12 6 less 33.3%

The Biter Bitten
Two tramps of the fighting order lie in ambush for a seemingly unsuspecting cyclist, who, cuter than they counted, dodges them into belabouring each other,

and completes their discomfiture by returning with a savage dog to accelerate their flight.

Charles Urban Trading Co. Ltd.: catalogue no. 1415, February 1905. 50 feet.

A Boating Accident
Depicting an incident that happened to a picnic party

Pretty scenery

(Permission to exhibit in South Wales must be obtained from Messrs. Haggar & Sons.)

Gaumont, catalogue no. 344, February 1906.   Length 130 ft., Price £3 5s.

Brutality rewarded
A beggar woman solicits alms from a passing pedestrian, who not only refuses them, but turns on the woman and handles her roughly. Others quickly gather, and he finds himself belaboured on all sides and attempts with difficulty to escape. He is pursued to the river bank, seized, and flung ignominiously into the all-encircling waters.

Urban, catalogue no. 1385, February 1905.   75 feet.

D.T.'s or The Effects of Drink
Permission to exhibit in South Wales must be obtained from Messrs Haggar and Sons.

A young man, who has just arrived home from his club much the worst for drink, is seen entering his bedroom where he at once proceeds to undress, but on taking off his coat and throwing it down it assumes the shape of a dog and walks off; he then fancies that the images on the mantelshelf have turned into owls, and he gets a broom to clear them off, but on striking them he only succeeds in smashing all the vases. He goes on like this for some time, fancying he sees all manner of things, which on him smashing into only prove to be hat, sticks, chairs, demons and grotesque monsters etc. He at last succeeds in getting into bed, but immediately he lies down the bed shifts its position to the other side of the room, leaving him on the floor; but he quickly picks himself up and gets in once more, but this time the bed turns into a dreadful monster, which takes him round the room on its back, finally disappearing in a cloud of smoke and sending him sky-high. By the time he reaches earth once more and finds that he is all there, he has made a resolution "that he will never get drunk any more".

A capital trick film, splendid subject for showmen

Length 220 ft., Price £5 10s.

Gaumont, catalogue no. 331, November 1905.

A Dash for Liberty, or, The Convict's Escape and Capture
(arranged and photographed for us by Messrs. W. Haggar & Sons)

A splendid sequel to our film no. 1034, "A Daring Daylight Burglary".

Scene 1 – Stone quarry showing convicts at work while the warder mounts guard. Two of these convicts have determined to make a desperate dash for liberty, and upon the return of the warder one of them pretends to have hurt his foot with the pick he was wielding. While the warder stoops to inspect the injury, the convict at work on an upper ledge of rock prostrates the warder with a blow from a large stone flung at him. Both convicts now make for liberty.

Scene 2 – Two warders seeing the fleeing "jail-birds" give chase. The latter, in their blind desire to get away, run into a quarry working from which there is no outlet. Cornered like rats, they defend themselves against the onrush of the warders. One succeeds in wrenching the gun from his pursuer, and is about to brain him with his weapon, when another warder arrives in time to stop this crime by shooting the culprit, while the other one gets away, still pursued.

Scene 3 – The escaping convict, on reaching a road leading past the quarry, espies a farmer driving along. He follows, dodging about awaiting his opportunity to mount the cart, forcing its owner into the road, and escapes by whipping up the horse, while the two warders just coming over the brow of the hill are soon joined by the farmer, who points out the direction taken by the convict. The pursuit now becomes hot, but the convict stops at the first place likely to offer him temporary safety.

Scene 4 – He espies a line from which hang various articles of female wearing apparel, does not stop long to consider, and proceeds to don the woman's clothes, thus disguising his appearance, so that when the officers rush up to the supposed old lady and breathlessly enquire as to the whereabouts of the convict, he puts them off on the wrong scent, and rushes away in the opposite direction.

Scene 5 – Exhausted and worn out, the convict laboriously works his way over the downs. He just reaches the crest of a hill when the warders overtake him, and he is shot down. During the struggle and hand-to-hand conflict which now ensues between the desperately wounded man and the two warders, the former is gradually overcome and re-captured. Pinioned between the two, he is seen staggering out of the picture, his face contorted with pain and hatred.

An exciting subject, natural scenery, and enacted by men who know their business. Splendid quality.

Urban, catalogue no. 1153, Supplement no. 1, January 1904.Length 300 feet. Price £6 6s.

A Dash for Liberty (second version)

A Dash for Liberty is an exciting number of this firm's manufacture. First we have the arrest of two cracksmen by detectives, then their confinement in adjacent cells in one of the convict settlements. From the cells they are marched out to assist in moving some iron girders and one of them seizes the opportunity to make a dash for liberty. He is recaptured and taken back to his cell, but both convicts take advantage of another opportunity, overpower the warder, and again escape, and then follows a series of exciting episodes until they part, and then we follow each convict's adventures. Struggles with the warders take place under various circumstances, ending with the shooting of both of the convicts. A good scene shows the men boarding a moving train. Warders follow in a motor car which runs on the rails by the side of the train.

The Walturdaw Company, in 'Review of Latest Productions' in the *Kine Weekly,* 19 March 1908.

Length 750 ft.   Price £18 15s. less 33.3%

Dick The Kisser

Walturdaw are responsible for a boisterous rough and tumble comic entitled Dick the Kisser. The hero is a young man with so strong a devotion to the other sex that he cannot allow a member of it to pass without attempting to imprint a kiss upon her cheek. He succeeds in taking several young ladies, of varying degrees of attractiveness, by surprise, parts a lover and his lass and kisses the latter, and attempts familiarity with an old apple woman, who retaliates by bringing her basket down on his head. Meanwhile the previous victims have been following him, and a chase is set up, in the course of which another young lady comes into view. She looks so dainty from the back that Dick follows her for some distance, but as he attempts to embrace her, she wheels round and reveals a countenance of such unattractive character that he takes to his heels. A skirmish in a horse pond follows, from which the hero escapes, but is surrounded and runs on to a bridge across a brook. His pursuers follow from either side and their weight brings down the bridge and drenches the whole party. Dick again gets free and the chase continues until he is cornered in the neighbourhood of a barrel of tar, stripped and tarred and feathered by the enemy.

Walturdaw, in 'Review of Latest Productions' in the *Kine Weekly*, 25 June 1908.

Length 355 ft.   Price £5 18 4 (less 33.3%).

Family Jars

Having acquired the negative of this amusing film, we are including it in the present list of films, as we have always found it possess those sterling qualities which establish for it a steady sale. To those of our customers who are still unacquainted with its merits we append a brief description. It happens through the master kissing the servant. All would have been well had the mistress not seen it all. Enough, she goes for him! A great fight takes place, in which the woman holds her own for a time and then resorts to the protection of the police. She calls an officer from the street. Her husband simply thrashes him. She calls another constable. The husband treats the pair like puppets. A whole batch of policemen are summoned to the rescue, and the husband is carried bodily from the house, kicking and screaming frantically.

The mistress sits down on a chair and gives way to tears. The servant, hearing her sobs, rushes into the room and attempts to console her by fanning her with her apron and with comforting words. This adds insult to injury. The mistress is roused once more to a desperate degree. Clutching the servant by the hair of the head, she shakes her violently for some moments. The servant retaliates, and a fight as only women can fight ensues, terminating with more policemen and further arrests.

A rattling comic picture.

Gaumont, catalogue no. 206, October 1904 Length 65 ft., Price £1 12s. 6d.

Flynn's Birthday Celebration

A very laughable account of how Flynn is being visited by his friend, whose greeting of Mrs. Flynn is certainly very cordial, goes for a refresher, and having partaken not wisely but too well, returns to celebrate the birthday. The series of episodes, and the havoc wrought in the Flynn household by their enactment is brimful of laughter, and the final and somewhat unconventional disappearance of Mrs. Flynn, wrong end up, through the window, means thus a proper scream.

Urban, catalogue no. 1414, February 1905.   125 feet.

Fun at the Waxworks

Permission to exhibit in South Wales must be obtained from Messrs. Haggar & Sons

Nobody would think that the waxworks were not all that they were supposed to be, neither were they until two sportive young men appeared on the scene, who, thinking the show rather dull, resolved to enliven it, which they did by removing two of the waxwork images and substituting themselves on pedestals. Armed with a bladder on a string, they caused considerable excitement among the spectators, who were struck from all sides, but were unable to discover the source. They looked around them, but could only see the apparently innocent figures of the waxworks. The fun soon becomes fast and furious, culminating in a melée, in which all hands join, but none could stand against the onslaughts of our friends with the bladders, who were soon left in undisputed possession of the battlefield.

Bubbling over with hearty mirth from start to finish

Gaumont, catalogue no. 334, November 1905. Length 225 ft., Price £5 12s. 6d.

The Gladiator's Affianced Bride

The Gladiator's Affianced Bride, another of Messrs. Tyler's subjects, tells a love story of ancient Rome. The promised wife of a gladiator is annoyed by the attentions of one of his companions, and a duel ensues between the two men – one armed with a sword and shield and clad in armour, the other carrying only trident and net. The latter (the girl's lover) is successful after a very well represented combat.

Walter Tyler, in 'Review of Latest Productions', in the *Kine Weekly*, 3 September 1908.

Length 410 ft. Price £10 5s. (less 33.3%). Colouring 7/6 extra, net.

Mary is dry

Permission to Exhibit in South Wales must be obtained from Messrs. Haggar & Sons.

The interior of a Public-house bar is shown, and two or three customers are having drinks, and all is peaceful. Mirthful Mary enters, and soon all is chaos, for feeling dry she picks up some of the customers' beer and drinks it off. When they remonstrate with her, however, she picks up a soda-water syphon and thoroughly drenches them. Not content with this, she upsets the tables and smashes the glasses, finally jumping on the counter and wrecking the whole place.

Turn-out subject for Showmen, and a continuation of our celebrated "Mirthful Mary" and "Mary in the Dock" series.

Gaumont, catalogue no. 342, October 1905.   Length 94 ft., Price £2 7s.

The Meddling Policeman

Here we see a too oppressive police officer interrupt a pair who are evidently diagnosing the contents of a picnic basket; they return the attack, wind the guardian of the law in strings of sausages, deluge him with flour and other condiments, until his appearance is less picturesque than pitiable.

Urban, catalogue no. 1386, February 1905.   125 feet.

A Message from the Sea

Scene 1 – The Home of a Jolly Tar.

Harry Mainstay was a British Tar, adored by his mates, and worshipped by the women; every inch a sailor, his song was always the cheeriest, his laugh the heartiest, of all the crew – and his dancing sent the girls almost crazy with delight. He had been on many a voyage ere our story opens, and now, as well as the old folks, he has a wife and child to cheer the weeks of his furlough.

When our picture opens, Harry is bidding farewell to his folks; his father and mother, from the door of the cottage, wave their hands as he departs. His wife and little girl escort him to the garden gate, and beyond it. After a touching scene, the sailor departs, and in another scene we see him join his ship, and start on what proves to be the most adventurous voyage he has ever had.

Scene 2 – Wrecked in Mid Ocean.

"The sea could tell" of the awful catastrophe which overtook the vessel in which our hero sailed; no detailed report was ever published. "Foundered with all hands", the papers said – and strong men wept.

But all were not lost. Harry Mainstay, another sailor, and a cabin boy escaped on a raft. For days they drifted; but their signals of distress were never sighted – no vessel came near. The three are now in a perilous plight. A few drops of fresh water only remain, and our hero raises the bottle to the parched lips of the boy. The other sailor checks his hand and tries to seize the bottle; Harry Mainstay retains his hold, and with all his remaining strength he lets fly at the man, who would see the boy die of thirst, and sends him into the sea. The boy's thirst is quenched, and there are now only two occupants of the raft. The boy sleeps. The sailor thinks of home and kin, his darling wife and child, his dear old parents. Can it be true that he will never see them again? It seems too true: he cannot hold out many hours now. Will succour never come? He must die, alone, and the World will never know. But stay! The World shall know. The bottle shall be the messenger. Our hero hastily scribbles a note, puts it in the bottle, and fixes the stopper. The bottle is hurled into the sea, and Harry Mainstay sinks exhausted.

Whither will the message drift? The sea could tell.

Scene 3 – At the Seaside.

Our hero's child is paddling, and her mother is close at hand. The child spies a bottle washed up by the tide. "Oh, Mamma, look!" And mamma comes to see what new wonder the child has found. The bottle is examined, curiosity releases the stopper; but curiosity turns to bewilderment and despair when the mother reads, "Shipwrecked, alone on a raft, no hope, God bless you, farewell. – Harry Mainstay."

Scene 4 – Midnight on the Ocean.

The lights of a vessel in sight. Our hero makes a last desperate effort – he waves his jacket and shouts with all the voice he has left. Joy! They have seen;

a boat is being lowered, and sturdy sailors are manning it. The joy is too great. Harry Mainstay sinks on the raft, and the sea tosses the frail craft mercilessly. The lifeboat crew from the "Man-o'-War" soon assist the helpless derelicts into the boat, and are soon rowing with powerful strokes back to the vessel.
Scene 5 – A Churchyard.
A widow and her little girl are arranging flowers on a newly erected monument. We recognise them, although the mother, in particular, is much changed. A figure emerges from the shrubbery – 'tis Harry Mainstay. The mother sees him. They meet, but do not speak. No language could describe such a homecoming. The widow's cap is thrown away, the jolly sailor's 'kerchief adorns the comely head of the mother, who is now a wife once more.
Titles are inserted throughout the film, which is partly tinted blue to augment effects.

This picture is splendid. Its simple pathos will appeal to all.

Announcement Title Slide, 6d. each.　　　　　　Length 420 ft., Price £10 10s.
Gaumont, catalogue no. 349, October 1905.

Mirthful Mary, A Case for the Blacklist

The Landlord is standing at the door of a country inn when Mary arrives, already the worse for liquor. She is refused admittance, and becomes abusive and loquacious. A policeman is called in and, after a brief struggle, loses his temper and strikes her with his truncheon. Mary, however, secures this article, and repays the blow with interest. Another policeman arrives on the scene, and finally a third very small one, who stands pompously on the inn steps and directs operations, during which he falls over crash (sic). Finally a handcart is fetched, and the united police force place Mary on it, despite her desperate struggles, and she is wheeled off close past the camera.

This is a really A1 comic.

Gaumont, catalogue no. 82B, June 1904.　　　　　length 120 ft., Price £3.

Mirthful Mary in the Dock

Sequel to Elge film, No. 82, "A case for the Black List".
It is evident that, as she takes up her position in the prisoner's dock, Mirthful Mary bears visible traces of her recent arrest: an arrest, by-the-by, which created such sensational interest, and which was chronicled in bold type on the screen of every theatre of note throughout the kingdom.
Hundreds of thousands of persons have watched this case from the commencement, and it would appear that outside the courthouse, which has for the nonce been cleared of the general public – owing to the volubility of the mirthful one – there are thousands more of these interested persons thirsting for every scrap of news concerning the trial about to take place, and which begins with the prisoner refusing to be sworn, and her calling the magistrate "An ould thief".
A Policeman raises his hands in protest, and the next moment he has occasion to raise his body from the floor – having caught the full force of an elbow "hook" from the amazon in the dock – he stares about him in a dazed condition, with a mouthful of loose teeth. A wild gleam is in the once blue eyes of Mary, as the Clerk of the Court calls aloud for "Order!" His fate is sealed.

With as much of a spring as her ponderous weight will allow, Mirthful Mary, despite the efforts of several policemen to restrain her, gets over the dock rail and stands unsteadily in the centre of the room. With a couple of stalwarts hanging on to her, she makes a bee-line for the table where sits the Clerk, with a look of disgust upon his face. Clearing her path and releasing herself from her assailants with a series of vigorous half-arm jambs (sic), she reaches her goal – the Clerk.

As Mary seizes him, a whirlwind of disorder sweeps through the court. Books and papers fly in all directions, "Coppers" fall like skittles. The magistrate's order to "Seize her!" is entirely ignored, and Mary proceeds with the slaughter with undiminished fury. Lifting the officer who caused her arrest, from the witness-box where he stands to give evidence, she dashes him bodily against the front line of attack, and it is when Mary slips her foot here and falls, that one can see at a glance she is still wearing the same conspicuous costume as when arrested.

However, she is soon on her feet again, the mistress of the situation. She now thrusts her nose up in the air, and makes threatening gestures towards the magistrate. Evidently the venerable unpaid one displeases her, for she bears down upon him, only being stopped at the clerk's table by the united efforts of six policemen. Another minute, and she has again outclassed all opposition, and is standing on the table, throwing everything that is handy at the magistrate. Books, pens, rulers, &c., follow each other in quick succession, till at last, seeing nothing else worth throwing, bang goes the inkpot at his head.

The result can be imagined. The magistrate's right eye is completely closed by contact with the inkpot, and is a fitting companion to the left one, which was already in mourning through the clumsy aiming of one of the officers earlier in the fight: the courthouse is almost wrecked, and justice defeated.

Later, Mary obeying her woman's instincts, gave way to tears, and was led back to her cell to await further developments; but the fun had ended, and so has one of the funniest pictures ever seen.

One hundred and fifteen feet of hilarity. A roof raiser.

Gaumont, catalogue no. 212, October 1904. Length 115 ft., Price £2 17s. 6d.

Pongo the Man Monkey
A MASTERPIECE OF MONKEY MISCHIEF AND APISH ANTICS
Quality Stereoscopic

Uncle Jack is coming home from the tropics and is bringing a great treasure home with him. Outside and inside the house, all is bustle and excitement. Uncle Jack arrives and speaks mysteriously of his priceless treasure. Everyone is on the tiptoe of expectancy. Shortly, Uncle Jack's luggage arrives, and with it is a large hamper, bearing the legend, "Uncle Jack's Treasure". The inquisitive servant girls flock around, and cannot restrain their curiosity. They lift the lid, and out leaps a mammoth ape of the baboon species. Pongo is the incarnation of mischief. He leaps at the girls to embrace them; they fly, shrieking. Then a chase follows, for Pongo, who eludes every attempt at capture, sows consternation everywhere.

While Aunt Jane is snugly asleep in bed, Pongo creeps into the bedroom and gets into bed with Auntie, who flies in terror when she starts up and finds Pongo by her side. Pongo then dresses himself in Aunt Jane's nightcap and gets into bed in her place. Soon Uncle comes in and, after undressing, gets into bed and bends over to kiss Auntie, when Pongo sits bolt upright, and poor Uncle is scared out of his wits. A chase round the bed follows, and a most comical scene in the bedroom results.

Again, Pongo makes his way to a laundry, and scatters the laundry-maids and defies his pursuers by flinging soap-suds over them. Poor Uncle, thinking to capture him, comes off rather rough. At another time, Uncle and Auntie are spooning in the garden, and Pongo creeps up behind them and puts his handsome face in between theirs, just when they are about to enjoy a lip-tickle. They start apart in surprise, and before they can recover themselves, Pongo leaps round in glee and upsets seat, Uncle, and Auntie in a most laughable manner. Pongo's escapades are too many to mention here.

After a most exciting chase, in which Pongo outwits his pursuers at every turn, he is captured, but not until he has held his would-be captors at bay, and flung them, as though they were so much matchwood, in all directions. Then he is seen in charge of half-a-dozen stalwart men and policemen, who get in each other's way, thus frustrating their purpose, in a most ridiculous manner, in their eagerness to capture Pongo.

Gaumont, catalogue no. 489, October 16th, 1906.　　　　Length 535 ft., Price £13 7s. 6d.

The Red Barn Crime, or Maria Martin

Messrs. Walter Tyler issue a film with the title, The Red Barn Crime, in which the leading incidents of a murder which created a great sensation at the time of its perpetration in the early part of the last century are set out in an effective way. Probably most of our readers are acquainted with the main details of the murder of Maria Martin, which has been re-enacted on the stage of many a travelling theatre. The girl was taken away from home by William Corder, a farmer who had promised to marry her but instead shot her in a barn and buried the body. The father and stepmother of the murdered girl both dreamed that they found her body in the barn, although they had been told that she was living happily with Corder in London, and at last the anxiety of the old man led him to dig in the floor of the barn, where the body was duly discovered. Corder was arrested at the Boarding House where he lived with his second wife – obtained through a matrimonial settlement – and at last confessed the crime, over 7000 people being present at his execution.

Walter Tyler, in 'Review of Latest Productions', in the *Kine Weekly*, 30 July 1908.

The farmer, his victim (Maria Martin, to whom he proposed marriage), the lonely farm. The murder is discovered, after a lapse of some months, by the father of the victim, the body is exhumed and the culprit arrested. He appears in the dock, well dressed – in fact, quite a dandy – he denies his guilt and concocts a false account of the deed. Finally he is sentenced to the extreme penalty, and a little while before the execution confesses guilt. This film is of splendid quality, and nothing like it is on the market – it is a triumph of film production.

Walter Tyler, advert in *The Stage*, 30 July 1908.

　　　　　　　　Length 685 ft.　　Price £17 2 6 (less 33.3 %).

The Rival Painters
Permission to Exhibit in South Wales must be obtained from Messrs. Haggar & Sons.

Two rival painters are at work. One is using black paint and the other white, they are having a few words and are apparently very angry with each other. Their anger reaches the climax when their work meets, and blows with the paint brushes ensue; not content with smothering each other with paint, they endeavour to spoil each other's work by slinging paint all over it. A Bobby arrives and endeavours to arrest them, but the result is indescribable confusion and chaotic disorder, in which painters, policemen, paint-pots and brushes, helmets and truncheons are ingloriously mixed.

A very funny film

Gaumont, catalogue no. 302, November 1905.   Length 90 ft., Price £2 5s.

Rivals
An amusing comedy, opening with a young man and woman spooning in the grass. From behind, another girl approaches rapidly, and having evidently a claim upon the young man's affections, she throws herself upon her rival. The young man makes off, while his erstwhile love tears her rival's hat up; a battle royal ensues, in which hair is pulled down, hats ruined, and faces scratched. A policeman runs up to intervene, when both viragoes turn upon him and punish him severely, pulling off the sleeves of his coat and likewise the legs of his trousers. Bobby whistles for help, and two other policemen run to his rescue and eventually secure the infuriated damsels, who are marched past the camera still struggling.

> Capital comic. Quality A1.   Length 70 ft., Price £1 15s.

Gaumont, catalogue no. 94B, July 1903.

Salmon Poachers: a Midnight Melée
This film not to be exhibited in South Wales without the permission of Messrs. Haggar & Sons.

The scene opens in a picturesque spot, where we see the salmon-poachers busy at work with the nets; but the authorities getting wind of their depredations arrive on the scene in a boat. The poachers, hastily gathering up their catch of eight or ten fine fish, make off. They are met, however, as they climb up the bank by two policemen, but after a struggle the policemen are flung into the river. They escape; but the minions of the law are upon their track and soon come upon them. A realistic fight takes place and the poachers make off again, but leaving their fish behind them, which a corpulent policeman promptly gathers up and takes away. The chase continues and they are eventually run to earth, and after some difficulty placed in a boat to be taken to the lock-up. They are not at the end of their resources, however, and make another bold bid for freedom while in the boat, and succeed in pitching their captors into the water, beating them off with the oars. They finally escape in the boat, leaving their discomfited pursuers struggling in the water.

Magnificent quality throughout, and beautifully tinted. This is the most realistic "moonlight effect" picture we have ever issued.

Gaumont, catalogue no. 346, November 1905. Length 274 ft., Price £6 17s.

Snowballing

The scene is in a country lane, where many of the young people of the village are congregated, with rosy cheeks and smiling faces, on this typical winter morning. The surrounding country is covered with a thick layer of new-fallen snow, and a mischievous twinkle in the eyes of the girls bespeaks fun and frolic. A handful of soft, fleecy snow deftly placed inside a fellow's collar starts the game. Sides are chosen, and a battle royal is soon in progress. Ammunition being plentiful, snowballs are rained in upon each team fast and furiously, many, of course, lodging themselves firmly in the ears of opponents.

During a temporary cessation of hostilities, the whole crowd observe some pedestrians and a cyclist coming down the road in their direction. In a few moments, miniature arsenals are completely full of cold shells. The pedestrians approach, heedless of the warm welcome awaiting them; and coming within range, are met by a tremendous fusillade from the small fortress. Here the animation of the picture is splendid, and the snow battle lasts until the pedestrians and cyclists have, not without difficulty, fought their way through the storm-swept centre; while the crisp air rings again with laughter.

This over, fresh conquests are sought for. The army moves off and, when near the village, an unexpected and well aimed snowball hits the leader of the party square on the nose. This causes some consternation, which is quelled when the enemy is discovered to be ONE strong, and that one to be none other than a big, powerful female, who had the reputation of being but seldom sober, and who went under the peculiar but euphonious name of "Mog the Fireman." A terrible rout takes place: Mog is bombarded upon every side: and the picture finishes with her fighting gamely in various and interesting attitudes with astonishing vigour.

Highly recommended. Splendid quality.

Gaumont, catalogue no. 288A, January 1905. Length 115 ft., Price £2 17s. 6d.

The Three Tramps

In this, the cleverst and funniest of all "Tramp" pictures, we are treated to a big slice of real broad comedy. It is a film which the up-to-date showman cannot afford to be without, and it is a grand subject to wind up a performance with, for the spectators – even the "Cheerful Charlies" – must of necessity give vent to something of a chuckle. A prime comic.

Gaumont, catalogue no. 277A, April & May 1905. Length 236 ft., Price £5 18s.

The Tramp and Baby's Bottle

Taken by Messrs. Wm. Haggar & Sons, from whom permission to exhibit in South Wales must be obtained.

Nurse comes into the park with her infant charge in a perambulator. She is followed by Corporal Atkins of the Royals, who in full regimentals looks very dashing. Dusty Rhodes, the tramp, is an interested spectator of the animated conversation which takes place between the Nurse and Atkins as they sit on the bench. His tender heart is touched by the neglected condition of the baby, which he sympathetically inspects – finding the baby's bottle and nipple, he samples the contents. The said contents prove to be tasty, and D. Rhodes is thoroughly enjoying them when he is detected by the nurse. Nurse sets the soldier on his track, and the military man, after chasing him round the bench three or four times, catches him, lifts him in the air, and throws him on the perambulator – which gives way, the baby being squashed beneath the weight. The struggle is continued for a short time, during which the bench is also demolished; then Dusty Rhodes makes off, closely followed by the soldier; while the nurse, gathering up her flattened charge, also follows suit.

Good comic subject of capital quality.

Gaumont, catalogue no. 133, June 1904.   Length 100 ft., Price £2 10s.

The Tramp and the Washerwoman
A Tragedy of Suburbia

Bridget, the maid-of-all work, is hanging out the clothes, a varied collection, in the plot of waste ground behind a suburban semi-detached villa. The job finished to Bridget's satisfaction, she departs, leaving the garments, many of which are of the nature "born to blush unseen", flaunting in the breeze. Dusty Rhodes, the tramp, who has been making sundry calls in the district, comes on the scene, and, espying the clothes, comes to the hasty conclusion that there are some which might be of service to him. Without more ado, he divests himself of his outer garments, and substitutes them with some from the line, which have seen less wear. This done, he suddenly remembers an urgent appointment in another district, but is too late, as the vigilant Bridget has seen him. She rushes after him, catches him, and drags him back by the ear.

She then takes the law into her own hands, giving him a sound thrashing, and relieving him of the stolen garments in a very forcible manner. So much taken up is she with her task that she fails to notice the approach of a cyclist, and runs right into his path, causing general confusion. Dusty Rhodes emerges from the melée and before the others can recover themselves, has mounted the bicycle and ridden off. Bridget and the cyclist give chase, but they are too late, and the tramp, though minus some very necessary articles of apparel, has a very valuable asset in the bicycle.

Really funny. Recommended.

Gaumont, catalogue no. 132B, June 1904.   Length 100 ft., Price £2 10s.

The Two Orphans

WE CAN THOROUGHLY RECOMMEND THIS AS BEING OF SUPERB QUALITY RIGHT THROUGH. THE PHOTO QUALITY IS STEREOSCOPIC. IT IS ACKNOWLEDGED BY ALL WHO HAVE SEEN IT TO BE ABSOLUTELY HIGH CLASS – A SPEAKING PICTURE, FULL OF LIFE.

Scene 1– Destitution. A garret showing every sign of the direst poverty. The walls bare, a ladder in place of a staircase, draughts blowing across the floor in all directions. The occupants of the room, a brother and sister. The boy lies on an old bed, dying; a few old rags suffice as bedclothes. The girl, Elsie, is devoted to her brother. A poor woman brings in a little food. The girl picks up the paper in which the food is brought. She sees an advertisement for an errand boy, and decides to apply for the place. She disguises herself as a boy in her brother's clothes and goes on her venture.

Scene 2 – Little Elsie seeks Employment. Elsie, who makes a charming boy, presents herself for the position of errand boy. Her fragile appearance at first goes against her, but her pleading overcomes the shopkeeper's objections.

She is employed and sent out with a heavy basket of goods.

Scene 3 – A policeman who had to do his duty. Struggling along in the heat of the day, the child's puny strength gives out under the heavy load. She sits down to rest at the base of a statue situated in a thoroughfare bearing every sign of well-to-do comfort. She is moved on by a tender-hearted policeman, who evinces every sign of reluctance to do his duty.

Scene 4 – Little Elsie tells her story. Elsie moves on, showing every sign of weariness. She finally reaches her destination, and sinks upon the step, thoroughly fatigued. The child is taken in and laid on the sofa. She is given some nourishment, and, being revived, tells her story. The kind people are interested in the girl's story, and decide to visit the poverty-stricken home.

Scene 5 – Alone in the world; a Christian act. Elsie, accompanied by her kind friends, reaches the old home only to find the brother whom she idolises has no longer any need of her help and self-sacrifice. She is led away by the kind people who have evinced so much interest in her. They adopt her as their own child, and provide for burial for the boy.

Finally, a quiet and calm graveyard scene. Elsie, unrecognisable as the puny weak child of the slums, is seen placing flowers on a neat grave, which holds all the remains of her much-loved brother.

Gaumont, catalogue no. 471, August 1906.   Length 560 ft., Price £14.

Vengeance is Mine

In Vengeance is Mine, Messrs. Tyler have succeeded in inventing a story of great dramatic quality, and particularly well suited to living picture representation. A blacksmith's wife is annoyed by the approaches of an old flame, while carrying her husband's lunch to his workplace. She angrily repulses the man's attentions, but later he comes to the place when she is alone, and a quarrel occurs, ending in the woman being killed by a blow from a walking stick. The little daughter takes the news to her father, who follows and overtakes the villain, and carrying him to the smithy, binds him to a plank and is about to put out his eyes with a hot iron when a lightning flash descends and takes the vengeance from his hands by killing the murderer.

Walter Tyler, in 'Review of Latest Productions', in the Kine Weekly, 3 September 1908.

Length 530 ft.   Price £13 5 0 (less 33.3%)

Wanted: a Wife

In **Wanted – a Husband** (not a Haggar film, but marketed by Gaumont in 1905), Young Smith, who is in bachelor's diggings, decides to play a practical joke on the public. He decides to insert an advertisement, "Wanted a Husband", and to receive the applicants himself, disguised as a woman. He does so, with marvellous results.

Wanted – a Wife was Haggar's riposte to this. It is not in the film catalogues, but Lily Richards describes it thus: 'A bachelor wanted a wife and he advertised, and all this flock of women came, and he had to treat everyone differently. It was a farce really. My father made that set on a truck, a flat lorry. The girls had a set of steps to go up, knock at the door and go in. The winner disrobes, taking out her glass eye and teeth, pulls off her wig, unscrews her wooden leg, etc.'   Lily Haggar, interview

Weary Willie and Tired Tim turned Barbers

Fun of the wildest order. Turning the legitimate barbers out of their shop, W. W. and T. T. commence operations on two unsuspecting customers who drop in for a shave. Being lathered too copiously, the customers vigorously resist. Police rush in to their assistance, when all turn upon them. Soapsuds fly, and one of the Bobbies is extinguished with the lather pot – while the other comes off just as badly.

Good broad comedy, highly suitable for showmen.

Gaumont, catalogue no. 93B, June 1904.   Length 118 ft., Price £2 19s.

Whitewashing the Policeman

A gentleman is sitting on a seat in the park when up comes Dusty Rhodes, who sits on the other end of the seat. Both fall off to sleep. Two small boys who have hidden behind the fence at the back then pop up their heads and commence tickling the gent with a feather. The gent wakes up, and seeing the tramp accuses him, but on being told it was not so, they both console themselves by another nap. No sooner has the tramp settled himself comfortably than the other boy jumps up and jams his hat down over his eyes, also striking him two or three blows. Up jumps our knight of the road, and seeing no other person about, he not unnaturally assumes that his sleeping companion is the author of his trouble, he wakes him up and demands an explanation. This not being to his satisfaction, they come to blows.

Two or three labourers, one of whom is carrying a pail of whitewash, come on the scene. The whitewash is placed on the ground while the men stand watching the fun. The gentleman seeing the pail, picks it up and throws the contents over what he takes to be Dusty Rhodes, but the entire contents go over a policeman who has just arrived on the scene, covering his beautiful blue tunic with the best whitewash. Seeing what he has done, the gent turns and rushes away, followed by the crowd.

A short scene of the ensuing chase is then given. Down the hill rushes the poor panting gent, and close at his heels comes the whitewashed bobby, followed by the crowd, with Dusty Rhodes bringing up the rear.

Very laughable comic. Quality A1.

Gaumont, catalogue no. 175, June 1904.   Length 65 ft., Price £1 12s. 6d.

The Young Ladies' Dormitory

A great joke is carried out in this film. Two tramps of the Weary Willie type, seeing the main door of a young ladies' school wide open, march right in with blazing effrontery and proceed to "inspect" all the best rooms in the place, just to see if any loose jewellery has been left lying about. They are just about to leave the dormitory of certain ladies when they hear footsteps on the stairs. They are hidden under separate beds in an instant. The footsteps happen to be those of the young ladies on their way to that very room where the tramps lie hidden. The weary ones, not being noticed, and judging by the supreme happiness on their faces, seem to be content with their lot while the girls undress, but the chuckle that escaped one of them led to their discovery. The girls drag them out from under their beds, and give them a sound thrashing, finishing off their resources of indignation by a direct attack with bolsters, which

146

give way and allow the feathers to escape all over the room.

A great "roar" for showmen.

Gaumont, catalogue no. 304A, August 1905.   Length 250 ft., Price £6 5s.

Appendix 4: 'The Maid of Cefn Ydfa': analysis

Title	Scene no. / description	Action
1. The Love Story of Ann Thomas, the Maid of Cefn Ydfa.		
2. Produced by Mr. & Mrs. Will Haggar Jnr and their Dramatic Company.		
3. Introduction	1 In the countryside	The whole cast passes by Will and his harp.[1]
4. Festivities at Cefn Ydfa. Ann falls in love with Will Hopkins	2 Outside a large house	The cast dance and joke. There is a fight between Will and Maddox. The whole scene is at a distance and difficult to understand.
5. Ann visiting the poor: the lovers meet.	3 Outside a cottage	Ann visits. Will is up a ladder, thatching. Distant, then close-up, with good movement. Cut to distant: Maddox arrives, and departs with Ann.
6. Cefn Ydfa. Mr. Maddox instructs his son Anthony to propose to Ann. He does so, and is refused.	4 Ann's house – interior	The cast of 5 act on stage, speaking their lines theatrically.
7a. Ann sets out for Bridgend Fair. Anthony follows	5 Outside a stables	Ann sets off on horseback; Maddox follows.
8. Scene at Bridgend Fair. Ann is insulted by Anthony. Will Hopkins thrashes him. Anthony hires two ruffians to kill Will Hopkins.	6 Outside an inn (The Farmer's Arms)	Distant shot. Cast argue – some fun by Lewis Bach and Gwenny: unintelligible. Ann arrives, followed by Maddox, who manhandles Ann. Will knocks him down. Gwenny taunts him. He and the ruffians go into the inn.
9. The betrothal of Will and Ann	7 In an orchard	Will and Ann embrace in close-up. Maddox and the ruffians are in the background.
10. The attack on Will Hopkins	8 In a lane, and at a gate	Will and Ann say goodbye – the camera moves during this. Maddox and the ruffians approach: Maddox strikes. A dog runs past.
11. Will's body is thrown into the water, but he is rescued by Morgan the Seer.	9 At the weir	The ruffians lay Will at the top and push him over the weir. Morgan drags him to the side. They approach the camera, with much comic business. The camera moves, to a close-up.
12. Lewis Bach, drunk, being wheeled home by Gwenny	10 In a lane (2 positions)	More comic business. They embrace. Enter Morgan carrying Will. Jump or bad cut to.....
13. Lewis promises not to get drunk any more. Morgan enlists his services to convey Will to his hut.	10 cont'd: another part of the lane	

Title	Scene no. / description	Action
(? missing title)	11 Interior of Morgan's hut (outside location: note shadows)	Morgan revives Will. Jump or bad cut to.....
	12 Ann's house – interior	Close-up of note from Will's death. Enter Ann, who receives the note from her mother, and swoons. Tableau.[2]
14. Ann accuses Anthony: she is ordered to her room.	(title interposed)	Ann accuses Anthony. All exit except Maddox. Morgan enters and holds up letter. Cut to chamber. Ann sees the letter being held up. Cut to Morgan holding up letter; cut to Ann grasping it. Cut to Morgan exiting.
15. Outside Ann's chamber. Morgan delivers a letter from Will.	13a Exterior of house 13b Ann's chamber – interior	
16. Maddox makes a false copy of the will. Morgan steals the real one.	14 Ann's house – interior	Maddox is writing. Morgan enters and theatrically steals the will. Close-up of the "Last Will & Testament of Evan Thomas".
17. Morgan takes Ann to see Will Hopkins. Anthony and his father follow them.	15 Exterior of house	Morgan and Ann depart, followed by the Maddoxes – distant shots.
18. Morgan's hut. Affectionate meeting of the lovers.	16 A road: two views	The two pairs walk along the road, around a corner, and the camera moves to follow them.
	17 Morgan's hut	Morgan shows Ann in to Will: they embrace. Maddox arrives. Scene is close to camera. A piece of paper blows past.
19. Will escorts Ann home. Mrs. Thomas orders him away.	18 A lane leading to a wall and gate.	Slightly confusing scene – Mrs. Thomas is escorted home; then Will and Ann arrive; Will is ejected; he knocks Maddox down.
20. Cefn Ydfa. Ann is asked to sign a marriage contract between herself and Anthony Maddox. She refuses. Maddox tells her she will be disinherited, but finds that Morgan has the real will.	19 Ann's house – interior	A stage scene involving most of the principals with some unintelligibility – interrupted by a close-up of the contract. Maddox threatens Morgan.
21. Ann's chamber. Stormy scene between Mother and Daughter. Ann is made a prisoner in her own house	20 Ann's chamber – interior	Ann, her mother and a maid act the scene.
22. Will Hopkins sings to Ann	21a Ann's chamber – interior 21b Outside the house	Balcony scene between Ann and Will, complete with harp. Six cuts between the two scenes.
23. Ann writing on the leaf, her blood for ink, a hairpin for a pen.	21c Ann's chamber – interior 21d Outside the house	Ann in close-up, writing, followed by close-up of the "leaf": "Will, Will, I am a prisoner here, save me." Cut to interior. Cut to exterior, where Will catches the leaf.
24. Morgan's Hut. Will Hopkins signs an agreement to go abroad for two years.	22 Morgan's Hut	Will, Morgan and Lewis Bach read the letter about the agreement. Close-up of letter.

Title	Scene no. / description	Action
		Will signs and Lewis witnesses the agreement – close-up.
25. Cefn Ydfa. Maddox receives the agreement. A villain's trick.	23 Ann's house – interior	Maddox receives the agreement, shows it (close-up) to Mrs. Thomas, then tears it in two: cut to.....
26. "Now read it"	(title interposed)	Close-up of torn half (dark background). Exeunt.
27. Ann's chamber. Her consent to marry Anthony is won by fraud.	24 Ann's chamber – interior	Maddox senior brings the agreement to Ann. Close-up. Anthony proposes. She swoons.
28. The wedding of Ann Thomas to Anthony Maddox	25 Outside the church - two views	The wedding party approaches the camera, which moves and pans to the church door. Lewis Bach carries Gwenny across the threshold.
29. Will Hopkins arrives too late.	(title interposed)	Will arrives, in despair. Morgan consoles him. The wedding party comes out. Will and Ann embrace. "Farewell for ever!" Tableau.[3]
30. Will Hopkins leaves his native land		Jump straight to next title
31. Lewis Bach setting out to find Will Hopkins	26 (scene missing) Outside a cottage	Lewis bids farewell to Gwenny and three children (time has passed!). He advances into close-up with baby. Lewis strikes a pose.
32. Farewell England, Farewell Wales! Heres off to the Rhondda Valley!	(title interposed)	Jump to next title
33. The murder of Morgan the Seer. Maddox regains the will.	27 (scene missing) Ann's house – interior	Stage act: the Maddoxes carouse and quarrel, and Ann intervenes. Ann laments theatrically.
34. LATER: a drunken quarrel between father and son. Ann interposes.	(title interposed)	
35. Ann's troubles. The loss of Will Hopkins, her marriage, a drunken husband, and the death of her child drive her to madness.		
36. Ann at the grave of her child, calling for Will Hopkins	28 In the churchyard	Ann in close-up, laying the dead child on the grave, and lamenting.
37. Ann takes off her wedding ring saying, "It hurts like the sting of a snake." She replaces it with the one given her by Will Hopkins, saying, "Will, Will, why don't you come to me".	(title interposed)	Ann gesticulates, taking the dead child in her arms. Cut to distant, indistinct shot of Ann seen against the church. She walks away. (End of the film).[4]

Notes:
1. A play-opening procession by the cast was conventional in the Victorian theatre.
2. A tableau at this point would have ended the first of the three reels.
3. A tableau here ended the second reel.
4. A third tableau is likely to have been staged at the (lost) end of the last reel. Such tableaux were conventional in the nineteenth century, the stage play ending with the Maid being received into heaven by an angel.

Appendix 5: The opening of the Kosy Kinema

Haggar's Kosy Kinema – Opened by the High Constable

ON MONDAY EVENING COUNCILLOR Haggar's New Picture Theatre in Market Street, Aberdare, was opened by the High Constable, Mr. Chas. Kenshole. There was a tremendous crowd present when the High Constable, accompanied by his lady, was presented by Mr. Gwilym Davies (Messrs. John Morgan & Son. Ltd) with the opening key. Mr. Kenshole just spoke a few words declaring the place open, and Mr. Gwilym Davies then presented Mrs. Kenshole with a handsome shower bouquet of malmaison carnations, white sweet peas and asparagus fern and smilax. The lady bowed her acknowledgments. Invitation cards had been sent to the ladies and gentlemen of the town, and a representative company stood up to sing 'The King', accompanied by Mr. Carroll's orchestra.

The High Constable then rose and addressed the audience. He said it was the first occasion that he had been called upon to open a theatre. He, however, felt justified on that occasion in coming forward to open Mr. Haggar's beautiful place of amusement for several reasons. Mr. Haggar had resided in Aberdare for many years, and had associated himself with everything that was for the welfare of the town, and especially had he come forward in the cause of charity. He (the speaker) felt it was his duty to come forward and give what support he possibly could. Mr. Haggar had provided a building worthy of the town, which they would agree with him had not been too fortunate in that respect. When they looked round they found they had got everything desirable in the way of comfort. He felt sure that whatever Mr. Haggar put on the screen there would be nothing objectionable, and everything to meet the most fastidious tastes. He ventured to hope that this venture of Mr. Haggar's would prove a success, and that he would be spared for many years to cater for the amusement and education of the people of Aberdare. (Cheers)

A Description of the Building

The designer of the building is Mr. Geo. Kenshole, M.S.A., of Aberdare and Bargoed, and it is the ninth building of the kind to be erected to his plans. The front is constructed in stucco in the Grecian style, with columns and enriched by festoons of laurels, with a canopy of steel and coloured lead lights, lit up by hundreds of coloured electric globes, which give a very pleasing and grand effect. On either side of the mosaic vestibule, a stone staircase leads to the balcony which is considered to be the finest in the provinces and seats 350. The balcony front is beautifully enriched with cherubs and festoons of fruit and flowers, and the proscenium with a magnificent design in carved wood and gilded in fine old English gold. There are emergency exits and the whole place can be cleared in two minutes. The sliding roofs for hot weather are the latest obtainable, and ensure to patrons the highest comfort.

Aberdare Leader, 28 August 1915

Appendix 6: 'Men at the wheel'

MR. WILLIAM HAGGAR (SENIOR), ABERDARE (by D.T.L.)

SOME WEEKS AGO THERE was an animated discussion in a London morning newspaper as to what sort of life a person must lead before he or she becomes entitled to burial in Westminster Abbey. The question was not satisfactorily answered either way, but it is possible that the same point has arisen in the minds of readers of this journal as to what qualifies a man or woman for inclusion, whilst still alive, in this popular series of articles. The answer to this question is that there are no hard and fast rules save that the persons dealt with must have proved their value as citizens to the community.

The name of Haggar has been before the public for nearly half a century, and who in the mining valleys of South Wales has not at one time or another heard the name. There are very few. When I was a boy, the name was one to conjure with, and the announcement that Haggar's show would visit our village kept adults and juveniles in an excited state for weeks on end, and I, for one, made many stolen visits and came home thrilled as only a boy can be thrilled with what we then looked upon as the finest entertainment ever given.

And now Mr. Haggar has retired after spending nearly 60 years as a public entertainer, and resides in Abernant Road, Aberdare, amongst the people he loves so well. When I called to see him a few days ago, I was courteously received, and during the course of our chat I was provided with enough material to fill several columns of this journal. 'You want to know about my ups and downs, do you, laddie?', asked Mr. Haggar. 'Well, I can tell you there's been more downs than ups.' And he proceeded to relate a story – the story of his life – which proved of absorbing interest, and gave me a vivid impression of the many hardships the old actor had passed through. But always there was a smile on his face, and I formed the opinion that Mr. Haggar owes much of his present success to the fact that he was able to meet his 'ups and downs' as he put it with unfailing cheerfulness.

He was born at a little village called Dedham in Essex, and received his early education at the village school, his parents paying the master one penny a week for the purpose of having their son 'educated'. When eleven years old he went to work in the dockyard at Wivenhoe, and later drifted to Southwold, where he was apprenticed to a watchmaker. Whilst in this Suffolk village he learnt to play the cornet and founded a brass band which, it is interesting to note, is still in existence. He was only 17 years old at this time, but the formation of that band undoubtedly influenced the course of his life. When the band were able to play properly, it happened that a travelling theatre visited Southwold and Haggar and his colleagues were engaged to play thereat. The proprietor was so impressed with young Haggar's ability that he invited him to join the company, an invitation which was promptly accepted. This was his first introduction to show life. With this company he travelled the whole of the Eastern Counties and Lancashire and Yorkshire, meeting with many misfortunes, but always displaying a cheery optimism. Before he was 20 years old he was married to a member of the same company, and Mr. Haggar told me that when he returned from the marriage ceremony he and his wife had exactly twopence-halfpenny between them. 'But,' he added, 'Saturday night was in front of us, when we knew that the share out would take place.'

Still an optimist, he remained with this company for a number of years, visiting every county in England, until the day came when he had saved sufficient to launch out on his own, and one Saturday night he and his company and portable theatre arrived at Ebbw Vale. They were absolutely penniless, but before the night was out the Ebbw Valians showed that there was a welcome awaiting him. The company were elated with their success and acted as they had never acted before. From that night Mr. Haggar never looked back, and for thirty years his theatre was a welcome visitor in every town and village in the Principality. He himself always took low comedy parts, and many of my readers will no doubt recall with pleasure his impersonation of many famous characters and his singing of popular songs.

Then, 24 years ago, moving pictures were discovered, and Mr. Haggar, quick to realise the possibilities of the new invention, transformed his theatre into a picture theatre. He was a pioneer of the movement in Wales, and took his 'pictures' to village fairs and like places, where people rushed to see the wonderful discovery. For the outside of his show he had a magnificent organ built in Paris, and it made its first appearance at Aberdare fair. After a time restrictions were imposed on travelling shows which crippled them as an industry, and Mr. Haggar settled down at Aberdare. During his residence at Aberdare he has proved very popular with the townspeople and has become noted for his generous disposition.

In 1913 he was elected as a member of the Aberdare Urban District Council, and also of the Merthyr Board of Guardians. On both bodies he served with distinction until pressure of business compelled his resignation in 1919. He is also a Governor of the General Hospital. Mr. Haggar has had 11 children, and he has 40* grandchildren and three great-grandchildren. He is now in his 74th year and presents an appearance of bluff heartiness and joviality which seems to make him certain of reaching his century.

Aberdare Leader, 9 August 1924

* There is confusion in these numbers: see family tree and note 31 on chapter 9.

Appendix 7: William's obituaries

DEATH OF MR. WILLIAM HAGGAR, ABERDARE.

THE WELL-KNOWN FIGURE OF Mr. W. Haggar will be keenly missed in Aberdare and district. He passed away yesterday (Wednesday) after a short and severe illness at the home of his son and daughter-in-law, Elm Grove, Aberdare. A member of the theatrical profession all his life, he had a wonderfully interesting and varied career. In the pre-Cinema days Mr. Haggar owned a portable theatre, and moved about from place to place, staying six months or so here and there in various towns and villages. When in his prime he was a splendid actor and first-class comic singer, possessing a resonant and clear voice that carried to the limit of the building. As a rule the part he took in the various plays presented was that of comedian, and he was an unqualified success. His first wife also took part (a humorous part as a rule) in the majority of plays.

A few months ago in conversation with the present writer, Mr. Haggar said he knew by heart about 50 or 60 plays, and could repeat not only his own part but the parts of the other actors as well. His company back in the 80's and 90's would have a repertoire of over 100 plays, and it was a fairly heavy strain on the memory to present a different play night after night. Among the dramas he took part in were **Dead Beat, Llewelyn the last of the Welsh Princes, Proof, Dumb Man of Manchester, Maria Marten, The Orphans, Alone in London, Lights of London,** and a host of others including many Shakespearian plays. And his company was a singularly good one too, including as it did his eldest son, Mr. William Haggar and the latter's wife. For the nimble 3d. in those days one could see a first-class play well acted, followed by two comic songs, 'to be concluded by a laughable sketch entitled ————'. And many people, besides the writer, have confessed that they have since paid 7s. 6d., aye and even 10s. 6d. to see a worse show.

But the old things went by and the silent stage took the place of the speaking stage. Old Haggar did not go out of business and lament that like Othello his profession was gone. He took up his place in the film world, and became one of the pioneers of living pictures in South Wales. He converted his portable theatre into a cinema, and for many months it was situated in Market Street, adjoining Aberdare Market. Later he erected a permanent structure opposite. Old Haggar had a good word for Wales. He was born in Dedham, Essex, but had a very chequered career until he stepped on Welsh soil. Here he made good and never turned back. Seventy-three years of age, he was twice married. His second wife – née Miss May Davies, Bird-in-Hand, Aberdare, passed away a few months ago. He leaves a grown-up family.

Aberdare Leader, 7 February 1925

Just over forty years ago, he came to South Wales, and the Welsh people received him with open arms, and from that time he never looked back. In course of time, he became proprietor of several large picture palaces and, settling down at Aberdare, he served for some years on the District Council and Education Committee. He was of a bright and generous disposition, and had hosts of friends throughout the district. It is only a few months since his second wife passed away, and from that time, the old gentleman gradually sank, until the end came as stated. As the funeral procession left the house, a terrific storm was in progress, but this did not prevent hundreds of people assembling to pay their last tribute of respect. The officiating minister was the Rev. James A. Lewis, B.A., R.D., vicar of Aberdare.

Mr. Editor, – There has just 'passed on' a very familiar and beloved personality whom some called 'Old Haggar' and some who were more familiar with him in his later and more private life called 'Dear old Willie Haggar'. Both were terms of endearment: he loved all and was beloved of all. As we say, he has 'passed on', but has he not left to many of us of this generation food for thought? And if we do but think, we shall see that he has – unconsciously perhaps – left us some lessons that we may well lay to heart. Perhaps one is most important and it is this: that he who is upright in all his dealings and who endeavours to bear the burden of the day – however heavy that burden may be – must succeed in life.

Mr. Haggar's life commenced in very humble circumstances, and it was always delightful to hear his reminiscences, and to gather therefrom the cheery manner in which he must have faced and overcome hardships such as are not often encountered by many in these days. The experience of those days of trial toughened an already strong 'Will to attain', and he did attain and to a good purpose. Mr. Haggar in his experience encountered many vicissitudes, and whilst he was meeting and overcoming them he became imbued with a great love for his fellows, and a longing to be of help to those not so able as he was to overcome the difficulties of the strenuous life he and they were leading. Many have lived and still live to thank and bless the hand that was held forth to help them. The dear departed sought competence not for its own sake, but rather for the good it enabled him to do. He was generous, not merely in the worldly meaning of the word – that of giving money (his purse was always open in a good cause) – but in the higher sense. There ever emanated from his spirit that 'something' which impelled him to do good. And in the latter days, Mr. Editor, when he became settled amongst us, there beamed forth, apparent to all, those noble qualities with which Nature had endowed him: that glorious and lovable simplicity; that ever readiness to advise and do good to all and sundry. And to those who knew him intimately, there are brought to mind many acts of kindness on his part that have lifted some who were in despair out of the depths into a brighter and more hopeful outlook upon life.

Such very shortly were Mr. Haggar's attributes. May Mr. Haggar's family and friends be comforted in the thought that although he has 'passed on', his memory will be cherished and held in love and reverence by all. I am, Mr. Editor,

K.

Aberdare Leader, 14 February 1925

Appendix 8: Sources

THE FOLLOWING IS A list of the books and other sources of information used to prepare, or quoted in this book:

Aaron, Wil: *Hen Bictwrs Bach* in *Barn*, October 1975

Asquith, Anthony: *The Tenth Muse Climbs Parnassus* in the *Penguin Film Review*, 1946.

Berry, David: *Wales & Cinema: The First Hundred Years* (University of Wales Press, 1994).

Berry, David: *William Haggar* (Unpublished lecture script).

Berry, David: *William Haggar* and **The Sheep Stealer** (1908) in *The Showman, the Spectacle and the Two-Minute Silence*, Flicks Books, 2001.

Blow, Sydney: *Through Stage Doors, or, Memories of Two in the Theatre* (W. & R. Chambers Ltd., 1958).

Borrow, George: *Wild Wales* (John Murray, 1923).

Bowen, F.W.E.: *Queen Elizabeth's Hospital, the City School* (Clevedon Printing Co., 1971).

Brewster, Ben and Jacobs, Lea: *Theatre to Cinema* (Oxford University Press, 1977)

Brook, Donald: *The Romance of the English Theatre* (Rockliff, 1945).

Buchanan, Andrew: *The Art of Film Production* (Pitman, 1936).

Cameron, David Kerr: *The English Fair* (Sutton Publishing Ltd., 1998).

Ceram, C. W.: *Archaeology of the Cinema* (Thames & Hudson, 1965).

Chanan, Michael: *The Dream that Kicks* (Routledge, 1996).

Clothia, Jean: *English Drama of the Early Modern Period 1890-1940* (Longman Group Ltd, 1996).

Davy, Charles (ed.): *Footnotes to The Film* (Lovat Dickson Ltd., 1938).

Ensor, Sir Robert: *England, 1870-1914* in *The Oxford History of England* (Clarendon Press, 1987).

Evans, J. Emlyn: *William Haggar, Welsh Film Pioneer* (Unpublished, Aberdare Library).

Fay, Arthur: *Bioscope Shows and their engines (Locomotion Paper No. 31)* (Oakwood Press, 1966).

Featherstone, Ann: *Victorian Provincial Entertainment* (Phd Thesis 1999).

Finler, Joel W: *Silent Cinema* (B.T. Batsford Ltd., 1997)

Gifford, Denis: *The British Film Catalogue, Volume 1 – Fiction Films 1895-1994, and Volume 2 – Non-Fiction Films 1888-1994* (Fitzroy Dearborn Publishers, 2000).

Golden Treasury Album of the Screen, The (Odhams Press, 1930s)

Gray, Richard: *Cinemas in Britain* (Lund Humphries Publishers, 1996).

Greville, Father P.R.: *Famous Travelling Bioscope Shows* (1967).

Gwyndaf, Robin: *Welsh Folk Tales, No. 56 – Llangynwyd* (National Museums and Galleries of Wales).

Haggar, Roy: *William Haggar: The Travelling Theatre, Film-making, and the Bioscope* (Unpublished essay, 1968).

Haggar, Walter: *Recollections: Early days of Show Business with a portable theatre in South Wales,* in *Dock Leaves,* Spring 1953.

Haggar, Walter: *Recollections: An account of the early bioscope* (Unpublished, June 1953).

Hepworth, Cecil: *Came the Dawn* (Phoenix House Ltd., 1951).

Hibbert, H.G.: *A Playgoer's Memories* (1920).

Hill, Geoffrey: *William Haggar, Pioneer of the Cinema in Wales,* in *Old Aberdare,* Volume 6 (Cynon Valley History Society, 1989).

Hunter, William: *Scrutiny of the Cinema* (Wishart & Co., 1932)

Kinematograph Year Book for 1915

Kingsbridge History Society: *The Great Blizzard of March 9th and 10th 1891 in the South Hams of Devon* (republished 2002).

Leigh Williams, Julian: *The Murder Stone* (Neath Library).

Lindgren, Ernest: *The Art of the Film* (George Allen and Unwin, 1950).

Low, Rachael & Manvell, Roger: *The History of the British Film, 1896-1906* (British Film Institute and British Film Academy, 1948).

Low, Rachael, *The History of the British Film 1906-1914, and 1914-18* (British Film Institute and British Film Academy, 1948).

Manvell, Roger, with Baxter & Wollenberg, editors: *The Penguin Film Review, Nos. 1 - 5* (Penguin Books, 1946-1948).

Manvell, Roger (ed.): *Cinema 1950* (Penguin Books, 1950).

Manvell, Roger: *Film* (Penguin Books, 1944).

Manvell, Roger: *The Film and the Public* (Penguin Books 1955).

Matthews, David: *I saw the Welsh revival,* (Ambassador Publications, 2004).

McKernan, Luke (ed): *A Yank in Britain: the Lost Memoirs of Charles Urban* (Projection Box, 1999).

Meyrick, Betty: *Behind the Light* (Hutchison, 1975).

Pitman, Gerald: *Sherborne Observed* (Abbey Bookshop, 1983).

Price, Cedric: *Portable Theatres in Wales, 1843-1914,* in The National Library of Wales Journal, Vol. IX/1 (1955).

Prior, Lorna A. E.: *Great and Little Chishill – a tale of two villages* (Prior, 1999).

Ramsaye, Terry: *A Million and One Nights* (Frank Cass & Co., 1926, reprinted 1964)

Reed, Stanley: *How Things Developed: The Cinema* (ESA Ltd., 1959).

Richards, Lily: *Biography of William Haggar, Actor, Showman and Pioneer of the Film Industry* (Unpublished, 1969).

Richards, Lily: Transcript of interview conducted by Dennis Pope and Frank Sharp of the Canton Film Appreciation Group (1971).

Robson, E.W. & M.M.: *The Film Answers Back* (John Lane, 1939)

Rotha, Paul & Richard Griffith: *The Film Till Now* (Vision Press Ltd., 1949).

Rotha, Paul & Manvell, Roger: *Movie Parade: A pictorial survey of world cinema, 1888-1949* (London and New York, 1950).

Scrivens, Kevin & Smith, Stephen: *The Harry Lee Story* (The Fairground Society, 1996)

Scrivens, Kevin, & Smith, Stephen: *The Travelling Cinematograph Show* (New Era Publications, 1999).

Seldes, Gilbert: *Movies for the Millions* (B.T. Batsford, 1937)

Speed, F. Maurice: *Movie Cavalcade* (Raven Books Ltd., 1944).

Spencer, D. A. and Waley, H. D.: *The Cinema Today* (Oxford University Press, 1939).

Steptoe, Brian: *Jump On, Jump On* (Navigator Books, 1994).

Talbot, F. A.: *Moving Pictures – How they are made and worked* (Heinemann, 1914).

Talbot, F.A.: *Practical Cinematography* (Heinemann,1913)

Thomas, Haydn: *Haggar's Cinema, Pontardulais* (Unpublished).

Toulmin, Vanessa: *Randall Williams, King of Showmen* (The Projection Box, 1998).

Toulmin, Vanessa, *Telling the Tale* in *Film History, Volume 6* (John Libby & Co., 1994).

Warren, Low: *The Film Game* (T. Werner Laurie Ltd., 1937).

Warren, Patricia: *British Cinema in Pictures*, (B.T.Batsford, 1993).

Wollenberg, H.H.: *Anatomy of the Film* (Marsland Publications Ltd., 1947)

Wood, Leslie: *The Miracle of the Movies* (Burke Publishing Co., 1947).

Newspapers:
The Aberdare Leader, dates between 1907 and 1925.
The Bioscope, 1908.
Cynon Valley Leader, 1997.
The Daily Telegraph, 20.2.1998.
The Era, 1869-1910.
The Essex Standard, 4.3.1870.
The Kinematograph and Lantern Weekly, 1907-8.
The Monmouthshire Beacon, 1905.
The Optical Lantern and Cinematograph Journal, 1904-7.
The Showman, 1901.
South Wales Echo, 1938-1971.
The Stage, 1907-8.
The Western Telegraph, 4.1.1995.
The World's Fair, 1909-1939.

Parish records for Badley and Barking (Suffolk), and Epping, Frating and Langham (Essex).

Proceedings of the British Kinematograph Society:
  No. 21: *Reminiscences of the British Film Trade* by Colonel A.C. Bromhead.
  No. 38: *Before 1910: Kinematograph Experiences*, by R.W. Paul, C.M. Hepworth and W.G. Barker.

Notes: Chapter 1

1. WILLIAM'S BIRTH WAS NOT registered (registration was not yet compulsory), so no birth certificate exists. The date of 10 March 1851 is given on William's baptismal certificate, and was entered by the curate, G.H. Weston, in the Frating church baptismal register (now at Essex County Record Office, Chelmsford).

2. William's great-uncle William Hagger, a gardener by trade, lived near the tollgate in Stratford Road, Dedham. Baptised at Badley, Suffolk, on 2 May 1798, he married Hellen Southgate at Langham, Essex on 30 June 1824, his brother James being a witness at the wedding. They had two daughters, Eliza Hellen and Mary Ann. At the time of the 1851 census, their household included their son-in-law Nehemiah Nevard, a carpenter, and his daughter Agnes (his wife Eliza being already dead), and their niece Elizabeth with her two-week old son William (named Arthur Hagger in the census return).

3. William was baptised on Sunday 14 March 1852. Mothering Sunday, on which by tradition girls in service living away went home to their Mother Church, seems the likely reason for the choice of that date.

4. The Hundred Rolls are included in the report, made in 1275, of the Royal Commission set up by King Edward I to enquire into the working of local government, hunting, and rights to hold fairs and markets at the time. The Hundred Rolls give the names of land-holders in each Hundred, the old Saxon unit of local administration, still in existence then. From the Roll for Suffolk emerge the names of Ivo, Ralph and John Acgard, the first Haggars known to dictionaries of genealogy and likely ancestors of present day Hagars, Haggers, Haggars and Haggards.

5. Sir Henry Rider Haggard (1856-1925) is chiefly remembered as the author of the novels *King Solomon's Mines* (1886) and *She* (1887).

6. The story of the Haggers of Great and Little Chishill may be found in Lorna E. A. Prior's *Great and Little Chishill – A Tale of Two Villages* (Prior, 1999). Henry and Edward Hagger were churchwardens in the 1550s when they certified the church plate. George Hagger presented his accounts as Overseer of the Poor at a Vestry meeting in April 1787. The family is found in the Post Office directory for 1855 as farmers and shopkeepers, and in Kelly's Directory for 1886 as farmers, drapers, grocers and at the village Post Office. In 1912 Eric Hagger was Clerk of the Parish Council, and during the 1930s Chris and Emily Hagger kept the village shop

7. On the day of the 1881 Census, Queen Victoria was at Windsor Castle, along with HRH Prince Leopold, HRH Princess Beatrice, ex-Empress Eugenie of the French, Prince and Princesses of Edinburgh Alfred, Maud, Victoria and Alexandra, aged 6, 5, 4 and 3 respectively, eleven principal Lords and Ladies in Waiting, and 167 staff, including Elizabeth Hagger, scullery maid. Elizabeth's father Henry, an Epping farm worker, was the grandson of James and Mary Hagger, one of the families at Badley in the 1790s. According to the census, Elizabeth was also at home with her parents: no doubt Windsor Castle had given the census enumerators a list of employees, but Elizabeth had gone

home for the weekend.

8. Gloria Haddock, Rose Haggar's granddaughter, wrote from Moorooka, Australia, to Peter Yorke that her cousin David Moses had told her that 'we had an ancestor Elizabeth who worked at Buckingham Palace and had a child and was paid a pension for her lifetime.' Gloria had written to Buckingham Palace, but was told that they had no records of her working there (letter from Gloria Haddock dated 28 November 1997). The tale of a pension for life was also told of William's mother Elizabeth.

9. In the church register of Badley, now at Suffolk County Record Office, it is recorded that William and Mary Hagger had their son William baptised on 2 May 1798; that James and Mary Hagger had three children baptised there between 1800 and 1804, and that Joseph, son of Joseph and Mary Hagger was baptised on 25 January 1807. These are the only Hagger family entries in that church register: this may indicate that the Haggers were itinerant agricultural labourers. Badley was a hamlet which has since disappeared.

10. For the four generations of Haggers from Badley to William, see the family tree.

11. James Hagger did not remember, in his answers to the census enumerators, when or where he was born: he gave three different answers to the three censuses of 1841, 1851 and 1861. However, it can be established that his brother was William Hagger the gardener of Dedham (James' daughter Elizabeth being stated to be William's niece in the 1851 census). That William, baptised in 1798, would have been James' elder brother if, as was usual, William, being the eldest son, was named after his father. James, then, will have been born about 1800, but was not baptised in Badley. James changed the spelling of his surname, and hence that of his grandson William, from Hagger to Haggar in time for the 1861 census.

12. Nowadays the village is called Frating Green. Frating is a dot on the map a mile or so away, its church now a private house. The Post Office Directory for Essex (1862) states that Frating was an ancient village and parish in Tendring Hundred, 1237 acres in extent and with a population of 235.

13. The Directory names 20 residents of Frating: Rev. Richard Duffield BD, the curate, 11 farmers, the publican of the King's Arms, a grocer, a maltster, a blacksmith and letter receiver, a bricklayer, an Inland Revenue officer, and 'Hagger Jas. wheelwright and carpenter'.

14. Samuel, baptised at Frating in February 1827, seems to have been the first of several Haggers not to use his first name: in the 1841 census he appears as James. His sister Elizabeth was baptised Mary Elizabeth in May 1830, but was always called Elizabeth; she had a younger sister Mary.

15. The sources for Sarah and her children are the 1841 and 1851 censuses, and the Frating church baptismal and burial registers.

16. The *Essex Standard*, published at Colchester on 4 March 1870, reported James' death and the coroner's verdict of death by natural causes.

17. By her great-granddaughter June Bilous, in conversation with Peter Yorke on 6 September 2002.

18. Lily Richards, unpublished *Biography of William Haggar*.

19. Lily Haggar (1891-1973), William's fourth and youngest daughter, married Bertie Richards in Aberdare in September 1912.

20. Reported by June Bilous, Lily Richards' youngest daughter, in conversation with Peter Yorke.

21. The sources for Elizabeth's marriages and family are birth, marriage and death certificates for the Bridgstocks, and the 1881 census for Prittlewell, Essex.

22. Arthur William Haggar, always known as Will Junior, (1871-1935), William's eldest son.

23. Lily Richards, *Biography.*

24. Rose Haggar (1885-1967), William's second daughter, married Sidney Moses at Rhymney in 1908.

25. Jennie Haggar, Will Junior's eldest daughter, born 1893.

26. Censuses for Kilburn for 1891 and 1901.

27. Source: George Haggar's birth certificate. When Rose married Sidney Moses in 1908, George became known as George Haggar Moses.

28. According to George Haggar Moses' daughter Gloria Haddock, in a letter to Peter Yorke dated 28 November 1997.

29. At the time of the 1861 census, Martha was keeping house for her father James, and looking after William and her own 6-year-old daughter Ellen.

30. For an article entitled 'Men at the Wheel' published by the *Aberdare Leader* on 9 August 1924 (see Appendix 6).

31. The full title of Lily Richards' work is *Biography of William Haggar, Actor, Showman and Pioneer of the Film Industry, written by his daughter Mrs. Lily May Richards.* Composed when Lily was living at June Bilous' home in Cardiff, it was completed in 1969, before Lily moved to the home of another daughter, Eileen, in Southsea, where she died in 1973. Lily also gave, in 1971, a tape-recorded interview to Dennis Pope and Frank Sharp of the Canton Film Appreciation Group, a transcript of which is held in the National Fairground Archive.

32. Walter Haggar (1880-1953), William's fifth son, married Ada Rosina Roberts (1883-1969) at Aberdare in 1906. Ada was one of a family of thirteen, two of her sisters, Frances and Lily, marrying brothers Edgar and Bill Symonds, and thus relating the Haggars by marriage to many Fairground families, including the Locks, Booths and Shufflebottoms, members of which families have spoken to Peter Yorke about this family relationship. Shortly before his death, Walter composed memoirs about his days with the travelling theatre, and with the travelling cinema. The second of these is entitled, *Recollections: an account of the early bioscope, by Walter Haggar, as dictated at Alderholt, Hants in 1953.* It was never published, or even corrected, and exists in 31 pages of typescript. A copy was lent to Lily by Walter's son Len Haggar.

33. Lily's Biography too is in typescript as June Bilous left it: June's account in conversation with Peter Yorke on 6 September 2002.

34. 'Which, it is interesting to note, is still in existence' (*Aberdare Leader*, 9 August 1924).

35. Walter Haggar's wife Ada, in conversation with her grandson Roy Haggar, and reported by him.

36. Lily Richards, *Biography.* Unfortunately for this narrative, the Salvation Army was not founded until 1878. Ada told her grandson that it had been a local church band. In her interview, Lily said that her father had come from farming stock. He had been by trade a carpenter, 'a very handy man'. Her mother had taught William all he knew about acting. Cedric Price, in *Portable Theatres in Wales,* in *The National Library of Wales Journal* (1955) reports that William had been a cabinet maker. If Lily's 'uncle who owned a sawmill' did not

exist, William will have learnt carpentry and cabinet making from his grandfather James the wheelwright.

37. Lily Richards, *Biography*.

38. Hemming was her real name, which she used on her daughters Rose' and Violet's birth certificates (hence it is quoted also on Rose's death certificate). But she got married as Sarah Walton, the family being well-known as 'The Waltons' in the theatrical world. In her interview, Lily said that her mother's people had been theatricals 'as far back as she could remember'. Advertisements in *The Era* (the newspaper of the stage, published from 1865 to 1939) in the 1870s called them 'The inimitable and unrivalled Walton Family' – they went in for pantomime and spectacular dancing shows. See also the obituary of William Walton (Hemming) in *The Era*, 16 July 1904: 'Mr. Walton was well known in the theatrical world as the younger member of the famous Walton Family so popular a few years back.' Sarah's father 'Watty' and her sister Louie were among many who sent wreaths.

39. Sources: William and Sarah's marriage certificate, and the census for Fakenham for 1871, taken two days after the wedding. Fakenham was in the Walsingham Registration District. The witnesses to the wedding were not family members, but Walter Rose, Beerhouse Keeper, landlord of The Sun where William and Sarah lodged, and Emily Goree, wife of James Goree, proprietor of Goree's Portable Theatre.

Notes: Chapter 2

1. WALTER HAGGAR, RECOLLECTIONS – *EARLY Days of Show Business with a portable theatre in South Wales*, published in the magazine *Dock Leaves*, spring 1953.

2. Lily Richards, *Biography*.

3. In later life, Walter Haggar used to lick his plate. When rebuked by his second wife, he used to say, 'you haven't starved!' (Roy Haggar, Walter's grandson, in conversation with Peter Yorke).

4. Lily Richards, *Biography*.

5. For example, 'Wanted: for the Prince of Wales Theatre, a few Useful People. Those used to Portable Theatres preferred; also a gentleman for outside business. Terms: shares. Houses checked. Address to Mr. R. Walton, Prince of Wales Theatre, Monmouth.' (*The Era*, 30 August 1868) Terms: shares' and 'Houses checked' refer to the so-called 'Commonwealth' method of paying actors.

6. Walter Haggar,*Theatre recollections*.

7. Ada Haggar, quoted by Roy Haggar in conversation with Peter Yorke.

8. Sydney Blow, in *Through Stage Doors, or, Memories of Two in the Theatre* (W. & R. Chambers Ltd., 1958) amusingly recalls Will Haggar Junior's theatre in 1912. He and Edmund Gwenne went to Wales to find Welsh actors for **Little Miss Llewelyn** which they were to put on in the West End. 'We heard of a possible comedy old lady, Louie Walton, playing in a Mr. Haggar's portable theatre up the Rhondda Valley. We found it. We were tired and hungry, having great difficulty locating it as it moved from one mining village to another. We arrived about half an hour before they rang up the curtain on **Maria Marten** (of the Red Barn). We knocked on the stage door, which was up some ricketty steps, more like a fowl-house ladder than a stage door. Mr. Haggar himself opened the door, and to our surprise he said to Teddy Gwenne, 'Thank the Lord you have come. Why didn't you send a telegram? I paid for your reply.' It transpired that Will Junior was expecting Tom Hughes from Cardiff, to replace his previous pianist who had eloped. They had to disappoint him, and Louie Walton disappointed them by refusing to leave Wales, even for a part on the London stage.

9. James Goree placed adverts in *The Era* on various dates from 30 April to 31 December 1871, giving addresses including Norwich, Lowestoft and Braintree. In 1874 Goree's theatre was at High Wycombe, and in 1881 in Belper.

10. Edward Ebley, aged forty-seven in 1871, had a touring theatre, 'Edward Ebley's Palace of Varieties', in South Wales in the 1890s. In 1904, he appeared before the Blaina magistrates in a test case, to determine whether his 'Olympia' portable theatre was a building within the meaning of the local bye-laws, which he needed planning permission to erect: the bench decided it was not (*The Era* on 29 October 1904 reported the case and applauded the outcome). Later still, he ran a bioscope for a few years.

11. Census for Fakenham, 1871.

12. Compare the census for Tredegar in 1891, which lists twenty-nine

musicians and actors lodging there then. They came from Windsor and Wigan, Woolwich, Wolverton and Woking, Wales, Scotland and Ireland.

13. By Ann Featherstone, in her thesis, *Victorian Provincial Entertainment* (1999), commended to Peter Yorke by Paul Lawrence Newman, great-grandson of Tom Lawrence, proprietor of Lawrence's Great Allied Theatre.

14. *The Era*, 22 September 1872.

15. *The Era*, 3 April 1870.

16. *Ilkeston Pioneer*, 2 May 1861.

17. *The Era*, 5 May 1868.

18. *The Era*, 6 February 1870.

19. *The Era*, 6 February 1870.

20. *The Era*, 6 February 1870.

21. Donald Brook, *The Romance of the English Theatre* (Rockliff, 1945), p. 80. Cedric Price, in *Portable Theatres in Wales, 1843-1914* (National Library of Wales Journal, 1955) states that the portable theatres regarded themselves as the heirs of the old strolling tradition, and maintained theatrical customs such as 'sharing' long after they had died out elsewhere.

22. **The Strollers**, Breval, 1727.

23. Donald Brook, *Romance*, p. 81.

24. Roy Haggar, *William Haggar, the travelling theatre, film-making and the Bioscope* (unpublished essay, 1968).

25. *The Era*, 22 August 1887.

26. Roy Haggar, essay. Will Junior became an accomplished actor. Cedric Price, *ibid.*, reported that the rival merits of Ted Ebley (Edward Ebley's son) and Will Haggar had been a great subject for debate.

27. Walter Haggar, *Theatre recollections*. In the 1950s the Ebley family still possessed a manuscript copy of the script of **The Maid of Cefn Ydfa**.

28. Roy Haggar, *essay*.

29. Walter Haggar, *Theatre recollections*.

30. The Lloydalls were said by Paul Lawrence Newman to have been working with Tom Lawrence in the 1860s (telephone conversation with Peter Yorke, 1999).

31. George Butler married Dulciebella Lawrence in Pontypridd in 1895, thus becoming Paul Lawrence Newman's great-uncle.

32. Doris Hare made her stage debut at the age of three, in the Alexandra Theare's production of **Current Cash** at Bargoed (her mother, Kate Tansley, being married to Bert Breamer, the Alexandra's proprietor). She went on to take many London parts, and to tour in revue as far afield as South Africa and Australia. During the Second World War she broadcast regularly as presenter of **Shipmates Ahoy**, and received the MBE for services to the Merchant Navy.

33. The cast of **The Test of Truth** is given in a souvenir programme printed on silk, and preserved in Chepstow Museum.

34. William Desmond, born Walter Mannion in Dublin in 1878, crossed the Atlantic in 1915, and became a star of Hollywood westerns, both silent and 'talkies'. Cedric Price, *ibid.*, mentions Jack Desmond, and cites the memories of Mr. Ernest Meadows, a member of Will Junior's company.

35. Will Fyffe (1885-1948), who can be seen as Lewis Bach in **The Maid of Cefn Ydfa**, made his London stage debut in 1916, went on to achieve fame in the Music Hall, and also made several films. In 1934, he became King Rat of the Grand Order of Water Rats, the stage and screen stars' charitable

organisation, and was later awarded the CBE. While with Will Haggar Junior's company, he was remembered by Haydn Thomas, conductor of the world-famous Pontardulais Male Voice Choir, as 'a certain Will Fyffe, who acted as a general handyman, and was the local bill-poster for the Haggar's cinema pictures. He was the person who eventually became top of the bill in London and provincial Music Halls. He was delighted to meet any of us at any time, who could talk to him about Pontardulais. He never forgot the steps by which he did ascend.' (Haydn Thomas, *Haggar's Cinema*, *Pontardulais*, unpublished typescript).

36. Roy Haggar, in conversation with Peter Yorke.

37. George Bernard Shaw, prologue to *Plays Unpleasant*.

38. Jean Clothia, *English Drama of the Early Modern Period, 1890-1940*, (Longman Group Ltd. 1996).

39. Fred Bertram, an actor, who joined Hendry's booth in Liverpool in the 1850s, quoted in Ann Featherstone's *Victorian Provincial Entertainment*.

40. Walter Haggar, *Theatre recollections*.

41. One stock play, **The Crossroads of Life**, was always performed on the opening night: 'it always went with a swing' according to Walter Haggar. It was filmed by D W Griffiths for Biograph in 1907.

42. See Appendix 1 for a list of plays put on by the Alexandra Theatre at Monmouth during a ten-week stay in 1905. Forty-nine plays were advertised. Cedric Price, *ibid.*, lists seventeen plays for which Will Junior had 'the sole fit-up rights'.

43. A play-bill for **The Fair Maid of Neath**, advertising a performance by Will Haggar and Miss Jenny Lindon's Select Players, survives: it reproduces the so-called Murder Stone in St. Catwg's churchyard at Cadoxton near Neath, the tombstone of Margaret Williams. A popular girl from Carmarthenshire, she worked at Gellia Farm. Having confided to a friend that she was expecting a child by Owain Thomas, a labourer on the same farm, she went out one morning to take the cows to graze, and never returned, her mutilated body being found in a ditch. Owain was suspected, but was acquitted for lack of proof. But the villagers held him guilty, and a local antiquary composed the wording on the stone: 'the cry of blood will assuredly pursue him to a certain and terrible righteous judgment. Vengeance is mine, saith the Lord: I will repay'. Owain emigrated to America to escape the gossip. (From *The Murder Stone* by Julian Leigh Williams, courtesy of Neath Library). Cedric Price, *ibid.*, names this play **Margaret Williams**, and says that Will Junior and Jack Desmond wrote it, and the company gave its first performance in Neath.

44. **Llewelyn, the last prince of Wales** is mentioned in the announcement of William's death in the *Aberdare Leader*, 7 February 1925. Geoffrey Hill quotes other Welsh dramas in *William Haggar, Pioneer of the cinema in Wales* (Cynon Valley History Society, 1989). Cedric Price, *ibid.*, mentions **The Maid of Sker**, possibly based on a novel by R.D. Blackmore.

45. Walter Haggar, *Theatre Recollections*.

Notes: Chapter 3

1. OTHERWISE KNOWN AS WILL Junior – see note 22 on chapter 1.
2. For the whole of William and Sarah's family, see the family tree.
3. Frederick Charles Haggar (1873-1913), married Catherine Waldron (1873-1906) in 1892.
4. George Haggar (1875-9), not the George Haggar said by Geoffrey Hill, in *William Haggar, Pioneer of the cinema in Wales* to have been born in Preston in 1884, who was unrelated. George died in Bexley Heath, a few days before his fourth birthday, of pneumonia; his father thought it was because he had recently been vaccinated, and vowed that he would not allow it to happen to any other child of his.
5. Ellen Elizabeth Haggar (1877-90).
6. James Richard Haggar (1879-1925), always known as Jim. He married Kate Silverton, his brother Will's sister-in-law, in 1900. After managing his father's theatre in Llanelly, he emigrated to Australia, where he died shortly after his father.
7. So described in the 1881 census.
8. Lily Richards, *Biography*.
9. When registering Nell's birth, William described his address as 'Stoke Newington', his mother Elizabeth's home, and gave Ellen Elizabeth his mother's name, a sign that he had now mended fences with her. It would have been at about the same time that Will Junior was sent to Elizabeth for schooling.
10. Archie was named after Archibald Carlyle in **East Lynne** (Lily Richards).
11. On Rose and Violet's birth certificates alone, Sarah is named as 'formerly Hemming', her proper name. On all her other children's birth certificates, she is named 'formerly Walton'.
12. Violet Alice Haggar (1887-1979) married Cyril Sydney Yorke (1887-1959) in Aberdare in 1912. The surname under which Cyril married was again a stage name, from his mother's maiden name: his parents were William Hardwick, a coal miner from the Forest of Dean, and Clara Amelia York. Violet and Cyril's son Cyril Haggar Yorke (1913-1994) married (1) Dorothy Hutchison in 1937, and (2) Joy Thorne in 1952.
13. Walter Haggar, *Theatre Recollections*.
14. His name, spelt Jas. Hager, is no. 630 in the school register in Poole Museum. He had previously been to school in Weymouth.
15. According to June Bilous, in conversation with Peter Yorke. Sixty-two years later, Walter recalled taking Violet back to the Quay to show her where she was born: they were very close to one another.
16. From where William advertised for a Leading Lady in *The Era* on 9 May 1887.
17. Where, Walter recalled, the streets were lined with tables for the general celebrations and the tea for the children. Queen Victoria's Golden Jubilee was celebrated in June 1887.
18. Walter Haggar, *Theatre Recollections*.

19. Elementary education, introduced nationwide in 1870, had become compulsory in 1880, but did not become free until 1891.

20. *The Era*, 22 August and 17 September 1887, advertising for a 'Leading Lady and Gent, also Leader of Band'.

21. Sir Robert Ensor, *England 1870-1914*, (Oxford, reprinted 1987), pp. 115-9: England was then in the grip of a major agricultural depression. Unlimited imports of American wheat had bankrupted many farmers: between 1871 and 1885 the area under wheat dropped by a million acres (nearly one-third), and in 1881 there were 90,000 fewer farm workers than in 1871. In addition, there had been a succession of wet summers, and in 1883 there was a severe outbreak of foot-and-mouth disease. As Ensor put it, 'for 20 years, the only chance for any young and enterprising person in the countryside was to get out of it.'

22. Walter's chief recollection of Thornbury was 'terrific toothache and the penny dinners in school.' Ever afterwards, Walter remembered the places where he got penny dinners, and pointed them out to his grandson, Roy Haggar. At Swindon, the Great Western Railway workers, about to produce the famous 'Dean Singles', distinguished by their single enormous 7 ft. 8½ in. driving wheel, tried to help the Haggars when their theatre truck's horse refused to budge, but only succeeded in pushing the horse over (Walter).

23. William Ewart Gladstone, Prime Minister 1868-74, 1880-5, 1886, and 1892-4.

24. Henry Percy Haggar (1889-1945), managed the Haggars' cinema in Merthyr Tydfil, never married, and died after falling from the balcony of a cinema in Birmingham.

25. Walter Haggar, *Theatre Recollections*.

26. By 1905, Campbell's steamers were no longer calling at Chepstow, but in *The Monmouthshire Beacon* they advertised sailings from Newport to Clevedon and Weston, with special excursions to Portishead, to Penarth and to Ilfracombe. At Weston, passengers could connect with the Bristol boats, which continued to steam up the muddy river Avon at high tide until the last two ships in the 'White Funnel Fleet', the *Bristol Queen* and the *Cardiff Queen* were scrapped during the 1960s.

27. The Chepstow Weekly Advertiser advertised, on 3 May 1890, 'Sloper's Family v. Chepstow C.C. A Novel Match between Mr. Haggar's Theatrical Company, in complete Sloper costume, and the above club will be played on the Chepstow Cricket Ground on Wednesday next, May 7th. commencing at 2.30. Admission to field: 6d. Enclosure: 1s. At intervals, a few comic songs will be given from the pavilion by Mr. Haggar.' The editorial column of the *Advertiser* repeated the notice of the game and asserted, 'plenty of fun may be expected', but, unfortunately, the next week's edition carried no report of the game. The cartoonist David Low described Ally Sloper as 'that absurd figure with bulbous red nose, Micawber hat, baggy gamp, facetiousness and ribald slapstick' (D. Low, *British Cartoonists*, Collins 1942).

28. The Alexandra Theatre gave a charity performance of **Charley's Aunt** during its run in Monmouth in 1905.

29. The programme is preserved in Chepstow Museum. William, Sarah, Will Junior and Fred all took part in **The Test of Truth**.

30. William, now in his late thirties, had developed a large repertoire of comic songs; over 100 of them according to Walter, including many of Dan Leno's

latest hits. He was still singing them in charity concerts in Aberdare twenty years later.

31. *The Chepstow Weekly Advertiser* on 7 June 1890, from which all of the following passage is taken.

32. George Borrow, *Wild Wales* (John Murray, London, 1923), pp. 683 and 687.

33. *Wild Wales*, p. 689.

34. Sir Robert Ensor, *England 1870-1914* pp. 108 and 298-9.

35. *The Era,* 10 September 1904. The Town Hall Theatre at Maesteg is described as 'another coming Eldorado'.

36. Walter Haggar, *Theatre Recollections*. Betty Meyrick, in her book, *Behind the Lights*, (Hutchison, 1975), about her grandfather, a lighthousekeeper, recalls another version of the story about 'sticking to the coal' Recalling 'Haggar's Electric Coliseum' 'in brightly lit misspelt letters across the elaborate wooden front of the travelling cinema in Puss Hall's field at the top of Frederick Street in Neyland, symbolising, along with the other Haggar's travelling shows, the epitome of sophisticated entertainment far and wide' she wrote that 'they had always been a travelling theatrical family back to the time of the strolling players, when a soothsayer had foretold to them when they were touring, none too successfully, around the Severn Valley near Gloucester, that if they wanted to make a success of their profession, they should "follow the coal".' Her memory of the travelling show dates from 1914-18 when it was being operated by Walter Haggar at Neyland, after his traction engine had been requisitioned for war work.

37. Cedric Price, *Portable Theatres in Wales*, 1843-1914, in *The National Library of Wales Journal*, Volume IX/I, 1955.

38. According to *The Daily Telegraph* on 20 February 1998. For three days from 7 March 1891, the southern half of the country was swept by a ferocious snowstorm. 220 people died, mostly at sea where 65 vessels were lost in the Bristol and English channels. Fourteen trains were stranded by snowdrifts in Devon alone. Kingsbridge, Devon History Society republished in 2002 a contemporary account, *The Great Blizzard of March 9th and 10th in the South Hams of Devon*, describing the effects of an average depth of snow of two feet. In Tredegar next morning, Walter says, the houses could not be seen for snowdrifts, and passages had to be cut to doorways for people to leave their homes.

39. Lily says, to Scotland. However, their children Frederick William and Robert were born in Tonypandy and in Leek, Staffs, respectively, and in 1901, at the time of the census, they were in Raunds, Northants.

40. The Coal Yard, Brynmawr, is the address given on Lily's birth certificate. Her daughter, June Bilous, named her 'Coalyard Lil', in conversation with Peter Yorke.

41. Lily Richards, *Biography*.

42. This 'Castle Theatre' was built new in 1896, but the name had been used before. Walter Haggar, in *Theatre Recollections* mentions such names as 'Haggar's Pavilion', 'Star Palace of Varieties' (which, as the 'Star Theatre' has already been encountered in adverts in *The Era*), and 'Theatre Royal', at Chepstow in 1890.

43. Lily Richards, *Biography*, p. 11. She wrote that some of these photographs were still in her possession. A copy of this one was given to Peter Yorke by

Lily's granddaughter, Caroline Hill.

44. Sometimes Jenny Linden, perhaps a reference to Jenny Lind, the so-called 'Swedish nightingale': Jane Emily's mother's maiden name was Lynde.

45. Walter Haggar, *Theatre Recollections*.

46. Lily Richards, *Biography*.

47. At this point, Walter Haggar closes his *Theatre Recollections*, and continues in his unpublished *Recollections: an account of the early bioscope* (see note 32 on chapter 1).

48. Lily Richards, *Biography*.

49. It has been pointed out that *Focus* was not yet published. Walter means its predecessor.

50. It was a 'triunial' lantern, as it was three lanterns in one: two for dissolving one lantern slide into another and the third for the moving pictures. Thus it was easy, in those early years, to alternate between films and lantern slides when necessary.

51. Limelight had been invented by Sir Goldsworthy Gurney in 1825. Walter was keenly interested in the equipment needed for taking and showing films, and describes it in some detail in his recollections.

52. Walter Haggar, *Bioscope Recollections*.

53. A perennially popular subject, the first such film having been made by Robert Paul in Newcastle in 1896. (Denis Gifford, *The British Film Catalogue, Volume II – Non-fiction films*, Fitzroy Dearborn Publishers)

54. Lõie Fuller was a well-known music hall artiste, whose 'serpentine dance' was filmed very early. On 8 October 1904, *The Era* announced that 'La Lõie' was giving her 'Fire and Lily' dance at the Camden Theatre.

55. Perhaps Robert Paul's film **Goods Train emerging from Highgate Tunnel** of 1895; but many such films were made. (Gifford).

56. The gentleman had been to the pictures before: films were made of rough seas at Brighton and Ramsgate in 1896, and continued to be popular. (Gifford)

57. Walter Haggar always spells 'cinematograph' thus, as the Lumière Brothers spelt it when they exhibited their machine in London in February 1896. In 1907, the *Kinematograph and Lantern Weekly* devoted an article to proving that it should be spelt with a 'K'.

58. **All Hell!** is not otherwise known.

59. Walter Haggar, *Bioscope Recollections*.

60. Harry Studt's fairground at Aberavon according to Walter Haggar. Kevin Scrivens and Stephen Smith, in *The Travelling Cinematograph Show* (New Era publications, 1999), although acknowledging that the new show was built at Aberavon, state that William Haggar exhibited moving pictures for the first time whilst open on William Symonds' ground at Lydney.

Notes: Chapter 4

1. *OPTICAL MAGIC LANTERN JOURNAL*, 15 November 1889, quoted in Leslie Wood's *The Miracle of the Movies*, p.84, (Burke Publishing Co. Ltd., London, 1947).

2. There is a photograph of Friese-Greene in school uniform, facing the title page of Low Warren's *The Film Game* (Laurie, 1937). In 1949, Friese-Greene's invention was commemorated by a plaque over a shop in Queen's Road in Bristol: 'On this site, W. Friese-Greene, the inventor of the Moving Picture Camera, served his apprenticeship as a photographer from 1869-1875'. Peter Yorke, who, like Friese-Green was a boarder at Queen Elizabeth's Hospital, attended a service for the centenary of Friese-Greene's birth in 1955. His subsequent career and death is told in detail in *The Miracle of the Movies*, p. 86ff. The United States courts eventually ruled that Friese-Greene, not Edison, had invented the movie-camera.

3. The story of Edison's kinetoscopes is told in *A million and one nights* by Terry Ramsaye (Simon & Schuster, 1926), in *The Miracle of the Movies*, chapters vi and vii, and in *Movie Cavalcade*, by F. Maurice Speed (Raven Books Ltd., London, 1944), where it is stated that 'Mary Irwin's exhibition of osculation in **The Kiss** brought shrieks of protest from the ultra-puritanical and a demand for censorship.' Walter Haggar, in his *Bioscope Recollections*, recalled seeing them in the Moss Empire in Cardiff in 1898. He commented that 'it was soon realised that to run a film for 2d. did not pay, so Kinetoscopes had a very short life'.

4. *The Miracle of the Movies*, and *Movie Cavalcade*.

5. 'Persistence of vision' is described in most of the film histories written in the 1940s and 1950s: but Michael Chanan, in *The Dream that Kicks* (Second Edition, Routledge, 1996), pp. 62-6, disputes this, explaining it instead in terms of the brain's perception of movement. He wrote: 'Film depends on the interaction between the perceptual threshold of duration and the statistical periodicity of projection.'

6. Robert W. Paul (1869-1943), a scientific instrument maker of Hatton Garden in London, became the most prolific of the early film-makers, until he retired in 1909 to concentrate on his instrument business, which later became part of the Cambridge Instruments Company. He made, in his studio at Muswell Hill, topical films, and short comedies and trick films, with titles such as **Come along, do!**, and **The ? Motorist**, which survives. There is a detailed description of Paul's 'maltese cross' method of projection, and its superiority over the 'claw' method (which the Lumières used) in *The Cinema Today* by D. A. Spencer and H. D. Whaley (Oxford University Press, 1939).

7. Cecil Hepworth (1874-1953) became the doyen of the early British film-makers, in a career lasting from the 1890s until his bankruptcy in 1924. The most famous of his early films was **Rescued by Rover** (1905), which sold 395 copies. Starring himself, his wife, his baby and his dog, it cost £7 13s. 9d. to make. He made the first British one-reeler (1000 feet), **Dick Turpin's ride to York**, and by 1913 was turning out over 100 films a year from his studio in

Walton-on-Thames. His autobiography, *Came the Dawn*, (Phoenix House Ltd., London) was published in 1951.

8. Cecil Hepworth, recounting how he visited Robert Paul to sell him his arc lamp, in his lecture to the British Kinematograph Society – see note 20 below.

9. This film is in the East Anglian Film Archive, at the University of East Anglia, Norwich.

10. Charles Urban (1867-1942), an American citizen, came to Britain to work for the firm of Maguire & Baucus, selling Edison's products. He set up the Warwick Trading Company, and then his own Charles Urban Trading Company, to sell equipment, and films which he commissioned or bought from other film-makers, including William Haggar. He left an unfinished diary, published as *A Yank in Britain – the lost memoirs of Charles Urban*, edited by Luke McKernan (Projection Box, 1999), and gave his archive to the Science Museum.

11. A.C.Bromhead gave an extended interview to the *Optical Lantern and Cinematograph Journal* in February 1905, and recalled his setting up the firm which later became known as Gaumont-British, in his own lecture to the British Kinematograph Society – see note 33 below. Cecil Hepworth joked that 'Gaumont-British has penetrated every walk of society. Why, half the motor cars you see on the road today are labelled GB!' Bromhead, like Urban, sold Haggar films.

12. The count of 64 films is from Dennis Gifford's *British Film Catalogue: Volume 2 – Non-fiction Films*, 1888-1994 (Fitzroy Dearborn Publishers, 2000).

13. This account is from Robert Paul's lecture to the British Kinematograph Society in 1936. Others give greater figures for deaths. Leslie Wood in *The Miracle of the Movies* says 'dozens of titled people perished, and so did a party of nuns.' *Movie Cavalcade* puts the death toll at 180, of whom 'more than 130 were of the French nobility or people holding high positions, quoting a circumstantial account in chapter 31 of Ramsaye's *A million and one nights*.

14. Esme Collings of Brighton made, according to James Williamson (quoted in *The History of the British Film, 1896-1906*, by Rachael Low and Roger Manvell, published by George Allen and Unwin in 1948) thirty short films in 1896; but he did not go on to make a living by making films. Another similar early film-maker was Arthur Cheetham of Rhyl, who made films of topical and local interest, twelve of which survive, between 1897 and 1903, and advertised as a 'Living Picture Entertainer' in the *Kinematograph Weekly* in September 1907.

15. This quotation is from *Charles Chaplin* by Louis Delluc, quoted in *Incunabula Cinematographica* by R. K. Nielson Baxter, in *Cinema 1950* (Penguin).

16. In *The Era* on 30 January 1904, Charles Urban took a whole-page advertisement to announce that he had won the case. Mr. Justice Joyce, in the High Court Chancery Division, had ruled that 'Bioscope' was not an invented word but a descriptive term in use since 1812, and could not be a good Trade Mark. The Plaintiffs had therefore no monopoly in it.

17. This count is from Denis Gifford's *British Film Catalogue: Volume 1 – Fiction Films 1895-1994* (Fitzroy Dearborn Publishers, 2000).

18. Apart from Robert Paul (note 6 above), Cecil Hepworth (note 7 above), Will Barker (note 22 below), and William Haggar, the other six were:
(i) James Bamforth, of Holmfirth in Yorkshire, who produced a few comedies in the early 1900s, and a series in 1913/4, a typical title being **Winky's Mother-**

in-law.

(ii) George Howard Cricks, in partnership first with H. M. Sharp, and later with J. H. Martin, made numerous short comedies in studios at Mitcham between 1901 and 1914.

(iii) Sagar Mitchell and James Kenyon, from Blackburn, made mainly topicals (the subject of a three-programme BBC2 Documentary feature in 2005), but also some fiction films, advertised as 'Norden Films' in *The Era* in 1904.

(iv) Frank Mottershaw, whose Sheffield Photo Company's most famous film was **A Daring Daylight Burglary** (1903). Leslie Wood in *The Miracle of the Movies* claims that Mottershaw sold 500 copies of the film, but this appears to be a mistake: Mottershaw's family account, quoted in *The History of the British Film, 1896-1906*, was that he sold the negative to Charles Urban for £50. Urban then exported the film to the USA, where, Michael Chanan claims in *The Dream that Kicks*, p. 255/6, it was distributed by Edison under the title, **Daylight Robbery**, and re-made by Edwin S. Porter as **The Great Train Robbery** – the film with which many film histories begin. Mottershaw also made **The Life of Charles Peace** in 1905, shortly after William Haggar had made his film of that name: until 1948 Haggar's surviving film was mistaken for Mottershaw's version.

(v) George Albert Smith made more than 100 films in Brighton from 1897 until 1903, and then went to work for Charles Urban, specialising in inventing new apparatus, and in particular developing the 'kinemacolour' process. Typical of his films were **Grandma's Reading Glass,** which employs cut-in close-ups, and **The Miller and the Sweep**, a 'black and white' slapstick comedy, which survives.

(vi) James Williamson, a chemist in Hove, made about 50 films a year from 1897 until 1909. His films, made with members of his own family, included **Fire!,** an early chase film, **Attack on a China Mission**, a 'newsreel' faked in his own garden, and **The Big Swallow**, a trick film in which a man opens his mouth so wide that he appears to swallow the camera. This and **Fire!** survive.

19. William Haggar was first mentioned by Leslie Wood in 1947 and by Rachael Low and Roger Manvell in 1948 (although they name him 'Walter Haggar'). See note 37 below.

20. 'Proceedings of the British Kinematograph Society: No. 38 – "Before 1910: Kinematograph Experiences" by R. W. Paul, C. M. Hepworth and W. G. Barker, delivered to a meeting of the British Kinematograph Society, held at Gaumont-British Theatre, Film House, 142 Wardour Street, W. 1., on February 3, 1936.' The complete series of these published lectures is held in the archives of the British Film Institute.

21. In his autobiography, *Came the Dawn*, p. 34.

22. William George Barker began film production in 1896. In 1901 he founded the Autoscope Company, operating with an open-air stage at Stamford Hall, London, and at first making mostly topicals: his best-selling film, of which 300 copies were made, was **Whaling in the Shetlands**, made in 1903/4. He then opened the first studio at Ealing, and in January 1906 took over as managing director of the Warwick Trading Company. From 1911 he began to make lavish and large-scale films, such as **Henry VIII**, the first British two-reeler (2000 ft.). In 1914 he made a series of war films, including **Chained to the Enemy, German Spy Peril,** and **Looters of Liège**, all shown at Haggar's Cinema in Aberdare. His final films were made in 1918, and included one of the first

'horror' films, **The Beetle**.

23. It was however rumoured that canny exhibitors kept films of the Boat Race for many years, merely retitling the final inter-title, 'Cambridge wins!' or 'Oxford wins!' as appropriate. (*Miracle of the Movies*)

24. These numbers are taken from Denis Gifford's *British Film Catalogues.*

25. In *A Review of the Cinematograph Industry* in *The World's Fair* in 1908, quoted by Vanessa Toulmin in *Telling the Tale* (*Film History, Volume 6*).

26. *The History of the British Film, 1896-1906.*

27. Information about the fairgrounds in the nineteenth century is excerpted from *The English Fair* by David Kerr Cameron (Sutton Publishing Ltd., 1998).

28. Quoted in *The True History of Pepper's Ghost,* by Melvyn Heard (Projection Box, 1996).

29. Randall Williams' story is told in *Randall Williams – King of Showmen*, by Vanessa Toulmin (The Projection Box, 1998)

30. Richard Monte masqueraded as Randall Williams at the British Kinematograph Society meeting in 1933, at which A. C. Bromhead gave his reminiscences. In 1946 Monte wrote in Randall's name to Rachael Low and Roger Manvell, who published his letter in *The History of the British Film*, 1896-1906 (appendix 2).

31. In *The Travelling Cinematograph Show*, by Kevin Scrivens and Stephen Smith (New Era Publications, 1999).

32. These are noted in *The Travelling Cinematograph Show.*

33. 'Proceedings of the British Kinematograph Society: No. 21 – Introduction and discussion on Colonel Bromhead's paper (*Reminiscences of the British Film Trade*), 11th December 1933.' Bromhead began by reminding his audience that 'the first year or two of my story is prior to the use of the typewriter or the motor car, as practical issues, and even the telephone was a rarity by no means in general use. Correspondence was all written by hand, and London conveyances were hansom cabs and horse 'buses. No wonder that the cinematograph, when it appeared, was regarded as at best a nine days' scientific wonder.'

34. 480 copies: Walter Haggar in his *Bioscope recollections* wrote: 'this particular film, **The Poachers** sold no less than 470 copies in one year, being marketed by Gaumonts. In fact, the success of this film prompted the remark by Charles Urban, "You should not help these little firms, Daddy!", this being addressed to my father.'

35. 'Dupes' were pirated copies.

36. **The Sign of the Cross** was advertised by Gaumont in *The Era* for six weeks, from 10 December 1904 to 14 January 1905, for sale at 700 feet @ 6d. a foot, £17 10s.

37. William Haggar is first noted by Leslie Wood (quoting Bromhead's lecture to the British Kinematograph Society) in *The Miracle of the Movies* (1947), p.112, as having made **The Poachers** ; and second in Low and Manvell's *History of the British Film, 1896-1906* (1948), where Rachael Low also quoted this lecture, and picked out information on his films from the surviving Gaumont catalogues, recognising them by the restriction that films should not be sold in South Wales without the permission of W. Haggar & Sons. Until Lily Richards, in 1948, recognised **The Life of Charles Peace** as her father's film, not Mottershaw's, no surviving films were recognised as Haggar's.

Notes: Chapter 5

1. Walter Haggar, *Bioscope recollections*
2. Walter and his cap were inseparable: he got married in it, as his wedding photograph shows.
3. Sir Robert Ensor, *England 1870-1914*, p.298ff.
4. Walter Haggar, *Bioscope recollections*
5. Walter Haggar, *Bioscope recollections*
6. Lily Richards, in her *Biography*, follows Walter in this anecdote, but refers it to Jack Scarrot, who also had a boxing booth and cinematograph show, rather than Bill Samuels.
7. Walter Haggar, *Bioscope recollections*
8. Walter explained that the Sunday Sacred Concert 'began with an opening hymn; then, with the use of the triunial lantern, we illustrated various songs, such as 'Star of Bethlehem', and fine dramatic recitations, finishing with a Passion Play on the bioscope, and another hymn. We were packed to suffocation for these Sacred Concerts and received great commendation wherever we went.' He then relates, as happening at a Sacred Concert in Tonypandy, the same story, of Lõie Fuller's dancing being said to be Salome dancing before Herod, as Cecil Hepworth had included in his autobiography: perhaps that story went the rounds in those early days.
9. See Chapter 4, note 10, for Charles Urban's *Lost Memoirs*.
10. William Symonds, known as 'Milky' because he had had a milk round before coming onto the fairgrounds, became one of the West Country's best known showmen. Having started with a set of swing boats, in 1892 he bought a steam switchback, and later a set of gallopers. Two of his sons, Bill and Edgar, were to marry Lily and Frances Roberts, thus becoming Walter Haggar's wife Ada's brothers-in-law.
11. Walter Haggar, *Bioscope recollections*
12. Lily Richards, *Biography.*
13. Walter Haggar, *Bioscope recollections*
14. Walter Haggar, *Bioscope recollections*
15. Walter Haggar, *Bioscope recollections*
16. 'Mr. W. Haggar opened at this town on Thursday last with his grand exhibition of animated pictures, giving scenes from the ceremonies of the late Queen's Funeral. It really is a good show, and should do well in Aberdare. The show is up-to-date in every way; the front is fitted with a good engine and electric light plant, six arc lamps supplying the illumination for outside. The splendid musical instrument is also out of the common, and has all the latest musical successes. A smart and clean exhibition, fit for visiting any town.' *The Showman*, 15 March 1901.
17. This photograph came early into the possession of the British Film Institute, and was used as an illustration of a Fairground Bioscope Show in Leslie Wood's *The Miracle of the Movies* (1947), Low and Manvell's *History of the British Film, 1896-1906* (1948), and Richard Gray's *Cinemas in Britain – One Hundred Years of Cinema Architecture* (Lund Humphries Publishers, London, 1996).

18. The 1901 Census records William, Sarah and Walter Haggar, in Travelling Van No. 3 on the Navigation Ground, Mountain Ash, with 19-year old William Reynolds boarding with them as 'Travelling Showman's Assistant Labourer'. Jim and Kate were in Crawley, Sussex, while Fred, Catherine and their children Fred Junior and Robert were 'visitors' at 114 Brook Street, Raunds, Northants. Neither the four younger Haggar children, Rose, Violet, Henry and Lily, nor Will Junior and Jenny and their children were counted in the Census.

19. Lily Richards, quoted in *William Haggar*, by Anthony Slide, in *Cinema Studies*, Vol. 2, No. 4, June 1967, 'believes that the first film her father made was of skaters on the lake in Aberdare Park.' That film would have been made on a winter's day – either in 1900/01 or, if Walter's timetable is correct, in 1901/2. William may have seen Cecil Hepworth's advert in *The Era* (4 May 1901), addressed to showmen, offering to photograph workmen leaving factories in towns which the showmen were about to visit, since 'A film showing workers leaving a factory will gain far greater popularity than the most exciting picture ever produced. The workers come in their hundreds with all their friends and relations...this is the greatest draw you can have.' William would have decided that he could do that himself.

20. *The Showman* reported on 9 August 1901 that at Swansea Fête and Gala, William Haggar had proved a big draw with views taken from his bioscope. According to the same newspaper (16 August and 27 September 1901), Haggar's show at Briton Ferry and Blaina included **The Dumb Man of Manchester**, which Walter remembered that Will Junior had wanted to make, probably for his dramatic *tour de force* as the hero struggling with the villain 'which used to whip the audience up into tremendous enthusiasm, but, of course, virtue always triumphed in the end' (Walter Haggar, *Theatre recollections*).

21. Walter is referring to the surviving film, **Desperate Poaching Affray**, the title under which it was sold in this country by Gaumont: made in 1903 (not 1904), it remained in the Gaumont catalogue, under the code word 'Poacher' from July 1903 to June 1904, selling, as Bromhead and Walter stated, 470 or 480 copies (see chapter 4, note 34). In the U.S.A. it was sold as **The Poachers**, and this was how it was always known within the Haggar family.

22. Walter Haggar, *Bioscope recollections*

23. **Outside the Works** is the only surviving instance of the many 'local films' which William made (see note 19 above), and can be compared with the Mitchell & Kenyon archive of such films. It was donated to The National Screen and Sound Archive of Wales in 1998 by Mr. Ron Bevan, who had worked in the Cosy Cinema (the name of Haggar's Kosy Kinema in its last years when owned by the Willis family) in Aberdare as a boy in 1944/46 before being called up. The boys there (Mr. Bevan recalled) would pinch pieces of film from old cans in a cubby hole and put bits of them in fags, to startle friends by singeing their eyebrows; another jape was to put a small roll in a tight wad of paper, light it, then stamp on it to make a smoke bomb. Mr. Bevan grabbed some film for this purpose, but fortunately did not burn it.

24. Lily Richards, *Biography*.

25. As Walter recalled that Mitchell & Kenyon of Blackburn had done.

26. Walter Haggar, *Bioscope recollections*

27. Walter Haggar, *Bioscope recollections*. Of these films, **Löie Fuller's Serpentine Dance** was a filmed music hall item, and would have been hand-

tinted. **The Last Cartridge** was a thriller set in the 1850s: a poster advertising it in Brighton (pictured in *The History of the British Film, 1896-1906*) proclaims it as 'A story of the Indian Mutiny, depicting the Bravery shown by a handful of Troops, who held the Fort until the last man and women, rather than fall into the enemy's hands, were about to take their own lives, but The Gallant Highlanders came in the nick of time and saved the fall of the fort.' The other three films were William Haggar's own, as Lily Richards confirmed in her *Biography*.

28. The opening stanza of a poem published in the *World's Fair* on 19 October 1907, and quoted in Kevin Scrivens and Stephen Smith's *The Travelling Cinematograph Show*.

29. Walter Haggar, *Bioscope recollections*. Reports in *The Era* bear out Walter's remarks, for example: 'Mr. Haggar stopped the week successfully at Carmarthen. His show is exceedingly good, a complete change of pictures being made every evening' (20 June 1904) and 'Llanelly Fair was held last week...Mr. Haggar with his Electric Bioscope was there, and as usual was quite up-to-date' (8 October 1904).

Notes: Chapter 6

1. *THE ERA*, 27 MARCH 1904. The engine was a Fowler A5 compound engine, no. 9386, reg. no. AX 2857. An official black and white works photograph, reproduced in *Fairground Engines in Focus*, shows the engine, its canopy legend simply 'W. Haggar, London'. In reality, the engine would have been resplendent in green, red and brassy gold. When the engine was delivered, it had a nameplate for *The Maid of Cefn Ydfa*, and also a brass nameplate on the back: 'Owners – W. Haggar & Sons, South Wales.' This caused, according to Walter, a mild sensation among the other showmen, because at that time the majority of their engines had the owner's nameplate hidden in some inaccessible corner. The nameplate, *The Maid of Cefn Ydfa* was retained by the family after the engine was sold to Johnny Butlin in 1914, and was later put up above the front door of Haggar's Cinema in Pembroke, then owned by Walter's son Len Haggar.
2. Walter Haggar, *Bioscope recollections*.
3. Lily Richards, *Biography*.
4. Gaumont used this letter as an advertisement in their catalogue in December 1904.
5. Walter Haggar, *Bioscope recollections*.
6. Walter names the two favourite tunes which the organ played as *The Village Blacksmith* and the *Halleluiah Chorus*.
7. According to Kevin Scrivens and Stephen Smith, in *The Travelling Cinematograph Show,* the organ was probably the first to be imported which was completely built and carved in Paris.
8. Lily Richards, *Biography*.
9. Henry Haggar, in an address entitled, 'My Job', given to members of the Merthyr Tydfil Rotary Club, as reported in the *World's Fair* on 27 June 1936.
10. Walter Haggar, *Bioscope recollections*.
11. Walter's Show became 'W. Haggar's Picture Palace' and was powered by yet another new engine, *King George V*, acquired in 1910. A picture of this engine thus labelled became widely available, and caused confusion as to whether the Show was William's or Walter's. In fact, it was owned by William, and run by Walter.
12. It was the Bioscope Lecturer's job to provide a commentary on the silent films in the Bioscope Exhibition, just as lantern slides had been used to illustrate lectures. J. Emlyn Evans of Aberdare remembered Cyril Sydney Yorke, as manager of Haggar's Shanty Cinema: 'Striding up and down the aisle, Cyril Yorke added the voice of Comedy and Drama when he thought it necessary (and that was often) in true thespian style: "Ha! How beautifully she sleeps. Little does she know who is around the corner. Who can it be? Why, it's the dastardly Sir Jasper!"'
13. According to the writer of Jenny Lindon's obituary in the *Pembroke Times* in 1954.
14. *World's Fair*, 23 October 1909 and 21 August 1909.
15. Roy Haggar in conversation with Peter Yorke.

16. Henry Haggar, 'My Job'.
17. Henry Haggar, 'My Job'.
18. Postcards in Peter Yorke's possession.
19. Lily Richards, *Biography*.
20. *The Monmouthshire Beacon and Forest of Dean Gazette*, 23 June 1905.
21. Printed in a special supplement about Neath Great Fair in *World's Fair*, September 10-16 1999. Father Greville described Dooner's Show, Wadbrook and Scard's Palace, Crecraft's Show, John Studt's Electric Pavilion, Edward Danter's Coliseum, and then the two Haggar shows: 'Walter Haggar's Royal Bioscope had been the first of the Welsh shows to have a big organ front, a grand Marenghi organ, covered with myriads of different coloured lights. Favourite tunes on this included "The Merry Widow", "Sousa's Marches", "The Village Blacksmith", and the songs, "I've got a bungalow, Little Girl, for you", and "We parted on the shore". There was a troupe of dancing girls. Wm. Haggar's Show front was truly magnificent with a 110 key Gavioli organ, and was entirely enclosed with sides and ceiling of beautiful panelling and gold carved work. Every tune on the organ was announced by means of a card placed on an easel. The paraders included Miss Violet Haggar and her troupe of dancing girls. Two popular songs featured on this organ in 1908 were "Bungalow in Borneo" and G. H. Elliott's "Sue, Sue, Sue".'
22. *The Bioscope*, 31 December 1908.
23. Geoffrey Hill, *William Haggar, Pioneer of the cinema in Wales*, in *Old Aberdare, Volume 6* (Cynon Valley History Society, 1989).
24. The Studts were a long-established fairground family, and were among the founders of the Showmans Guild in the 1880s. John Studt, known as 'Big John', possessed a powerful voice: it was not unusual to see hundreds of people standing in front of his switchback, from the steps of which he would sing "Land of My Fathers" to the strains of the organ. The family is still in show business in South Wales and Richard Studt conducts the Bournemouth Sinfonietta.
25. Cricks and Martin – see Chapter 4, note 18.
26. Leon Vint later built up a chain of enterprises, from Neath (the Electric Palace) to Llanelly and Aberavon (Vint's Palace) and as far afield as Loughborough (Leon Vint's Electric Hippodrome) – from adverts in *The Era* in 1910 and 1913.
27. Lily Richards, *Biography*.
28. Lily Richards' daughter June Bilous, in conversation with Peter Yorke, 6 September 2002.
29. Lily Richards, *Biography*, and the account of the funeral in *World's Fair*, 28 August 1909: 'The coffin was covered with choice wreaths and floral emblems (53 wreaths, crosses and sprays were received, in addition to five artificial wreaths), and a conveyance had to be requisitioned to convey the remainder to the cemetary.' The principal mourners, in six coaches, included, in addition to William and his children with their spouses, James Taylor, William's step-brother, Jennie and Robbie Haggar, the two eldest grandchildren, representatives of the Roberts, Studt, Dooner, Day and North fairground families, Mrs. Breamer (Doris Hare's mother, from the Alexandra Theatre), and the Leola Troupe – Nelly, Millie, Petty and Bertie, as well as the Kettley family from the Tanners Arms.
30. *The Era*, 21 August 1909. A short obituary was also published in *The*

Portable Times on 10 September 1909: 'Mrs. Haggar was well-known throughout Wales, where she and her husband had travelled for the past twenty years, and during which period she had endeared herself to all with whom she came into contact. Deceased was greatly loved by all her employees, who will feel her death very keenly. Her memory will ever remain green in the annals of Fair life.'

31. Lily Richards, *Biography*.
32. Cyril H. Yorke in conversation with Peter Yorke, 1988.
33. *World's Fair*, 12 September 1909.

Notes: Chapter 7

1. ACCORDING TO LOW & MANVELL, *The History of the British Film, 1896-1906*.
2. Lily Richards, transcript of interview conducted in 1971 by Dennis Pope and Frank Sharp of the Canton (Cardiff) Film Appreciation Group.
3. Walter Haggar, *Bioscope Recollections*.
4. According to Henry Haggar in his talk to the Merthyr Rotary Club in 1936, quoted in chapter 6.
5. Roy Haggar in conversation with Peter Yorke.
6. A list of all known Haggar films is given in Appendix 2, and synopses of lost films in Appendix 3.
7. Walter Haggar related that his brother Jim was always getting bitten by one particular dog.
8. When considering the films in the order in which William made them, it must be borne in mind that there may be many films of which nothing is known: for example, no surviving film or synopsis contains a scene in which a cyclist rides into a river, as Walter practised doing. In considering criticisms of the film-making of those days, the difficulties must be remembered: for instance, cameras were bulky and panning shots could at first only be accomplished by lifting the camera off its tripod and swivelling it, whilst continuing to turn the handle at the necessary steady speed. Close-ups could not be over-close since lenses could not be re-focussed from their scene-taking distance.
9. Walter Haggar, *Bioscope Recollections*: he states that at that time, film cost a shilling a foot, and they used sixty feet.
10. Lily Richards, quoted in *William Haggar*, by Anthony Slide.
11. Lily Richards, *Biography*: she comments that this performance needed great skill to avoid serious injury.
12. Roy Haggar, essay.
13. From Denis Gifford, *British Film Catalogue*. William continued to make films which were long for their time: for example, **The Sign of The Cross**, and **The Life of Charles Peace**.
14. Roy Haggar, essay, quoting Ada Haggar's memories.
15. In 'The Prompter's' review, quoted in the Preface, above.
16. Cedric Price, *Portable Theatres in Wales, 1843-1914*. A legendary figure, Twm was 'a Welsh Robin Hood'
17. Roy Haggar, essay.
18. These are the first films attributed to William in Denis Gifford's *British Film Catalogue – Fiction Films*. Puzzlingly, the Warwick Trading Company's Catalogue describes **The Wild Man of Borneo** as 'The combat between the Knight and the Hermit in the Forest.' Perhaps the hermit was likened to the proverbial 'wild man of Borneo' whom Charles Urban was proposing to film in 1903. An Internet Site, 'Classic Horror Movies' states that this film 'features an ape-man', but this may be a deduction from the title.
19. Warwick Trading Company, Film Blue Book Supplement No. 3, October 1902: dramatized series, numbers 6948-6951 (in the British Film Institute archives). They were advertised in *The Era* on 4 October 1902 with the note:

'The above pictures are furnished (by) our patrons with the proviso that they are not to be exhibited in Wales, where Exclusive Rights have been granted': the first instance of this prohibition.

20. Since their first meeting in 1899, described in chapter 5, William and Charles Urban had become firm friends. Walter, in the *Bioscope Recollections*, described an occasion in 1900 when William commended to Urban Paul's idea of a double-bladed bioscope shutter, demonstrating it with a sheet of violet gelatine. 'Charles Urban was delighted and, chewing his inevitable cigar, he said, "We will adopt it, Daddy"'. Henry and Lily do not complain about the terms of William's dealings with Urban, as they do in the case of Gaumont (see note 24). It may be that Urban's remark about **The Poachers**, 'You should not help these little firms, Daddy!' implies that he, too, thought that William had been unduly generous with Bromhead.

21. **The Weary Willies and the Policeman** is placed next to **True as Steel** in the Warwick Trading Company Supplement No. 3 (it is no. 6952), **Weary Willie and his pal on the rampage** is nearby at no. 6961, and **Unfair Exchange is Robbery** is no. 6975. Lily, in her interview, said that she had a list of her father's films. If she gave this list to Denis Gifford (who acknowledges her as 'Lilian Richards, actress'), it would explain how he was able to attribute to William films which were not marketed with the Wales prohibition (note 19 above), and are not ascribed to Haggar by any other source. Gifford also includes in *The British Film Catalogue* other details, such as casts of films, which are not mentioned by contemporary sources: these details too may have been in Lily's list. Lily said that the British Film Institute had films 'not under my father's name but the Warwick Trading Company and someone else'. She was to be proved correct: at that time, for example, **Desperate Poaching Affray** was listed as 'Gaumont', and **The Bathers' Revenge** was unattributed. Are there still others to be found?

22. Referred to in chapter 5.

23. Wearie Willie and Tired Tim were characters in a comic strip by Tom Browne. Other film-makers of the day made films about them.

24. Walter Haggar, *Bioscope Recollections*. Henry Haggar, in his talk to the Merthyr Rotary Club, claimed to have a letter from Gaumont 'stating that it was our films which gave Gaumont the big push they required in those days.' Bromhead acknowledged 'a considerable debt of gratitude to dear old William Haggar' – perhaps for this.

25. The film, no. 114B, appears in the Gaumont 'Elge' (the initials of Léon Gaumont) Lists for July 1903 and June 1904 (in the British Film Institute archives). Gaumont marketed it without reference to William Haggar.

26. Even Cecil Hepworth's **Rescued by Rover** sold only 395 copies. Both Bromhead and Walter Haggar independently cite **The Poachers** (this was the name by which, according to Roy Haggar, the family always knew **Desperate Poaching Affray**, and under which it was sold abroad) as selling 470 or 480 copies: see note 34 on chapter 4 and note 21 on chapter 5. When Rachael Low came to write her first volume of *The History of the British Film*, she did not know that the surviving **Desperate Poaching Affray**, which she lists in her appendix five as by 'Gaumont', was Haggar's. Confronted with Bromhead's statement (which she quotes) that **The Poachers**, a Haggar film, had sold 480 copies, she looked in the catalogues, found that the later, lost film **The Salmon Poachers**, was attributed to Haggar, and made the erroneous assumption that

it was the latter film which had sold 480 copies. Subsequent film historians have repeated this mistake: but there is no evidence that **The Salmon Poachers** achieved a wide sale – rather to the contrary, as it was advertised in *The Era* for just two weeks, 2 and 9 December 1905.

27. Robert K. Kepler, *Silent Films 1877-1996* (McFarland & Co. Inc., 1999).

28. Sid Griffiths was William's traction engine driver. Later, he too went into the cinema world, becoming manager of the Plaza Cinema in Swansea. His niece, Leita Griffiths, married Bill Haggar, Will Junior's son. Through this family connection, Sid obtained for a time in the 1950s the sole surviving copy of **The Maid of Cefn Ydfa** (see Chapter 10).

29. Gaumont's Elge List for June 1903.

30. Roy Haggar in conversation with the author. This may explain Walter's reference to the film (in his *Bioscope Recollections*) as being 450 feet long – twice its catalogue length.

31. Charles Urban Trading Company, Catalogue for 1903, Supplement no. 1, January 1904, film no. 1153. **A Daring Daylight Burglary** was Mottershaw's film which Urban had bought and successfully marketed in the USA (see chapter 4, note 18 (iv)). In *The Era* (14.11.03) Urban advertised the fact that **A Dash for Liberty** was made by 'Messrs. W. Haggar & Sons, the producers of "A Desperate Affray with Poachers"' – one of the very few times when credit was given by a film seller to the film maker.

32. *The Era*, 10 December 1904 to 14 January 1905.

33. Wilson Barrett had obtained the rights (except in Italy) for the theatrical adaptation of Henryk Sienkiewicz' epic novel *Quo Vadis*? Re-naming it *The Sign of the Cross*, he simplified the plot and changed the names of the principal characters, Lygia becoming Mercia and Marcus Vinicius, Marcus Superbus. The story was filmed three times: by William Haggar in 1904, by Frederick Thompson for Famous Players in 1914, and (with sound) by Cecil B. De Mille in 1932, his version becoming the stuff of legend for the Empress Poppaea's bath of asses' milk (Peplum: Images de L'Antiquité – Cinema).

34. David Matthews, *I saw the Welsh Revival – Centenary Edition*, (Ambassador Publications, 2004).

35. Geoffrey Hill, in *William Haggar, Pioneer of the cinema in Wales*, thought that both this film, and **DTs, or the effects of Drink** might have been made with the Revival in mind.

36. Jon Solomon, *The Ancient World in the Cinema* (Yale University Press, 2001), p. 4: 'A few sources also report a British **The Sign of the Cross** supposedly made by the same Sigmund Lubin who directed **The Great Train Robbery** that year.' Lubin is said to have pirated other films. The International Media Database (on the Internet) includes **The Sign of the Cross** as made in the USA in 1905, but with no further details.

37. *World's Fair*, 29 July 1939, reporting Walter Haggar's radio interview a fortnight before.

38. Who was Mog? No report of her survives. It has been suggested that this was a nickname made up from her initials – Mary Olwyn Griffiths, or some such.

39. Synopsis of film no. 212 in Elge List for October 1904.

40. Biograph catalogue entry, in American Film Institute Catalogue, *Film Beginnings – A work in Progress, 1893-1910* (Scarecrow Press, New Jersey, 1995).

41. Synopsis of film no. 288A, Elge List for January 1905. Gaumont advertised **Snowballing** in *The Era* on 4 and 11 February 1905: 'Our old friend Mirthful Mary gets snowballed. Extremely funny and highly recommended.' Film historians have not recognised this as the fourth in the Mirthful Mary series.

42. Synopsis of film no. 1384 in Charles Urban Trading Co. catalogue for February 1905.

43. Roy Haggar in conversation with Peter Yorke. In the National Film Archive, it was known as **Bathers Pull Couple into Water** (David Berry, *William Haggar*, unpublished lecture script).

44. See Appendix 2, Addendum. Pointers to what may be other Haggar films (now lost) may be found in the language of their catalogue synopses, and their positions in catalogues next to acknowledged Haggar films, which were often inserted in 'blocks' in the Urban or Gaumont catalogues. For one example, the synopsis of **Rivals**, film no. 94B in the Elge List for July 1903, includes 'a battle royal ensued' as in **Snowballing**, and they 'are marched past the camera' (a particular Haggar technique) as in **The Poachers** and **A Dash for Liberty**. Synopses of Haggar films in both Urban and Gaumont catalogues contain similar phrases, suggesting that they were written by the same person.

45. Walter Haggar, *Bioscope Recollections*

46. Lily Richards, *Biography*.

47. Roy Haggar in conversation with Peter Yorke.

48. Advertised by Gaumont in *The Era* from 23 September to 4 November 1905, alongside **The Life of Charles Peace** and, from 28 October 1905, **A Message from the Sea.**

49. *World's Fair*, 29 July 1939.

50. Synopsis of film no. 349, Elge List for October 1905. **A Message from the Sea** was advertised in *The Era* from 28 October to 18 November 1905. *The Optical Lantern and Cinematograph Journal* for November 1905 felt that 'genuine pathos and interest commend us to Gaumont & Co.'s "Message from the Sea", which is a splendid idea capitally worked out, and it is a wonder that the subject was not taken long ago.'

51. The film's purchase is recorded on its National Film Archive title index card. Among the first books in which stills appeared were *The Cinema Today* by D. A. Spencer and H. D. Whaley (Oxford University Press, 1939) and *Anatomy of the Film* by H. H. Wollenberg (Marsland Publications, 1947), in both of which the film was attributed to the Sheffield Photo Company's Mottershaw. When advertising Haggar's film, Gaumont included the statement that 'the latter' (**i.e. The Life of Charles Peace**) 'is the ORIGINAL and FIRST picture taken dealing with the life of the "Modern Ishmael", and must not be confused with another film of the same title issued by another firm some weeks after us' (*The Era*, 11 November 1905). (*The Optical Lantern and Cinematograph Journal* in November 1905 reported it as 'a matter of regret' that the Sheffield Photo Co.'s film 'should closely follow a film with a similar title issued by another firm, but these gentlemen inform us that they have been working on the subject for a considerable time.') Gaumont also advertised the film as 'specially suitable for Fair Ground business. Not recommended for Sunday School exhibitions' (*The Era*, 23 September 1905). They kept their adverts going for eight weeks, from 23 September to 11 November 1905.

52. When Lily Richards saw it in Rhiwbina cinema, in Cardiff, being shown as part of the celebrations for the half-century of the cinema. As it was attributed

to Mottershaw, she wrote to the British Film Institute pointing out that she was in it, her message arriving just in time to be included in Low & Manvell's *History of the British Film, 1896-1906*, published in 1948.

53. In some copies there is minor damage to the scene titles. They are among the first to have been made, and it is possible that William had not sufficiently realised the need to photograph them repeatedly, in order to allow time for them to be read. As a result, they flash hastily on and off the screen.

54. The affair quickly became the subject of popular melodrama. Charles Peace was still spoken of when Peter Yorke was at school in the 1950s.

55. Lily Richards, Interview. She claimed that it was made in 1904, when she was twelve (i.e. earlier than 2 June 1904, her thirteenth birthday), but this appears mistaken, since the film was not advertised for sale until September 1905. Roy Haggar in conversation added the details that they gave the woman who loaned her house two free tickets for the show. The railway station in the film was the Birdcage Halt, Pembroke Dock – it no longer exists.

56. *World's Fair*, 29 July 1939.

57. This cast list presumably came from Lily Richards. The Giddings were family friends, Frank Giddings being a guest at Violet's wedding. In an Internet Site (IMDb de William Haggar) listing William's films in a French translation, upon re-translation into English, Violet has changed to 'Purple Haggar'!

58. Ernest Lindgren, *The Art of Film* (George Allen & Unwin, 1950). The Elge List from which this synopsis presumably was taken is no longer in the British Film Institute Archives.

59. At this point, a dog which has been sitting under the table sidles up to and nuzzles a cat which has just appeared: a lovely touch to reflect the main action.

60. Lindgren uses **The Life of Charles Peace** to support his contention that such early films were made with a static camera, some distance from the actors, surveying the scene as if it were a theatre stage. This is to some extent true of the first three scenes of **The Life of Charles Peace**, but not true of much of the rest of the film. Perhaps Lindgren did not view the remainder of the film.

61. Michael Chanan, *The Dream that Kicks* (Second Edition, Routledge, 1996).

62. Chanan prefaces his account by remarking that the film is an outstanding example of the 'hybrid' story and chase genre when it was made. The use of title-cards is telling: they replace the lecturer. The National Film Archive holds a copy in which each scene is tinted a particular colour, according to what is deemed thematically or emotionally appropriate.

63. The roof set exhibits two chimney pots, which are smoking. They must have contained smoke flares or similar, since one gets knocked off, apparently accidentally, as it rolls around for a short time, and then disappears from view – perhaps it was grabbed by someone off shot – while Peace hurls the second one at a policeman.

64. A favourite gesture of Walter's in real life, according to his grandson Roy Haggar. With no script and only a sketchy scenario, it was probably spontaneous.

65. The row of cottages reflected in the carriage window remains stationary, although the train is meant to be moving.

66. Since Mottershaw specifically refused to film the execution (and his scenario survived), it is strange that William's film which includes the execution scene was attributed to Mottershaw between 1937 and 1948. Perhaps, like

Lindgren, they failed to view it.

Notes: Chapter 8

1. THE FIRM OF WALTURDAW took its name from its founders, Walker, Turner and Dawson, and seems to have been the first to hire out, rather than sell films: they advertised as 'The Oldest and Original Lending Library for Films' (*Kinematograph and Lantern Weekly*, 19 March 1908). Walter Tyler had begun by giving lantern slide lectures in the 1870s, and, his method of producing oxy-calcium limelight being suitable for church schoolrooms which did not have gas, he started selling lanterns, six or eight a month. This suggested to him starting a shop. From selling lanterns, and gas 'in customers' own bags at 8d. per foot', he progressed to selling, and subsequently hiring out lantern slides, and by 1906, his firm possessed a stock of 800,000, plus 50,000 readings. 'This number increases weekly by over a thousand.' To their slides business, they added selling and hiring out films. (Chats with Trade Leaders, No. 8 – Mr. Walter Tyler and his partners: *Optical Lantern and Kinematograph Journal*, October 1906.) Urban and Bromhead had sold their films at 6d. a foot: Tyler and Walturdaw nominally continued this, but allowed a standard discount of one-third, to reduce the price to 4d. a foot.

2. Second hand films were first advertised in the *Kinematograph and Lantern Weekly* on 4 July 1907 'at the request of several in the trade'. As examples, Pym, of 'Glen Mount', Lewes, advertised **The Poaching Affray**, 220ft., and **Daylight Burglary**, 267 ft., for 2d. per foot, in very good condition, on 4 July 1907. The Artograph listed **Wanted A Maid** (could this have been Lily's **Wanted – A Wife?**), **Tramps and Washerwoman, Tramp, Woman and Bike**, and on 2 July 1908, **Salmon Poachers** for 15 shillings. On the same date, "K" of Box No. 94 offered **Unfair Exchange is Robbery** for 1d. and **Two's Company, Three's None** for 1¼d. per foot.

3. **Desperate Footpads** was advertised by the Warwick Trading Co. in the *Kinematograph and Lantern Weekly* for three weeks beginning 26 September 1907, for £5. 5s. Six months later, on 5 March 1908, it could be had second-hand for £2 from Films For Hire, of Manchester Street, Liverpool.

4. The Western Cleddau, near Haverfordwest.

5. Lily Richards, Interview.

6. Lily Richards, quoted in *William Haggar*, by Anthony Slide.

7. **The Dumb Man of Manchester** in 1901, **The Maid of Cefn Ydfa** and the four scenes from dramas filmed in 1902, **The Sign of the Cross** in 1904, **The Squire's Daughter** and **The Life of Charles Peace** in 1905 are the known predecessors of these two films.

8. Lily Richards, Interview, for **Wanted – A Wife** (with Roy Haggar supplying the ending, in conversation) and **Spaghetti Eating.**

9. See notes on Appendix 2.

10.Many of these films were advertised in the *Kinematograph and Lantern Weekly*: **A Dash for Liberty** by Walturdaw on 19 March 1908; **Dick the Kisser** by Walturdaw on 25 June 1908; **The Red Barn Crime, or Maria Martin** by Walter Tyler on 30 July 1908, **The Sheep Stealer** by Walter Tyler from 10 September to 22 October 1908, **Bathing Prohibited** and **The Plumber and**

the Lunatics on 27 August 1908, and **Vengeance is Mine** and the **Gladiator's Affianced Bride** by Walter Tyler on 3 September 1908.

11. These two films were instanced as typical Haggar productions by the *World's Fair* on 8 August 1914. In *The British Film Catalogue*, **Dick the Kisser** is (wrongly, therefore) ascribed to Dave Aylott. The *World's Fair*, describing William's election to the Aberdare District Council, reminds its readers that 'not only in projecting does Mr. Haggar excel, but also in production. We wonder if many can remember such Haggar productions as **The Poachers** (which, by the way, we believe was the first chase picture ever filmed), **Message from the Sea, Maria Martin, Charles Peace, Dick the Kisser, The Sheep Stealer**, etc., and it may not be out of place in mentioning one that is to be shortly placed upon the market, **The Maid of Cefn Ydfa**, founded upon the Welsh historical story, taken on the exact spots, the acting is good, and the setting, dresses, etc., typical of the country.' This article is the main reference to William as film-maker in his lifetime.

12. **The Sheep Stealer** was discovered in the 1970s in a collection of films made by the Swiss priest, Abbé Joseph Joye, but was not identified as William's until thirty years later, despite his portrait being on the two inter-titles. See *William Haggar and the Sheep Stealer* by David Berry, in *The Showman, the Spectacle & the Two-Minute Silence* (Flicks Books, 2001).

13. The quotation is from Tyler's advertisement, in which the film is termed 'A splendidly staged dramatic and pathetic film, certain to be one of the biggest successes of the season' (*Kine Weekly*, 10 September 1908).

14. Walter Haggar, *Bioscope Recollections*. His grandson, Roy Haggar, made the fruitless enquiry of the Welsh National Museum.

15. To borrow more modern parlance, it was a 'long, hot summer', the temperature rising to a peak of 97°F in London on 11 August 1911. The events of that summer are described in Juliet Nicholson's *A Perfect Summer* (John Murray, 2006)

16. Walter Haggar, *Bioscope Recollections*.

17. Already noticed in chapter 5. The two incidents are described in the Swansea Industrial Museum.

18. The incidents at Fishguard were related by Walter's wife Ada to Roy Haggar. Ada had been in charge of the catering, and had fed the actors on 'a great stew'.

19. 'Pa filmed the lot – we used it later on the fairground for the Titanic.' (Ada, quoted by Roy Haggar in a letter to Peter Yorke: "Pa" was Walter). Poole's Myriorama of the loss of the Titanic was later advertised, in the *Aberdare Leader* on 11 January 1913, as NOT a cinematograph picture – perhaps in reaction to Walter's version.

20. Cefn Ydfa means, 'back of the wheat-field' – no doubt where the mansion was built.

21. *Welsh Folk Tales, no. 56* by Robin Gwyndaf (National Museums and Galleries of Wales). The play by J.C. O'Dowd, a member of John Hord's portable theatre company, was given its first performance in Aberdare on 21 April 1870 (*The Era*, 1.5.70).

22. World's Fair, 29 July 1939, and South Wales Echo, 16 April 1938. It is not known whether William edited in additions to the popular 1902 film, or entirely re-shot scenes from the play to produce a new film perhaps twice as long as its predecessor.

23. The details of the film-making included in his review by 'The Prompter' (see Preface) were handed down within the Haggar family, and probably had been told to Mr. Key either by Walter, whose film Mr. Key showed, or by Jenny Lindon, at that time widowed and living in Pembroke. Shooting outdoors when the sun shone meant that shadows could appear 'indoors' – as they do inside Morgan the Seer's hut. The exterior locations identified include St. Teilo's Vicarage, the Dulais Arms, and the former Farmer's Arms on the Swansea Road at Pontardulais, Bridgend, Bargoed, and the weir at Pontardulais or Llanelly (both have been claimed). Shots at these various locations may have been made because of, or may have had to await Will Junior's theatre company's engagements there.

24. William's horrified reaction was recalled by Ada, and passed on to her grandson Roy Haggar.

25. For some Victorian theatrical conventions in **The Maid**, see the footnotes to Appendix 4. Such conventions are described in *Theatre to Cinema* by Ben Brewster and Lea Jacobs (OUP, 1997).

26. Film historians, without the benefit of the family traditions, have ascribed the film to Will Junior, because the opening title states that it was 'produced by Mr. & Mrs. Will Haggar Junior and their Dramatic Company'. But Will was the actor, not the editor, and producer was not used in the modern idiom: the inspiration and use of the film medium was his father's. As well as in the *World's Fair* (note 11 above), the film was advertised in the *Kinematograph Year Book for 1915*, in its 'Personalities in Filmland' gossip column: 'August (1914) – Mr W Haggar started film production. The plot of the subject called "The Maid of Cefn Ydfa" was written by Mr Jas Haggar, manager of the Royalty Theatre, Llanelly, and was enacted by Mr & Mrs Will Haggar jnr. and their dramatic company.' In this column, William joined such personalities as "Pop" Lubin, D W Griffith, Mrs Carl Laemmle (stranded in Germany on the outbreak of war) and King Nicholas of Montenegro: possibly the greatest public accolade accorded him by the film world.

27. In the *Aberdare Leader*, from 17 October 1914, 'Coming shortly, the great Welsh story, The Maid of Cefn Ydfa' appears each week below the adverts for such films as **Adventures of a Midshipmite, Etta of the Footlights**, and **Won in the Clouds, or The Romance of a Zeppelin**. At last the great day arrived, and for greater effect, William advertised in Welsh: 'Rhagfyr 14, 15 a'r 16, 1914: Yr ystori enwog o garwriaeth Ann Thomas, **Y Ferch o Gefn Ydfa**. William Haggar Junior – Will Hopkin. Jenny Haggar – Ann Thomas. Be sure to see it. Extra to our usual big programme. No advance in prices.' The preview of the Mountain Ash showing (in the *Aberdare Leader*) was 'The centre of attraction for the latter end of the week is the long promised and long looked for Welsh drama, **The Maid of Cefn Ydfa**. The photo play meets entirely the spoken play. It has been staged locally and played by local actors, none other than Mr. William Haggar Junior and his wife. It is the best picture ever shown in South Wales and will excite an immense amount of enthusiasm while it is here. Don't forget, only three nights' (a previous trailer had explained that it was on for only three nights as other Welsh towns were clamouring for it). 'Continuous performance from 6.30. All the best comedy and drama pictures as well.'

28. A full list of titles and scenes is given in Appendix 4.

29. Not until 1911 had the first two-reel films been made: Will Barker's **Henry VIII** of 2000 feet, followed by his **Rob Roy** of 2560 feet. So when William

planned **The Maid** in 1912, nothing longer had been produced. But in 1912 Clarendon brought out **Lorna Doone** (4300 feet), and in 1913 Hepworth's **David Copperfield** was an enormous 7500 feet – over two hours long. By 1914, when **The Maid** was at last shown, 80 films were as long, or longer than it. (Statistics from *The British Film Catalogue*).

30. These films were reviewed by Rachael Low in *The History of the British Film*, 1906-1914. She criticises F. R. Benson's **Richard III,** which contains much wild histrionic gesturing, for being unintelligible and showing no appreciation of the possibilities of film-making. In Barker's **East Lynne**, the camera remains static, but the plot is well explained by the titles, and the acting is more restrained. Hepworth's **David Copperfield** is praised for its better use of the camera, involving panning, movement and dissolves.

31. Rachael Low comments that early readiness to take a camera out and about was largely forgotten. The exception was Hepworth's **Hamlet** of 1913, in which the then remote Lulworth Cove, in Dorset, stood in for Elsinore.

32. Walter Haggar states that the film was a very great success (*Bioscope Recollections*). When they showed it in their cinema in Pontardulais, Will Junior and Jenny Lindon would stand together behind the screen and speak the dialogue of the silent film: at the end of the last showing, they would go to the exit to wish their patrons good-night. (Roy Haggar, *Haggar's Cinema*, in the Town Guide to Pembroke, May 1999.)

33. Or, occasionally, with a modern musical accompaniment: but it should be noted that, since moving pictures were considered a development of lantern slides, lecturers such as Cyril Yorke provided a commentary on the film, as was done for the slides. It would only have been when intertitles told the film's story, from about 1908 onwards, that lecturers became redundant and music was provided instead.

Notes: Chapter 9

1.THE SHANTY CINEMA WAS recalled by J. Emlyn Evans of Aberdare, in a memoir held in Aberdare Library. 'Haggar was truly a pioneer. He filmed his own stories, with his family as "stars", and Aberdare Park provided all the scenery necessary. He built the "Shanty" cinema in the Market Yard, large enough to seat several hundred on backless wooden benches. The front of the building boasted an open stage facing the main road. Shows were preceded by open-air performances by scantily-clad high-kicking girls, surely the 1910 forerunner of the modern striptease show, just as provocative in its period, and much frowned upon by the many thousands of chapel-goers.' Emlyn recalled the double seats, the 'talking apparatus' which so frequently broke down, the 'Westerns' of Tom Mix, William S. Hart and Broncho Billy Anderson, and the serials, **The Perils of Pauline, The Black Box**, and **The Broken Coin**.

2. *The Era*, 7 July and 3 December 1910 for William's purchase of The Royalty, the skating rink at Pontardulais, and bid for the Old Post Office buildings in Llanelly (the newspaper headlines 'The Old'Un at Llanelly'). The Castle Cinema at Merthyr is said to have cost £3000.

3. *Aberdare Leader*, 20 January and 28 August 1912. Cyril Sydney Yorke's real surname was Hardwick, but he unblushingly assured the Registrar that it was Yorke. The *Leader* therefore reported that among the guests were his parents, 'Mr. & Mrs. Yorke, of Coleford.'

4. Under the heading, 'Cinema Companies' the *Kinematograph Year Book for 1915* lists Haggar's Circuit, its head office at Kinema House, Abernant Road, Aberdare, with cinemas at Llanelly, Aberdare, Mountain Ash, Pontardulais and Pontlottyn. Most of the family cinemas were known as 'Haggar's'. Lily owned that in Mountain Ash until the 1960s, although she leased it out from 1937: *South Wales Echo*, 13 May 1971.

5. *Aberdare Leader*, 23 March 1912. William's only friends at the wedding breakfast were his best man, Stanley Gower from Swansea, and his solicitor, T. W. Griffiths. On his marriage certificate, William understated his age by 3 years (declaring that he was 58 to his bride's 28), and stated that his father was (the non-existent) William Haggar deceased, Timber Merchant.

6. Lily Richards, *Biography*. The 46,000 ton ship's maiden voyage, begun on 10 April 1912, ended in disaster, when it hit an iceberg, and sank with the loss of 1635 lives.

7. Lily Richards, *Biography*.

8. Rachael Low, *The History of the British Film, 1906-14*.

9. *Aberdare Leader,* 27 January, 2, 9, 16 and 23 March 1912, and 20 December 1913.

10. The sermon was reported at length in the *Aberdare Leader* on 9 March 1912.

11. *Aberdare Leader*, 4 January 1913. The next week, William was advertising a singing competition for girls. By 1914, the British Board of Flm Censors had been introduced: this did not end the debate about the influence of the cinema.

12. Lily Richards, *Biography*. On 5 March 1971, the *Leader* printed a

photograph, brought in by a reader, of 'the ingenious and enterprising William and his wife and daughter outside Kinema House.' The picture shows a laughing William, in cap and waistcoat, with an older and a younger woman. Since neither bears any resemblance to Rose, Violet or Lily, it seems probable that the younger woman is May, and the older a visitor, perhaps her mother.

13. The political cartoon is shown, dated 12 February 1910, in Geoffrey Hill's *William Haggar*. William as Father Christmas was published in *The Bioscope* in 1910 with the caption: 'Picture Personalities: Mr. W. Haggar (The Old'Un).'

14. Lily Richards, *Biography*. The *Aberdare Leader* on 23 March 1912 published a letter in support of William from Robert Lewis, Branch Secretary, The Amalgamated Society of Railway Servants. They had always found Mr. Wm. Haggar and family sympathetic and kind to the Orphan Fund, to which their pictures had contributed nearly £50, for which they as railwaymen felt grateful. Mr. Lewis added that William had assured him personally that it was his wish and effort to keep his entertainments free from anything that would offend or cause a blush.

15. *Aberdare Leader*, 17 October 1914.

16. *Aberdare Leader*, 26 July and 2 August 1913.

17. *Aberdare Leader*, 25 October and 1 November 1913.

18. *Aberdare Leader*, 11 and 18 July, and 1 August 1914.

19. The *World's Fair*, 8 August 1914. The turn-out was 71% of a total electorate of 1802. 'Thus despite the aspersions of his opponents and the untiring efforts of the Free Church Council and the I. L. P.' (the Independent Labour Party, founded in 1893) 'the old showman was once again top dog.'

20. *Aberdare Leader*, 14 February 1925.

21. *Aberdare Leader*, 5, 12 and 19 September 1914. On 12 September, the film advertised was **The Great German Spy Peril**. 'See how a brave English lad tracks down a horde of German spies. See how he is captured. See how the spies attempt to blow up the Houses of Parliament. See how our hero foils them and blows them up instead. It's great – don't miss it.' Rachael Low, in *The History of the British Film, 1914-1918* (British Film Institute and British Film Academy, 1948) commented that this was one of a large number of films in which British secret servants toiled to outwit sly, but fortunately clumsy German cads, who had an habitual tendency to assault English girls. Not everyone had the good fortune of the hero of this particular film, who, walking down Whitehall one day, chanced to overhear a group of spies discussing their plans to blow up Parliament.

22. *Aberdare Leader*, 3 October 1914.

23. *Aberdare Leader*, 10 October 1914.

24. *Aberdare Leader*, 12, 19 and 24 December 1914: 'Continuous performance on Xmas and Boxing Days from 2.30 pm. Haggar's The Place for Good Goods.'

25. J. Emlyn Evans, *William Haggar, Welsh Film Pioneer*.

26. The adverts for the Kosy in the *Leader* begin on 7 August 1914, when the main film at the old cinema was **Thou Shalt Not – The Tenth Commandment**, and episode 14 of The **Master Key** was showing. On Saturday 14 August, the advert trumpeted, 'Opening Shortly, Councillor Haggar's New Cinema Hall, Aberdare.'

27. The account of the opening and description of the Kosy was published in the *Leader* on 28 August 1914. The full text is given in Appendix 5.

28. Cyril Haggar Yorke in conversation with his son, Peter Yorke, 30 May 1988.

29. *Haggar's Cinema, Pontardulais*: typescript memoir by Haydn Thomas – copy in Peter Yorke's possession. He recalls Will Junior's family and shows, Will Fyffe acting as general handyman and bill-poster, and the amateur operatic performances for which Will would close the cinema. The disastrous fire took place at about 10 p.m. in the late Spring of 1923: 'the building being almost wholly of timber, was within minutes, so to speak, a blazing inferno, and completely destroyed.' Walter Haggar, in his *Theatre Recollections*, described the fire as a severe misfortune, as the whole stock-in-trade of their original profession, the stage, was lost.

30. Roy Haggar, in conversation with Peter Yorke.

31. The full text of the article is given in Appendix 6. In making William have 11 children and 40 grandchildren, either the writer or William had become confused. In 1924 William had had 11 children and 29 grandchildren, plus four baby grandchildren who died at or a few days after birth. One more grandchild, Lily's youngest daughter June, was born after William's death.

32. According to Ada Haggar, quoted by Roy Haggar in conversation.

33. William's death was reported in the *Aberdare Leader* on 7 February, and his funeral on 14 February 1925. Will Junior, Walter and Ada, Rose and Sid, Violet, Henry, Lily and Bert followed the coffin, with William's mother-in-law, Jane Davies and other Davies relatives, and the family friends, Dr. Ogilvie, J.D. Hughes and A. Rhys Williams. The paper reported that 32 wreaths were received from close family and friends, among them the Roberts, Symonds and Butlin relatives, and, from other fairground families, Mr. & Mrs. Crecraft, Mr. R. Dooner, Mr. Harry Scard, and Mr. & Mrs. H. Studt; and the film magnates Sir William Jury and Colonel Bromhead. The film industry had not forgotten the pioneer.

34. A few days out, due perhaps to lack of documentation – although William's baptismal certificate, which gives the correct birth date, 10 March 1851, has been preserved.

35. Probate of the Will was granted on 27 March 1925 to Walter Haggar and William Thomas, the executors. The figure of £1000 per share of the residue was quoted by Roy Haggar in conversation. William left nothing to Jim and Kate, who were in Australia and sent a wreath, nor to Fred's surviving children. Part of William's savings had been in War Loan: this was not cashed, but parcelled out as part of the share of the residue. Some of it eventually came to William's great-great-grandchildren, in memory of Violet.

36. For the full text of William's obituary, and an appreciation by 'K', see Appendix 7.

37. Lily Richards, *Biography*.

38. *Aberdare Leader*, 20 January 1912.

39. Cyril Haggar Yorke, speaking to Peter Yorke on 30 May 1988. Ada Haggar, quoted by Roy Haggar, used the same words of her mother-in-law Sarah. Perhaps both were true: William would be the paterfamilias, but leave the children's upbringing to Sarah.

40. June Bilous, Lily Richards' daughter, in conversation with Peter Yorke, 6 September 2002.

41. *Aberdare Leader*, 14 February 1925.

42. H. H. Wollenberg, *Anatomy of the Film* (Marsland Publications Ltd., 1947).

43. Michael Chanan, *The Dream that Kicks* (Routledge, 1996)

44. Paul Rotha, *The Film Till Now* (Vision Press Ltd., 1930)

45. Unlike any of the other pioneer film makers, who made films to sell to others to exhibit, William depended for his livelihood on showing his own films to his fairground audiences. His films were, therefore, targeted at those audiences: the anti-authoritarian humour, the slapstick, the drama and the thrill of the chase were evidently what they wanted to see.

Notes: Chapter 10

1. WALTER SOLD THE KOSY to Captain Billy Willis, father of Welsh rugby international Rex Willis, who renamed it the Cosy Cinema. In August 1939, workmen renovating the cinema unearthed the original canopy, which showed 'Haggar's' in stained glass on both sides. In 1946 the cinema burnt down, the flames lighting up the Valley, according to Mr. & Mrs. Meredith, researching their family history in Aberdare Library in 1997, who remembered the fire and, even earlier, the proud boast that there had been 'no fleas at Haggar's!'
2. Despite the urging to the contrary of his son Roy Haggar Senior, who is not to be confused with his nephew and namesake Roy Haggar, the source of many quotations cited above.
3. According to Trevor Taylor, retired showman, in a conversation on Aberystwyth promenade in August 2004.
4. Walter had been deemed unfit to run the cinema, having been tricked by an entertainment tax inspector into allowing him into the cinema for a shilling without a ticket after the last performance had begun. Walter was prosecuted for not paying entertainment tax, of 8½d on a 1/9d ticket. He was succeeded by his son, Len, for whom his son Roy Haggar later had the job of buying entertainment tax stamps at the Post Office and sticking them on the tickets. Their glue tasted foul.
5. Walter had intended that the film should be given to the Museum, and perhaps had made the arrangement: but his brother Henry intercepted it, and it never arrived. According to Moya England, Jennie Haggar's daughter, in a letter to Peter Yorke in 2004, her half-brother Dai Thomas was taken as a small boy during the war by their mother, Jennie, to the Welsh National Museum to see the film, in which she had played the part of Gwenny; but when she asked about it, the Museum 'seemed to have it, but couldn't find it.' Jennie was furious.
6. The *World's Fair*, 29 July 1939, with the heading, 'Family who made early pictures: how the Haggars began, by "Gee-Gee".' See note 29 below.
7. See note 1 to chapter 2.
8. In *The Film Till Now*, first published in 1930.
9. F. Maurice Speed, *Movie Cavalcade* (Raven Books Ltd., 1942).
10. Dr. Roger Manvell (1909-1987) obtained his PhD from London University, and during the Second World War worked in the film division of the Ministry of Information. After the war, he became Research Officer of the British Film Institute, and, from 1947, first Director of the British Film Academy, a post he held for twelve years. He became Britain's leading chronicler of the art of film, his Penguin Book *Film* (1944) selling over a million copies. From the mid-1970s until his death, he was a personal friend of Betty Cullingford, later Betty Yorke. His archive is housed in the University of Louisville, Kentucky.
11. David Low, war cartoonist and creator of 'Colonel Blimp'. One of his most famous cartoons shows the ghosts of William Pitt the younger and Lloyd George welcoming Winston Churchill, their worthy successor as war leader.
12. The BFI had formed a History Committee, chaired by Cecil Hepworth, to

oversee the project. The first volume of *The History of the British Film (1896-1906)* is ascribed to Low and Manvell. Rachael Low's name alone appears as author of the succeeding volumes. The first three volumes formed her PhD thesis.

13. Lily had had a hard, and sometimes sad life. She had fallen in love with a greengrocer, only for her father to threaten to take a shotgun to him: he was not good enough for her. Her subsequent marriage to Bert Richards produced five children, but failed in 1937, Bert gambling their money away and incompetent at running their cinema. After the war Lily visited her sister Rose in Australia, but returned saying that there was 'too much livestock' in Australia. Settling for many years with her youngest daughter June and her husband Rudy Bilous, she eventually went to live with her elder daughter Eileen in Southsea, where she died in January 1973, aged 81, following a stroke. She had kept in touch with her sisters, Rose who died in Brisbane in 1967, and Violet, who outlived her, dying in Truro in 1979, the last of William and Sarah's children, shortly after her ninety-second birthday.

14. The footnote is on page 103 of *The History of the British Film, 1896-1906*: 'The Sheffield Photo Company's version of the *Life of Charles Peace*, a synopsis of which is reproduced here, was actually no more advanced than that of the lesser-known producer Walter Haggar, whose production in fact preceded the other by some months. It is Haggar's film, and not the S.P.C.'s as formerly supposed, which is preserved in the National Film Library.'

15. In his lecture to the British Kinematograph Society, quoted in chapter 4 above, which Rachael Low quotes repeatedly.

16. 'Walter Haggar was a travelling showman, well-known in the fairgrounds, especially South Wales.' (Low & Manvell, p. 21). William's portrait follows page 32, captioned, 'Walter Haggar'.

17. For Lily's *Biography*, see note 31 to Chapter 1. Roy Haggar told Peter Yorke that it was his father, Len's copy of Walter's Recollections which Lily had used: Lily in her interview said that it was her niece (presumably one of Len's sisters) who had loaned her the copy.

18. Anthony Slide in his article *William Haggar* quoted Mrs. L. M. Richards as his source.

19. Denis Gifford, in *The British Film Catalogue* acknowledged assistance from 'Lillian Richards, actress'. David Berry, in *Wales and Cinema: the first hundred years*, followed Gifford in mis-naming Lily as Lillian.

20. *South Wales Echo*, 12-15 May 1971.

21. The interview was tape-recorded: a copy of the transcript is in the National Fairground Archive at the University of Sheffield..

22. *Sunday Times Magazine*, 20 September 1970.

23. Roy Haggar, *William Haggar: the travelling theatre, film-making and the bioscope* (unpublished essay, 1968).

24. Published by the University of Wales Press in 1994.

25. Quoted in part in chapter 7 above.

26. Geoffrey Hill, *William Haggar, Pioneer of the cinema in Wales* (from *Old Aberdare, Volume 6*, Cynon Valley History Society, 1989).

27. According to Roy Haggar, who had often barked his shins on such boxes in Haggar's in Pembroke.

28. It was Roy Haggar's understanding that Henry had the film. Henry died as a result of falling from the balcony of a cinema in Birmingham. Bill Haggar, Will

Junior's son, a Swansea bus driver, was close to his uncle Henry.

29. Walter Haggar's obituary was published in the *World's Fair* in 1954. The writer, signing himself 'G.G.' stated: 'Prior to the last war, Mr. Walter Haggar broadcast the family story in a BBC feature production written by G. Griffiths and produced by Wynford Vaughan Thomas.' Since that radio broadcast had been reported in the *World's Fair* by 'Gee-Gee' (note 6), it is likely that 'Gee-Gee', 'G. G.' and G. Griffiths were the same. In Walter's obituary, G.G. wrote that the oldest living member of the family was 80-year-old Mrs. Will Haggar, and that the only copy of **The Maid of Cefn Ydfa** was then in the possession of Mr. Sid Griffiths, manager of the Plaza Cinema, Swansea, who in his younger days was closely associated with the Haggars (he had been one of **The Poachers**). Probably only a member of both families could have known these facts: Bill Haggar had married Leita Griffiths, thus becoming related both to Sid and G. Griffiths.

30. In her Canton interview, Lily said that it was Bill's brother-in-law, Mr. Griffiths, who had the film. She had written to him when she first started her biography, 'and begged him to send it to the British Film Institute, so that they could preserve it if possible, because it was really worth doing, a very good film. And he never replied to me.'

31. Jo Haggar, Will Junior's youngest daughter, wrote to her niece, Moya England, telling her that Phyllis had found the film when turning out a cupboard. 'So John Haggar and a man who is writing a history of the cinema in Wales sent the film to the British Institute of Films in London, it was in very good condition being 70 years old so they are working on it....Really the film belonged to Mother, and as John said I have the right to claim it, but he said it was now a national heritage, but I'm really glad it has been brought to light.' Both Geoffrey Hill (in *William Haggar*) and David Berry (in *Wales and Cinema*) state that the conserved film lasts 26 minutes, when, in fact, it lasts 38 minutes.

32. **A Penny For Your Dreams** was written by Ken Howard and Gwenlyn Parry for BBC Wales and Landseer Films (Howard's company).

33. **The Magic Caravan** starred Tony Robinson as William Haggar.

34. The ceremony was reported in the *Cynon Valley Leader* on 16 January 1997, David Berry writing the feature article on p. 21.

35. Patricia Warren, *British Cinema in Pictures* (B. T. Batsford, 1994).

36. Joel W. Finler, *Silent Cinema* (B. T. Batsford, 1997).

37. Richard Gray, *Cinemas in Britain* (Lund Humphries Publishers, 1996).

38. **Hamlet** by Hepworth in 1913; **Romeo and Juliet** by Gaumont in 1908; **East Lynne** by Barker in 1913.

Notes: Appendix 2

1. WALTER HAGGAR, *BIOSCOPE RECOLLECTIONS*.
2. Lily Richards, quoted in *William Haggar* by Anthony Slide
3. Walter Haggar, *Bioscope Recollections*.
4. Walter Haggar, *Bioscope Recollections*.
5. Walter Haggar, *Bioscope Recollections*.
6. Roy Haggar, essay.
7. Roy Haggar, essay, and David Berry, *Wales & Cinema*, quoting reports in *The Showman*, 16 August and 27 September 1901.
8. Walter Haggar, *Bioscope recollections*.
9. Roy Haggar, essay. In 1908 D.W.Griffith filmed **Ingomar the Barbarian**, 13 minutes long, with a cast which included himself, Florence Lawrence (the 'Biograph girl'), and Mack Sennett as a barbarian (*IMDb, Internet*). It is for speculation whether that film was suggested or inspired by the earlier Haggar version.
10. Cedric Price, *Portable Theatres in Wales*.
11. Roy Haggar, essay.
12. Walter Haggar, *Bioscope recollections*.
13. Walter Haggar, *Bioscope recollections*.
14. Walter Haggar, *Bioscope recollections*.
15. Roy Haggar, review of Wales & Cinema in the *Western Telegraph*, 4 January 1995.
16. In the *British Film Catalogue*, this film is entitled, 'A Boating Incident', but its correct title is given in the Gaumont catalogue of February 1906.
17. Walter Haggar, *Bioscope recollections*. The *Kine Weekly* reported on 3 September 1908 that 'Messrs. R.W. Paul have secured a good picture of the wreck and survivors of the barque *Amazon*, which came ashore at Port Talbot. It was well received at the Alhambra, where it was on the screen for the first time Wednesday night.'
18. Walter Haggar, *Bioscope recollections*.
19. Walter Haggar, *Bioscope recollections*.
20. Lily Richards, interview.
21. Lily Richards, interview.
22. Roy Haggar, essay.
23. Lily Richards, quoted in *William Haggar* by Anthony Slide
24. Lily Richards, quoted in William Haggar by Anthony Slide
25. The *World's Fair* on 8 August 1914 quoted this as one of the most memorable of William's films. In the *British Film Catalogue*, it is ascribed to Dave Aylott.
26. David Berry, *Wales & Cinema*, quoting a report in the *Bioscope* in 1908.
27. *World's Fair*, 12 September 1909.
28. *Llanelly Mercury*, 21 December 1911
29. *Llanelly Mercury*, 24 August 1911
30. *Llanelly Mercury*, 14 September 1911
31. Presented to and preserved in the Llanelli Public Library, and noted in

Llanelly Mercury, 30 September 1911.

32. *World's Fair*, 29 July 1939, and Roy Haggar, letter to Peter Yorke of 3 April 2002.

33. *Aberdare Leader*, 21 August 1915.

34. There are many similarities of plot and style. For example, in the synopsis of **Rivals** (see Appendix 3), the 'infuriated damsels' are 'marched past the camera still struggling'. This was a particular trick of William's, as can be seen in **Desperate Poaching Affray**. See also note 44 on chapter 7.

35. In the *British Film Catalogue*, this is named 'Fair exchange is no robbery', but the correct title is given in the Warwick Trading Company's catalogue, October 1902.

36. In the *British Film Catalogue*, these three films are attributed to Alf Collins. William had already filmed, in 1902, a scene from *The Two Orphans*.

37. This film is still in existence, the action and overall look being very similar to William's, as acknowledged by David Berry in *William Haggar and The Sheep Stealer* (in *The Showman, the Spectacle and the Two-Minute Silence*, Flicks Books, 2001).

General index

Tonypandy 27-9, 169, 175
Toulmin, Vanessa 174
Trade Unionism 50-1
*Travelling Cinematograph Show,
The* 170, 174, 177-8
Trecynon 80, 103-6
Tredegar 13, 27-8, 46, 164, 169
Tree, Sir Herbert Beerbohm 17
Treharris 66, 82
Treherbert 26
Treorchy 29, 54, 57-8, 60
Trewen, Felicien 36-7
Trowbridge 10, 55
*True History of Pepper's Ghost,
The* 174
Truro 196
Twickenham 10
Twm Shon Catti 181
Tyler, Walter 91, 130-3, 187-8
Type-casting 13-14

United States of America 78, 80-1,
95, 100, 103, 117, 168, 183
University of East Anglia 172
Urban, Charles 37-9, 45, 55, 62,
72, 77-9, 82, 91, 103, 133, 172-5,
181-3, 187
Urban District Council, Aberdare
109-10, 112-3, 116, 154, 156, 171

Victoria, HRH Princess of
Edinburgh 160
Victoria, Queen 38, 52, 160, 167,
175
Victorian Provincial Entertainment
165-6
Village Blacksmith, The 64, 179
Vint, Leon 69, 179
Vitagraph (USA) 95

Wadbrook, Nellie 65
Wadbrook's travelling cinema 46,
52, 56-7, 60, 65
Wadbrook & Scard's Palace 179
*Wales & Cinema: the first hundred
years* 122, 124, 196-8
Wales, North 63
Wales, South 10-11, 25-27, 48, 50-
1, 58, 64, 69, 77, 109, 112, 154-5,
164, 174, 178, 189

Wales, West 69
Walsh, T.A. 37
Walsingham 163
Walter Haggar's Royal Bioscope
198
Walton Company, The Inimitable
11, 163
Walton, Louisa 9-10, 163-4
Walton, Richard (Julius) 8-10, 163-
4
Walton, Sarah 9-10
Walton (Hemming), William 163
Walton-on-Thames 172
Walturdaw Co. 91, 130, 133, 187
Ware, Herts. 4
Warren, Low 171
Warren, Patricia 123, 197
Warwick Trading Co. 39, 77, 127-8,
130, 132-3, 172-3, 181-2, 187, 199
Weary Willie & Tired Tim 182
'Weenie Paul' 126
Welsh Folk Tales 188
Welsh National Museum 1, 94,
119, 195
Welsh National Pageant 71, 94
Wentworth, Jim 63
Western Cleddau 81, 187
Western Telegraph 198
Westminster Abbey 154
Weston, G.H. 160
Weston-super-Mare 168
Weymouth 167
Whaley, H.D. 171, 184
Whitby 10
Wigan 165
Wild Wales 169
William Haggar 121, 176, 181, 187,
196, 198
*William Haggar, Pioneer of the
cinema in Wales* 166-7, 179, 183,
196-7
*William Haggar: The Travelling
Theatre, Film-making and the
Bioscope* 165, 196
*William Haggar, Welsh Film
Pioneer* 191-2
Williams, A. Rhys 193
Williams, Julian Leigh 166
Williams, Margaret 166
Williams, Randall 45, 174

Williams, Rev. W. Cynog 104-6
Williamson, James 122, 172-3
Willis, Captain Billy 195
Willis, Rex 195
Wiltshire 21, 54
Wimborne 22
Winchester 22
Windsor 165
Windsor Castle 4, 32, 160
Windsor Castle Biograph 32, 54
Wivenhoe, Essex 7, 153
Woking 165
Wollenberg, H.H. 184, 193
Wolverhampton 95
Wolverton 165
Wood, Mrs. Henry 126
Wood, Leslie 171-5
Woolwich 165
Wotton-under-Edge, Glos. 21, 23
World's Fair 65, 69, 96, 98, 109,
119, 177-80, 183-5, 188-9, 192,
195, 197-9
Wrench, John 55, 62
Wright, Maggie and Jessie 95
Wye, River 23-5

Yank in Britain, A 172, 175
York, Clara Amelia 167
Yorke, Betty Baker 195
Yorke, Cyril Haggar 71, 103, 112,
167, 180, 192-3
Yorke, Cyril Sydney 65, 98, 101-3,
112, 167, 178, 189, 191
Yorke, Peter John 161-2, 165-6,
171, 178-81, 183-4, 188, 192-3,
196, 199
Yorke, Violet Alice (née Haggar)
21-2, 28, 59, 65, 69-71, 85, 92,
102-3, 112, 114, 116-7, 130, 163-4,
167, 169, 176, 179, 192-3, 196
Yorkshire 19, 153

Zoetrope 11

Index of films and plays

Films are in bold type, plays in italics